Changing Models of Capitalism in Europe and the US

T0362150

The volume analyses the long-term trajectories of change in the capitalist models of the UK, Germany, Sweden, France, Italy, Hungary, Slovakia, and the United States. The case studies identify critical junctures and key periods of change in order to show how institutions are shaped by different sets of socio-political compromises and public policy. The case studies follow a common methodology, comparing change and linkages across six core institutional domains, thus facilitating a comparative understanding of the patterns and drivers of institutional change, as well as how liberalization impacts countries in similar and dissimilar ways. The historical perspective of the cases highlights the transformative effects of relatively slow and incremental changes. These case studies also make an innovative contribution to examining the linkages between four levels of institutions that regulate the economy – the international, macro (national), meso, and micro. The volume reveals both a common trend toward more liberal forms of capitalism but also variations on this overarching trajectory. Markets themselves create their own dynamics, which have varied effects on firms and other economic actors in historically diverse institutional contexts.

This book was originally published as a special issue of the *Journal of European Public Policy*.

Richard Deeg is Professor and Head of the Department of Political Science at Temple University, USA. He received his PhD from the Massachusetts Institute of Technology, USA. His publications include *Finance Capitalism Unveiled: Banks and the German Political Economy* (1999) and numerous articles on German and European political economy in various journals, including *Comparative Political Studies, Economy & Society, Governance, Journal of European Public Policy, Journal of International Business Studies, Publius: The Journal of Federalism, Small Business Economics, Socio-Economic Review, West European Politics*, and *World Politics*. His current research focuses on causes and mechanisms of institutional change in financial systems.

Gregory Jackson is Professor of Management at the Free University Berlin, Germany. He received his PhD in Sociology from Columbia University, USA, and has worked extensively on the comparative institutional analysis of corporate governance. His publications include *Corporate Governance in Japan: Institutional Change and Organizational Diversity* (edited with Masahiko Aoki and Hideaki Miyajima, 2007), as well as numerous journal articles spanning the fields of sociology, political science and business studies. He is currently Chief Editor of the *Socio-Economic Review*.

Journal of European Public Policy Series

Series Editor: Jeremy Richardson is a Professor at Nuffield College, Oxford University

This series seeks to bring together some of the finest edited works on European Public Policy. Reprinting from Special Issues of the *Journal of European Public Policy*, the focus is on using a wide range of social sciences approaches, both qualitative and quantitative, to gain a comprehensive and definitive understanding of Public Policy in Europe.

Towards a Federal Europe
Edited by Alexander H. Trechsel

The Disparity of European Integration
Edited by Tanja A. Börzel

Cross-National Policy Convergence:
Causes Concepts and Empirical Findings
Edited by Christoph Knill

Civilian or Military Power?
European Foreign Policy in Perspective
Edited by Helene Sjursen

The European Union and New Trade Politics
Edited by John Peterson and Alasdair R. Young

Comparative Studies of Policy Agendas
Edited by Frank R. Baumgartner, Christoffer Green-Pedersen and Bryan D. Jones

The Constitutionalization of the European Union
Edited by Berthold Rittberger and Frank Schimmelfenig

Empirical and Theoretical Studies in EU Lobbying
Edited by David Coen

Mutual Recognition as a New Mode of Governance
Edited by Susanne K. Schmidt

France and the European Union
Edited by Emiliano Grossman

Immigration and Integration Policy in Europe
Edited by Tim Bale

Reforming the European Commission
Edited by Michael W. Bauer

International Influence Beyond Conditionality
Postcommunist Europe after EU enlargement
Edited by Rachel A. Epstein and Ulrich Sedelmeier

The Role of Political Parties in the European Union
Edited by Björn Lindberg, Anne Rasmussen and Andreas Warntjen

EU External Governance
Projecting EU Rules beyond Membership
Edited by Sandra Lavenex and Frank Schimmelfennig

EMU and Political Science
What Have We Learned?
Edited by Henrik Enderlein and Amy Verdun

Learning and Governance in the EU Policy Making Process
Edited by Anthony R. Zito

Political Representation and EU Governance
Edited by Peter Mair and Jacques Thomassen

Europe and the Management of Globalization
Edited by Wade Jacoby and Sophie Meunier

Negotiation Theory and the EU
The State of the Art
Edited by Andreas Dür, Gemma Mateo and Daniel C. Thomas

The Political Economy of Europe's Incomplete Single Market
Edited by David Howarth and Tal Sadeh

The European Union's Foreign Economic Policies
A Principal-Agent Perspective
Edited by Andreas Dür and Michael Elsig

Changing Models of Capitalism in Europe and the US

Edited by
Richard Deeg and Gregory Jackson

LONDON AND NEW YORK

First published 2015 by Routledge

2 Park Square, Milton Park, Abingdon, Oxon, OX14 4RN
605 Third Avenue, New York, NY 10017

Routledge is an imprint of the Taylor & Francis Group, an informa business

First issued in paperback 2020

British Library Cataloguing in Publication Data
A catalogue record for this book is available from the British Library

ISBN 13: 978-1-138-80148-6 (hbk)
ISBN 13: 978-0-367-73987-4 (pbk)

Typeset in Adobe Garamond
by RefineCatch Limited, Bungay, Suffolk

Publisher's Note
The publisher accepts responsibility for any inconsistencies that may have
arisen during the conversion of this book from journal articles to book chapters,
namely the possible inclusion of journal terminology.

Disclaimer
Every effort has been made to contact copyright holders for their permission to
reprint material in this book. The publishers would be grateful to hear from any
copyright holder who is not here acknowledged and will undertake to rectify any
errors or omissions in future editions of this book.

Contents

Citation Information

The chapters in this book were originally published in the *Journal of European Public Policy*, volume 19, issue 8 (October 2012). When citing this material, please use the original page numbering for each article, as follows:

Chapter 6

The role of state in development of socio-economic models in Hungary and Slovakia: the case of industrial policy
Anil Duman and Lucia Kureková
Journal of European Public Policy, volume 19, issue 8 (October 2012) pp. 1207–1228

Chapter 7

Strategic transformation and muddling through: industrial relations and industrial training in the UK
Howard Gospel and Tony Edwards
Journal of European Public Policy, volume 19, issue 8 (October 2012) pp. 1229–1248

Chapter 8

The limits of liberalization? American capitalism at the crossroads
Richard Deeg
Journal of European Public Policy, volume 19, issue 8 (October 2012) pp. 1249–1268

Please direct any queries you may have about the citations to
clsuk.permissions@cengage.com

The long-term trajectories of institutional change in European capitalism

Gregory Jackson and Richard Deeg

ABSTRACT   The article provides a theoretical overview and empirical summary of the contributions to this collection. The collection makes four contributions to the literature on comparative capitalism. First, its analysis of institutional change adopts a long-term historical perspective that allows us to observe the potentially transformative effects of relatively slow and incremental changes. Second, it examines the linkages between four levels of institutions that regulate the economy – the international, macro (national), meso and micro. Third, the national case studies compare change and linkages across six core institutional domains. And fourth, the cases show how institutions are shaped by different sets of socio-political compromises.

1.   INTRODUCTION

The comparative capitalisms (CC) approach to political economy is concerned with the diversity and change of institutions across countries (Jackson and Deeg 2008). Institutional diversity is associated with distinct 'logics' of economic action that may yield comparative institutional advantages for different types of economic activities. At the same time, institutions are themselves a result of socio-political compromises built on a complex distribution of power among different economic actors and their interactions within existing political institutions. The early CC literature was largely focused on explaining the stability of such institutional arrangements rooted in path-dependent political legacies (Pierson 2000) and institutional complementarities across economic domains (Hall and Soskice 2001). But the analytical focus of the CC literature has recently shifted toward the attempts to document and explain institutional change in relation to European integration, liberalization, globalization and, most recently, financialization.

This collection presents case studies of selected European countries and the United States that document and analyse the trajectories of institutional change over the last 30 years – from roughly 1979 to the onset of the current financial crisis around 2008/9. The contributions identify critical

1

junctures and key periods in the change of each model, and examine the role of public policy in shaping these changes. The case studies follow a common methodology and approach intended to facilitate a comparative understanding of the patterns and drivers of institutional change, as well as how liberalization impacts countries in similar and dissimilar ways.

We believe this collection makes four contributions to understanding institutional change in the CC literature. First, the analysis of institutional change adopts a long-term historical perspective that allows us to observe the potentially transformative effects of relatively slow and incremental changes (Streeck and Thelen 2005). Even the radical liberalization policies of Britain's Thatcher or America's Reagan years were less coherent and more gradual in their effects than often assumed, and unfolded often through unintended consequences across different interdependent policy fields. Second, we examine the linkages between four levels of institutions that regulate the economy: external aspects of *international relations*; the *macro* level of national politics; the *meso* level of state policies and their effects in particular institutional domains; and the *micro* level of how firms and other economic actors cope with, enact, reproduce or modify existing institutions (Deeg and Jackson 2007). Third, all cases compare the changes and linkages across six institutional domains: finance; corporate governance and responsibility; industrial relations; education/skill formation; industrial policy; and the welfare state. Unlike most studies focused on specific domains, this scope provides a uniquely comprehensive analysis of all the key domains that constitute each national political economy. Finally, we highlight how institutions are shaped by different sets of socio-political compromises. Particular attention is given to the role of the state and regulatory policy in the process of institutional change.

2. DIMENSIONS OF INSTITUTIONAL DIVERSITY AND CHANGE

Comparative studies inevitably depend on a conceptual framework to map and benchmark the diversity of institutions and their change over time. The CC literature lacks agreement on the number of distinct types of capitalisms, the key institutional domains that constitute distinct types, and the conceptual dimensions used to compare institutions within those domains. Rather, the CC literature offers a number of competing theories about institutional change, the sources of socio-economic dynamism and the role of politics. This section briefly reviews existing conceptual typologies in the CC literature and summarizes our major findings regarding change in each institutional domain.

2.1. Limits of existing typologies

The 'varieties of capitalism' (VoC) approach (Hall and Soskice 2001) has been the most influential strand of the CC literature. This theory identifies two basic types of production regimes (capitalisms): liberal market economies (LMEs) and co-ordinated market economies (CMEs) based on the extent of market co-ordination through investment in transferable assets (LMEs) versus non-market or strategic co-ordination through investment in specific assets (CMEs). The degree of co-ordination is linked to the political strength of producer interests with regime characteristics: political systems that foster decision through consensus favour the policies and institutional stability necessary for asset-specific production strategies found in CMEs. Institutional complementarities in the mode of co-ordination across different domains also lend stability, coherence and economic efficiency to each model. VoC's explanatory strength and appeal lie in its parsimony, but the reduction of institutional diversity to a single dimension has also been its liability. The framework misses many differences in how co-ordination takes place within CME countries and faces trouble accounting for mixed cases lacking institutional complementarities. By subsuming too much diversity under a broad label, VoC have been criticized for over-emphasizing continuity and missing important aspects of institutional change.

Alternative CC frameworks stem from literatures on governance (Crouch and Streeck 1997; Hollingsworth and Boyer 1997), national business systems (Whitley 2007) or social systems of innovation (Amable 2003). These frameworks introduce a number of additional dimensions for understanding institutional diversity. For example, the governance approach uses a number of generic co-ordination mechanisms to describe how economic activity is organized in a particular domain and extends this to understanding national cases in terms of unique combinations. This framework describes CME countries in more rich and complex terms, where co-ordination takes place in inter-firm networks as in Japan, formal business associations such as sectoral unions and employers' associations as in Germany, or more community-based co-ordination as in the Third Italy. Other frameworks emphasize the varied role of the state in institutionalization (Whitley 2007) and the role of socio-political power relationships and coalitions among unequal actors with divergent interests (Amable 2003: 7–11). Moreover, new 'types' of capitalism emerging in transition economies such as Central and Eastern Europe (CEE) do not fit neatly into existing categories or typologies (Bohle and Greskovits 2007; Hancké et al. 2007). CEE countries have been described as 'dependent market economies' (DME) (Nölke and Vliegenthart 2009), whereby institutions have developed in ways very reliant on foreign direct investment and multinational enterprises exploiting relatively cheap labour.

While there are useful studies utilizing a quantitative approach to identify capitalist systems and change, the clustering of institutional variables into cohesive country groups is very sensitive to the institutional domains selected for the analysis and is unstable across different measures (Ahlquist and Breunig 2009). As a guide to empirical investigation, therefore, this collection takes a historical case study approach that draws loosely on Amable's (2003) distinction in Europe among the market-based model, Nordic or social-democratic model, Continental European model, and Mediterranean model. We focus on six institutional domains: finance; corporate governance; industrial relations and labour market institutions; the education and training system; the welfare state; and industrial policy (e.g., product market regulation). Rather than using a common dimension for each domain, we describe each domain in terms of institutional typologies drawn from specific literatures on each domain (Jackson and Deeg 2006), which are summarized in Table 1. To facilitate comparison, each country case study in the collection includes a table showing a basic political chronology of significant institutional reforms in each of these domains (Jackson and Wylegala 2012).

2.2. Change in what direction?

Quantitative analyses show that, while there is significant change within numerous institutional domains, there is a remarkable stability of institutional clusters across Organization for Economic Co-operation and Development (OECD) countries through 2008 (Becue *et al.* 2011). In Europe, these clusters conform closely to the market-based, Nordic, Continental and Mediterranean type of capitalism (Amable 2003). In other words, the *relative differences* between the countries included in this collection have largely remained stable across our selected domains. For example, Germany is often seen as a paradigm case of a co-ordinated market economy, and strategic co-ordination remains a remarkably stable feature despite the huge external shock of German unification and other institutional changes in the German model. In short, no overall convergence has taken place toward a single variety of capitalism.

Nonetheless, the contributions to this collection show how this picture of relative stability hides a larger and more important set of observations about

Table 1 Domains for political reform chronology

Institutional Domain	Typology	Examples of key areas for political reform
Financial systems	Bank/market-based/FDI dependent	Stock marketing listing rules; separation of commercial vs. investment bank activities
Corporate governance	Insider/outsider or stakeholder/shareholder	Board independence; executive compensation; share buy-backs; privatization
Industrial relations	Conflictarian/pluralism/corporatist	Board-level codetermination; works councils; recognition of unions
Education and skill creation	State/association/market/firm-based skill formation	Rules governing apprenticeships
Welfare state	Social democratic/conservative/liberal	Benefit levels and scope; eligibility rules
Industrial policy	*Dirigisme*/developmental state/neo-liberal	Product market regulation; subsidies; state ownership

change. In 1979, even liberal market economies such as the UK or USA were far less uniformly liberal and grounded in post-war social compromises of managerial capitalism, pluralistic industrial relations, and state regulation of markets. Both countries underwent a deepening of liberalization that created new institutional logics based on 'financialized' interdependencies between capital markets, corporations and the household sector (Krippner 2011). In contrast to the common imagery of the 'Thatcher revolution', Gospel and Edwards stress the incremental nature of many changes in the United Kingdom (UK), which involved policy drift and unexpected interactions across policy fields. Deeg also shows that the highly financialized United States (US) economy was not a linear process nor an inevitable result of neoliberal policies, as often presumed, but an emergent feature of how corporations and households redefined their interests over time. Similarly, co-ordinated market economies have undergone significant change: Schnyder documents how the exhaustion of the Swedish model after the 1970s underwent crisis and re-emerged with new forms of co-ordination based on a very different institutional logic. The continuity of Swedish institutions is thus closely bound up with how these institutions changed and developed new competitive strengths. Jackson and Sorge find Germany maintained many features of its co-ordinated model, but this model became far less encompassing over time and led to greater internal diversity in governing institutions. Amable *et al.* show how France underwent substantial liberalization, but successive policies reshaped political coalitions in ways that made changes incremental or partial in their effects. Rangone and Solari demonstrate how Italy adapted its model of family- and state-enhanced capitalism to a new and very different liberalized market environment in Europe, yet the result is an incoherent and politically intractable set of institutions.

Thus, our case studies point to very substantial institutional transformation. Looking across the cases two common patterns we find are a growing *liberalization* in relation to the role of the state and a growing *segmentation* (dualization) in terms of employment conditions and social protection. These trends create very different sets of challenges and responses within each country in relation to the diverse institutional starting points. In this section, we therefore highlight the common aspects to better situate the diversity of the cases in a common narrative framework.

A first trend over the past three decades is liberalization (Yamamura and Streeck 2003). While liberalization is often equated with the withdrawal of state intervention, it is not just about the degree of state involvement but the kind of state intervention. Liberalization may be defined 'as the politically implemented and politically legitimated delegation of allocation and distribution decisions to markets' (Höpner *et al.* 2009: 3). Regulatory liberalization refers to deregulation and privatization of public utilities, policies to increase competition among market actors, the strengthening of property rights, as well as the deregulation of labour markets (e.g., employment protection) and financial markets. Distributive liberalization includes reduction of transfer payments related to pensions, unemployment, subvention, and public spending. Thus, far from being a unified phenomenon, our cases show that liberalization occurs in different ways across institutional domains. Drawing on the contributions to this collection, Table 2 presents an overview of empirical findings across six domains.

Financial systems show substantial liberalization and growth of market-oriented activity with a corresponding weakening of long-term relational forms of bank–industry relationships. The UK and US have historically rather different approaches to financial market regulation, but both have moved toward a more liberal system and seen major developments toward highly 'financialized' patterns of growth. Other countries moved to a more complex mix of banks and markets. Sweden liberalized rapidly during the mid-1980s and, despite a banking crisis in 1991, remained on this path. France moved away from state-centred banking and other types of patient capital toward the most market-based system on the Continent. Germany maintains strong relational banking among co-operative and savings banks focused on *Mittelstand* firms, but has also seen a growth in stock market activity and changing strategic orientation of large private banks. Consequently, one can observe a bifurcation of financial arrangements in these countries between the older, bank-based and market-based mechanisms (Deeg 2009).

Corporate governance reform often came slightly later and partially as a response to financial market liberalization. The UK was an early mover, where shareholder-oriented corporate governance institutions were developed both through law and self-regulatory codes regarding the structure and duties of boards. Other countries followed with measures to strengthen shareholder rights and deregulate the use of corporate equity. Nonetheless, these policies had a less uniform effect on patterns of ownership and control of large firms. Insider-dominated corporate ownership has persisted in Sweden and Italy alongside a slowly growing influence of foreign institutional investors, whereas a greater dissolution of patient capital took place in France and Germany. Despite the dominance of liberal policies, a unified European market for corporate control has not emerged. Similarly, the role of stakeholders in European corporate governance remains diverse. Employee participation has remained a stable feature in Sweden and Germany, but these policies have not been emulated elsewhere.

Regarding *industrial relations and labour markets*, liberalization has occurred through the institutional layering and subsequent growth of newer, flexible forms of employment. Despite watershed industrial conflicts of the UK coal miners or US air traffic controllers, the weakening role of unions in liberal countries involved a long-term and slow decline. Even in labour-friendly Sweden, the highly centralized system of collective bargaining shifted to a more loosely co-ordinated pattern by 1990. Thus, many countries saw a gradual decline in the coverage of collective bargaining and shifts toward more decentralized, firm-level forms of bargaining. Meanwhile, employment arrangements outside the core were made much more flexible. For example,

Table 2 Trajectories of change across six institutional domains, 1979–2009

	Finance	Corporate governance	Industrial relations	Education and training	Welfare state	Industrial policy
UK	Deepening market orientation	Managerialist → shareholder-oriented	Pluralism → growing voluntarism	Apprenticeship → market-based → state-co-ordinated apprenticeship	Liberal → some strengthening of provision	Regulated markets → privatization, deregulated
USA	Deepening market orientation	Managerialist → shareholder-oriented	Pluralism → growing voluntarism	Market-based, fragmented, minimal apprenticeship	Liberal → toward residual benefits	Regulated markets, technology promotion → deregulated
Sweden	Bank-based → both banks and markets	Insider-dominated	Corporatism → limited segmentation	State-dominated, employer associations largely absent from vocational training system	State-dominated	Regulated markets → mix of developmentalist and deregulated
France	Bank-oriented → both banks and markets	Managerialist → some elements of shareholder value	Corporatism → increasing segmentation	State-based	State-dominated → some retrenchment, residual benefits	Highly regulated → deregulated with active state limited to certain sector-oriented
Germany	Bank-oriented → both banks and markets	Stakeholder-oriented → some elements of shareholder value	Corporatism → increasing segmentation	Association-based vocational training	Conservative → limited introduction of market elements, some retrenchment	Highly regulated → deregulated
Italy	Bank oriented, state-dominated → private banks and markets	Insider-dominated	Conflictarian → fragmented	Mixed system	Conservative → retrenchment	Highly regulated, active state → deregulated

(Continued)

Table 2 Continued

	Finance	Corporate governance	Industrial relations	Education and training	Welfare state	Industrial policy
Hungary	Bank-oriented → but also FDI dependent	Insider-dominated	Conflictarian	State/school-based	Weakly privatized pension system, welfare-workfare and state controlled health care	Active state
Slovakia	Bank-oriented → but also FDI dependent	Insider-dominated	Corporatism → pluralism	State/school-based	Strongly privatized pension system, welfare-workfare, state regulated healthcare with market elements	From protectionist paternalism → regulatory state

the French introduced substantial deregulation of contingent employment in 2005 – making it possible for French firms to adopt more dualistic human resource management strategies. To some extent, liberalization was counterbalanced by new types of state intervention that sought to strengthen the position of core workers in more co-ordinated countries or compensate for the growing vulnerability of peripheral workers in liberal economies. For example, the UK Labour government of 1997 introduced a National Minimum Wage. In Germany, left governments introduced reforms to facilitate the adaptation of works councils to changing forms of network-based organization. But as discussed below, these measures fit a larger trend toward greater *segmentation of rights and protections* across the workforce.

Liberalization was perhaps least uniform in the area of *education and training*. Institutions of collective skill formation represent a stunning variety of co-ordination modes, which reflect very complex political dynamics (Busemeyer and Trampusch 2012). Europeanization has spurred efforts to enhance the comparability and portability of qualifications across Europe, but not via a strict harmonization of rules. In some ways, states have been increasing their role in provision of remedial and higher education. Also, in the UK, government made efforts to institutionalize more co-ordinated forms of training and skill formation, although the effects were rather marginal to the overall context of liberal policies toward employees.

Welfare state reform presents a complex picture and the collection highlights two aspects: social insurance and pensions. Reforms to unemployment insurance and social benefits have led to substantial retrenchment in some countries, and often gone hand-in-hand with liberalization of labour markets for atypical employment under the rubric of 'flexicurity'. The combined effect of labour market and welfare state policies has been to vastly expand atypical and low-wage employment in the service sector, which is also associated with rising levels of inequality (OECD 2008). Meanwhile, reforms to public pensions have been rather less extensive. Private pension funds have become a common institutional feature, but their role remains relatively marginal in many countries. Across these domains, social protections have not disappeared but become more varied and less uniform. As will be discussed later, these changes also have longer-term destabilizing effects on core social protections.

Industrial policy reforms reflect a broad trend toward more liberalization of markets in public-relevant sectors of the economy, as well as far reaching efforts of privatization. While all countries engaged in privatization and market liberalization, they did so to different degrees and utilizing different approaches. Liberal countries underwent significant change in this domain as well, but the most regulated economies tended to change more while maintaining some important differences to the US or UK. Countries also differed greatly with regard to whether industrial policies focused on attracting foreign direct investment and maintaining suitable supports for multi-national firms – here, Ireland and the CEE countries showed certain similarities. Differences in industrial policy were also shaped by partisan politics. Right-wing governments tend to privatize more, whereas left-wing governments engage in more liberalization (Belloc and Nicita 2011).

A second common trend across our cases concerns how public policies influence the institutionalized forms of governance among private economic actors (see Thelen 2009). The case studies support the conclusion that European economies have become both *less co-ordinated and less solidaristic over time*. However, countries had different starting points and changed to different extents across these dimensions. The dimension of *co-ordination* is based on the presence of relationship-specific assets rather than liberal forms based on transferable assets. Co-ordination is often measured in terms of long-term patient capital, the level and co-ordination of collective bargaining, non-market co-operative arrangements between firms, or the duration of employment relationships (Hall and Gingerich 2009). In financial systems and corporate governance, for example, liberalization created new financing alternatives that eroded long-term co-ordination between firms and patient investors. Regulatory liberalization had a larger impact in countries, like France and Germany, where the state played a greater role in supporting private co-ordination through bank–firm and inter-corporate ties. By contrast, informal modes of co-ordination through families, as in Italy and Sweden, have proven to be surprisingly durable. Meanwhile, co-ordination generally remains very important in employment relations. Sweden and Germany have preserved co-ordination in employment relations via collective bargaining and co-determination in core sectors. Similarly, in Italy employment protection remains high, despite loosening of restrictions of non-regular employment and reinforcement of pre-existing dualism. In sum, the uneven unwinding of co-ordination across domains has resulted in a declining coherence of institutional arrangements. An open question is whether new institutional linkages will generate future complementarities or reinforce political deadlock, as in Italy.

While changes in co-ordination are significant, even greater shifts have taken place along the dimension of *solidarism* versus *segmentalism* (Höpner 2007; Swenson 2002; Thelen 2009). Solidarism implies universalistic mechanisms for redistribution to weaker market participants, whereas segmentation implies the exclusion of workers from rewards or benefits across industry lines or other groupings. Solidarity can be measured in terms of the coverage of collective bargaining, degree of labour market dualism, public spending in support of household income and universalistic forms of employment protection. As discussed above, industrial relations underwent incremental change that reinforced existing divisions between labour market insiders and outsiders. In short, core firms retain co-ordinated relations with their workforces, but the coverage of such institutions has become narrower in scope and thus less solidaristic (Palier and Thelen 2010). As market pressures have increased through liberalization, stakeholders often protected existing forms of co-ordination by reducing their scope and redistributing gains from co-operation across a smaller group of insiders. Thus, co-ordination faced a subtle form of erosion and reduction to a core group of industries and firms. The resulting shift toward more institutionalized segmentalism has long-term consequences for the socio-political dynamics of different forms of capitalism and the future dynamics of institutional change. These changes have been reinforced by the shift in welfare state arrangements to a dominant 'flexicurity' approach.

An interesting question remains as to development and change in Central and Eastern European countries. Despite obvious differences in the institutional legacies between Western European and CEE economies, we can still analyse the evolution of CEE economies utilizing the institutional dimensions developed in the CC literature. The contribution by Duman and Kurekova focuses on Hungary and Slovakia, which emerged from their socialist past as relatively advanced and internationally integrated economies. In terms of finance, bank-based finance still dominates, but the most distinguishing feature is their high dependence on foreign investment in fixed capital formation, a process encouraged by government policies. A spill-on effect for corporate governance is the large role of multinationals via control over subsidiaries, and the emergence of hybrid forms of state and foreign ownership among privatized state enterprises. Despite liberalization reforms, corporate governance remains a *de facto* insider-oriented affair, and both countries adopted at least a modicum of employee representation at the board level. Altogether, the overall trajectory of finance and corporate governance in these countries shares affinities with more co-ordinated models of capitalism.

Meanwhile, industrial relations institutions in these cases remain complex and politically contested. Hungarian unions remain more fragmented and politicized along the lines of the Italian model. Meanwhile, Slovakia adopted a more corporatist structure with state support (after 2001) to promote more co-ordinated and solidaristic collective bargaining. Both countries also legislated workplace representation by independent works councils. Turning to the situation in education and training, the relative involvement of social partners is the opposite – namely, extensive involvement in Hungary contrasts with a more state-centred approach in Slovakia. In sum, Hungary and Slovakia represent the novel mixtures of institutions that prevail in CEE and lack easy categorization into standard capitalist categories.

3. SOCIO-POLITICAL DYNAMICS OF INSTITUTIONAL CHANGE

What social and political factors can help explain both the growing liberalization and dualism across countries, but also the non-convergence of many institutions? Our contributors seek answers to these questions using a historical institutional approach that stresses how actors define their interests in relation to institutions, but also change institutions over time through their actions – these processes are ongoing and recursive (Thelen 1999). Our view of institutions does not assume path dependence but allows that incremental forms of change may also be transformative (Streeck and Thelen 2005). Institutions may create their own endogenous momentum for change over time, because even institutional persistence requires adaptation (Streeck 2009). Institutions also reflect broad socio-political compromises about the rules governing the economy. Studying their dynamics implies a complex analysis across different levels of the phenomenon and in this collection we consider four levels:– external influence of *international relations* and foreign dependence; the *macro* level of national electoral politics and coalition building; the *meso* level of policies toward particular institutional domains and how these interact with one another; and the *micro* level of how firms and other economic actors enact, reproduce, or modify existing institutions (Deeg and Jackson 2007).

At the *international level*, national socio-economic models are increasingly open to international influence triggered by the entry of foreign actors (e.g., institutional investors), the exit or relocation of activities (e.g., multinational corporationss) or transnational political processes enforced by non-state forms of authority (Djelic and Sahlin-Andersson 2006), and inter-state co-operation. Unlike the US or Asia, institutional change in Europe is now deeply intertwined through the dynamic of European Union (EU) integration where the politics of common rules and standards reduced the diversity of institutions through a wide-ranging liberalization push. However, the effects of this push across institutional domains and countries are *asymmetric*. The EU has larger influence in the area of financial markets relative to industrial relations or vocational training. Across countries, the liberalization policies of the EU have had a larger influence on the more co-ordinated models of capitalism, pushing them toward more rules-based and market-conforming forms of governance. This phenomenon of 'negative integration' has been widely document among EU scholars (Scharpf 2000). Meanwhile, countries with more co-ordinated forms of capitalism have been far less successful in exporting social protection at the EU level. The result has been a declining coherence of policies as policy-making is fragmented across a multi-level political regime (Callaghan 2010).

At the *macro level*, the role of politics in institutional change defies simple explanation using established CC concepts. In terms of electoral politics, the cases presented in this collection suggest it is very difficult to map the trajectories of reform onto simple left–right political ideologies and coalitions. In particular, the power of left political coalitions seems to have surprisingly little explanatory power in relation to differences in the degree or form of liberalization across countries. British 'New Labour', the US Clinton administration, French socialists and the German Social Democrats promoted reform of social protection and labour rights to changing circumstances, yet also furthered the agenda of financial market liberalization and policies that solidified dualism in the labour market. This 'party paradox' is apparent in a number of distinct policy areas (Cioffi and Höpner 2006). Meanwhile, the different traditions of centre-right political parties based on more Christian versus liberal approaches may help explain the more incremental nature of liberalization in countries such as Germany. The overall coherence and complementarities in a given institutional set-up is closely related to the particular socio-political compromise.

Another key variable in the CC literature has been the character of the political system, namely whether it is consensual or majoritarian. Consensual systems are thought to allow greater integration of producer groups in the policy process, shape more lasting types of social compromises between left and right parties, and facilitate more lasting forms of redistributive policies. However, the UK case shows that even in majoritarian regimes, radical shifts in policies often take the character of 'muddling through' where liberalization is worked out at meso and micro levels in ways that often involve counter-movements and shifting state action toward market regulation and a residual focus on compensating for market failures. Similarly, the fragmentation of state power played a major role in the competitive deregulation of finance in the US.

At the *meso level*, changes across institutional domains are often interconnected. While the stability of socio-economic models is often explained by institutional complementarities, interdependence may also imply that changes in one institution exert pressure to change other, related institutions. One important dynamic across countries has been renegotiating the relationship between more market-oriented forms of finance and corporate governance on one hand, and social protection in the labour market and through the welfare state on the other. The US case, for example, shows how financial market liberalization slowly evolved into financialization as households became increasingly dependent on private pension funds; these funds in turn promoted shareholder value forms of corporate governance, and even unions redefined their interests in relation to shareholder activism. In other countries, the link between finance and labour played out differently: Sweden has managed to largely maintain the egalitarian and solidaristic nature of its economic system, while solidarism has declined in important ways in Germany. Different types of corporate ownership and control may account for these divergent outcomes. In particular, the Swedish ownership structure has proven to guarantee a higher capacity for co-ordination and solidarism than the now demised bank-centred ownership networks in Germany. As discussed above, co-ordinated economies also reshaped the links between welfare states and employment regulations toward a 'flexicurity' approach that helped accommodate financial market pressures on firms, but reinforced segmentation of the labour market.

Finally, at the micro level, institutional change is shaped by how different types of organizations utilize, avoid, or otherwise strategically respond to, dominant institutions. These micro processes are important to institutional change where institutions are reinterpreted, contested or conflicts emerge over institutionalized rules. Institutions may thus undergo slow and often unintended processes of incremental change, rather than through large-scale collapse and replacement of institutions (Streeck and Thelen 2005). One important way in which liberalization shapes institutional change is by deinstitutionalizing some organizational forms and encouraging market-driven experimentation and competition with others (Crouch 2005). Liberalization thus frequently amplifies differences between large and small firms, owing to the different degrees of internationalization of operations, ownership and finance. More generally, as contributions to this collection demonstrate, liberalization is related to rising heterogeneity or internal diversity of organizations within national economies (Lane and Wood 2009). In the UK, for example, liberalized industrial relations led to more heterogeneous forms of human resource management (HRM) practices and divergence between firms pursuing high performance HRM relative to low-road strategies. This growing diversity has played out in a parallel fashion in more co-ordinated market economies. In Germany, market-oriented financing for large firms and bank-oriented finance for SMEs has created bifurcated patterns within the same national model (Deeg 2009). Similarly, multinational and domestic firms play very different roles and participate in domestic institutions in different ways within CEE countries.

4. THE FUTURE OF CAPITALISM IS CAPITALISM, OR IS IT?

Over the last 30 years, European forms of capitalism have moved toward a more liberal but in some ways more variegated set of institutions. Looking across a variety of countries and policy areas over a long period of time, this collection shows both the common trend toward a more liberal form of capitalism but also variations on this overarching theme. Markets themselves create their own dynamics, which have varied effects on firms and other economic actors in historically diverse institutional contexts. A crucial factor in understanding change is examining how actors seek to build complementarities across different institutional domains, either by following coherent strategies across them or seeking to compensate for the deficiencies of one sphere through complementary but different strategies in others.

In this regard, the financial crisis and resulting economic crises after 2008 represent something of a watershed moment where the existing logics and complementarities in different models of capitalism have reached a moment of exhaustion. Further liberalization of markets is unlikely to restore economic stability. In fact, the continued competitive strength of countries such as Germany or Sweden is strongly linked to the continuity of institutional co-ordination. Meanwhile, the crisis has exposed the growing tensions within the Italian model and unsustainable nature of financialization in the US and UK.

The role of the state and public policy has been an important driver of liberalization. But at the same time, liberalization itself calls forth political demand to re-embed markets within stable institutional arrangements that provide sufficient levels of collective goods for firms and sustain politically acceptable distributions of economic rewards in society. Unfortunately, our analysis also shows how the political foundations of solidarism within advanced capitalist economies remain weak. The growing economic segmentation that has resulted from liberalization has fragmented class-based interests between labour market and welfare state insiders and outsiders, as well as institutionalized the interests of finance within government itself (e.g., lobbying, public debt), firms (e.g., financialization of business activities), and households (e.g., consumer credit, mortgages, pension funds). This situation is further complicated by the multi-level nature of policy-making in the EU. While liberal capitalism will prove resilient to the current crisis (Crouch 2011), continued marketization stands in ever greater tension with the basic legitimacy of democratic public policy that must deal with its very real economic, social, political and ecological limits. The future of public policy will surely not just be more liberal capitalism.

Biographical notes: Gregory Jackson is Professor of Management, Chair of Human Resource Management and Labour Politics at the Free University of Berlin. Richard Deeg is Professor and Head of the Department of Political Science at Temple University.

ACKNOWLEDGEMENTS

The research in this collection was supported by the European Union's Seventh Framework Programme (FP7/2007-2011) under grant agreement number 225349 (ICaTSEM project).

REFERENCES

Ahlquist, J.S. and Breunig, C. (2009) 'Country clustering in comparative political economy', *MPIfG Discussion Paper 09 / 5*, Cologne: Max-Planck-Institut für Gesellschaftsforschung.

Amable, B. (2003) *The Diversity of Modern Capitalism*, Oxford: Oxford University Press.

Becue, M., Bouaroudj, V., Carrincazeaux, C. and Lung, Y. (2011) 'The future of socio-economic models in Europe: intermediary report', *EU FP7, Project number 225349*, Brussels: ICaTSEM.

Belloc, F. and Nicita, A. (2011) 'Liberalisation–privatization paths: policies and politics', *Working Paper No. 2011-32*, Milan European Economy Workshops.

Bohle, D. and Greskovits, B. (2007) 'Neoliberalism, embedded neoliberalism, and neo-corporatism: paths toward transitional capitalism in eastern Europe', *West European Politics* 30(3): 417–66.

Busemeyer, M.R. and Trampusch, C. (eds) (2012) *The Political Economy of Collective Skill Formation*, Oxford: Oxford University Press.

Callaghan, H. (2010) 'Beyond methodological nationalism: how multilevel governance affects the clash of capitalisms', *Journal of European Public Policy* 17(4): 564–80.

Cioffi, J.W. and Höpner, M. (2006) 'The political paradox of finance capitalism: interests, preferences, and center-left party politics in corporate governance reform', *Politics and Society* 34(4): 463–502.

Crouch, C. (2005) *Capitalist Diversity and Change. Recombinant Governance and Institutional Entrepreneurs*, Oxford: Oxford University Press.

Crouch, C. (2011) *The Strange Non-Death of Neo-Liberalism*, Cambridge: Polity Press.

Crouch, C. and Streeck, W. (1997) *Political Economy of Modern Capitalism: Mapping Convergence and Diversity*, London: Sage.

Deeg, R. (2009) 'The rise of internal capitalist diversity? Changing patterns of finance and corporate governance in Europe', *Economy and Society* 38(4): 552–79.

Deeg, R. and Jackson, G. (2007) 'Towards a more dynamic theory of capitalist variety', *Socio-Economic Review* 5(1): 149–80.

Djelic, M.-L. and Sahlin-Andersson, K. (eds) (2006) *Transnational Governance: Institutional Dynamics of Regulation*, Cambridge: Cambridge University Press.

Hall, P.A. and Gingerich, D.W. (2009) 'Varieties of capitalism and institutional complementarities in the political economy: an empirical analysis', *British Journal of Political Science* 39(3): 449–82.

Hall, P.A. and Soskice, D. (eds) (2001) *Varieties of Capitalism: The Institutional Foundations of Comparative Advantage*, Oxford: Oxford University Press.

Hancké, B., Rhodes, M. and Thatcher, M. (eds) (2007) *Beyond Varieties of Capitalism: Contradictions, Complementarities and Change*, Oxford: Oxford University Press.

Hollingsworth, J.R. and Boyer, R. (1997) *Contemporary Capitalism: The Embeddedness of Institutions*, Cambridge: Cambridge University Press.

Höpner, M. (2007) 'Coordination and organisation: the two dimensions of non-liberal capitalism', *MPIfG Discussion Paper*, Cologne: Max Planck Institut für Gesellschaftsforschung.

Höpner, M., Petring, A. and Seikel, D. (2009) 'Liberalisierungspolitik: Eine Bestandsaufnahme von zweieinhalb Dekaden marktschaffender Politik in entwickelten Industrieländern', *MPIfG Discussion Paper 09/7*, Cologne: Max Planck Institut für Gesellschaftsforschung.

Jackson, G. and Deeg, R. (2006) 'How many varieties of capitalism? Comparing the comparative institutional analyses of capitalist diversity', *Discussion Paper, 062*, Cologne: Max Planck Institut für Gesellschaftsforschung.

Jackson, G. and Deeg, R. (2008) 'From comparing capitalisms to the politics of institutional change', *Review of International Political Economy* 15(4): 680–709.

Jackson, G. and Wylegala, J. (2012) 'ICaTSEM reform database 1979–2009', *European Commission, FP7 Project no. 225349, Institutional Changes and Trajectoriesof Socio-Economic Development Models (ICaTSEM)*, available at http://icatsem.u-bordeaux4.fr/, accessed 14 May 2012.

Krippner, G.R. (2011) *Capitalizing on Crisis: The Political Origins of the Rise of Finance*, Cambridge, MA: Harvard University Press.

Lane, C. and Wood, G. (2009) 'Capitalist diversity and diversity in capitalism', *Economy and Society* 38(4): 530–50.

Nölke, A. and Vliegenthart, A. (2009) 'Enlarging the varieties of capitalism: the emergence of dependent market economies in East Central Europe', *World Politics* 61(4): 670–702.

OECD (2008) *Growing Unequal? Income Distribution and Poverty in OECD Countries*, Paris: OECD.

Palier, B. and Thelen, K. (2010) 'Institutionalizing dualism: complementarities and change in France and Germany', *Politics & Society* 38(1): 119–48.

Pierson, P. (2000) 'Increasing returns, path dependence, and the study of politics', *American Political Science Review* 94(2): 252–67.

Scharpf, F.W. (2000) 'Notes toward a theory of multilevel governing in Europe', *MPIfG Discussion Paper 00/5*, Cologne: Max Planck Institut für Gesellschaftsforschung.

Streeck, W. (2009) *Re-Forming Capitalism: Institutional Change in the German Political Economy*, Oxford: Oxford University Press.

Streeck, W. and Thelen, K. (eds) (2005) *Beyond Continuity: Explorations in the Dynamics of Advanced Political Economies*, Oxford: Oxford University Press.

Swenson, P. (2002) *Capitalists against Markets*, New York: Oxford University Press.

Thelen, K. (1999) 'Historical institutionalism in comparative politics', *American Review of Political Science* 2: 369–404.

Thelen, K. (2009) 'Institutional change in advanced political economies', *British Journal of Industrial Relations* 47(3): 471–98.

Whitley, R. (2007) *Business Systems and Organisational Capabilities: The Institutional Structuring of Competitive Competences*, Oxford: Oxford University Press.

Yamamura, K. and Streeck, W. (eds) (2003) *The End of Diversity? Prospects of German and Japanese Capitalism*, Ithaca, NY: Cornell University Press.

Like a phoenix from the ashes? Reassessing the transformation of the Swedish political economy since the 1970s

Gerhard Schnyder

ABSTRACT This contribution reassesses the evolution of the Swedish model since the 1970s across different institutional spheres. It addresses two questions. Firstly, why did a system that was based on strong complementarities undergo such extensive changes? Secondly, what explains Sweden's recent return to strong social and economic performance? The decline of the Swedish model is explained by the endogenous nature of change, which was sparked off by 'normative dissonances' that led actors to 'defect' from crucial institutions, leading to knock-on effects on other spheres through changing political strategies and macro-level political coalitions. It is further argued that the new complementarities that have emerged after 1995, while providing new sectors with institutional advantages, also contain sources of normative dissonances, which make the long-term viability of the 'new model' doubtful.

1. INTRODUCTION

For a long time, Sweden was considered a model business system, where internationally competitive companies thrived, workers' rights were well protected and social equality and living standards were extraordinarily high. The institutional set-up was perceived as strongly complementary, making for an ideal-typical co-ordinated-market economy (CME) with particularly coherent[1] institutions (Kenworthy 2006).

From a varieties of capitalism (VoC) perspective, coherence and complementarity between institutional spheres are crucial to economic performance and the main reason why we would expect a country's capitalist model to resist change (Hall and Soskice 2001). However, major changes since the 1970s have weakened the Swedish model to such an extent that by the 1990s many observers announced its 'failure' or 'death' (e.g., Meidner 1993; Peterson 2011; Pontusson 1997), the end of its welfare state (Lindbeck 1997) and of its insider-oriented corporate governance system (Henrekson and Jakobsson 2003).

Changes have indeed been profound in different domains. However, recent good economic and social performances have led increasing numbers of authors – often the same who announced the death of the model some 10 to 20 years ago – to consider that Sweden has emerged from three decades of turmoil, once again as a successful and functioning model. More strikingly, traditional social-democratic features, such as solidarism and universal welfare provision, which set the Swedish – and other Nordic – systems apart, appear surprisingly stable (Anxo and Niklasson 2008; Kristensen and Lilja 2011; Pontusson 2011; Steinmo 2010).

The questions that motivate this contribution are related to these empirical findings: if complementarities are a major source of stability in capitalist models, what explains that arguably one of the most strongly complementary systems experienced so much change over the last decades? Conversely, what explains the resurgence of a successful model since the mid-1990s and how stable can we expect this 'new model' to be?

Section 2 shows that despite a strongly complementary institutional set-up, there was a strong potential for 'normative dissonance' between the stated aim of the Swedish model and its (actual or perceived) impact on different actors. As a result, crucial actors defected from the institutional arrangements triggering their 'exhaustion'. The contribution then turns to explore the 'new complementarities' that recently permitted Sweden to return to a very strong social and economic performance (Section 3). I argue that some of the new institutional arrangements build in new sources of normative dissonances that make them vulnerable to 'exhaustion'. I therefore challenge the more optimistic accounts and doubt that the new institutional arrangements constitute a viable institutional configuration in the long run. A final section concludes.

2. THE SWEDISH MODEL AND ITS EXHAUSTION

The traditional Swedish model is most commonly associated with the Rehn–Meidner Model (RMM), developed in 1951 by two trade union economists, Gösta Rehn and Rudolf Meidner. Schematically, this model resided on four main policy goals: full employment; 'equal pay for equal work' and hence 'wage solidarity', but also relative income equality; the competitiveness of the Swedish export-industry; and the fight against inflation.

A complex set of institutional arrangements existed in order to resolve the contradictions between these policy goals. Contrary to a common sense conception of the Swedish model as a 'social democratic' model, state intervention in the private economy was remarkably limited. Indeed, since the signing between the 'social partners' of a neo-corporatist agreement in 1938 (the so-called Saltsjöbad agreement), an 'historical compromise' prevailed, which implied that the social-democratic dominated state and trade unions would refrain from interfering with private companies and respect the employers' 'right to manage'. In return, the employers would accept a generous welfare state and social policies to compensate workers for hardship (Korpi 1982).

As a result of this socio-economic compromise, the state did not intervene in the sphere of industrial relations, where a bipartite corporatist relationship between the umbrella organization of blue collar trade unions (the *Landsorganisationen* or LO) and the employers' association *Sveriges Arbetgivare Föreningen* (SAF) prevailed.

Similarly, the sphere of corporate governance was largely left to the powerful Swedish owner families, whose control over a large number of companies was actively favoured by successive social democratic governments in order to concentrate capital in a limited number of very large and highly productive companies (Henrekson and Jakobsson 2001).

Industrial policy was based on market mechanisms in the sense that wage solidarity, high profits tax and trade openness was used in order to put pressure on companies to 'rationalize' and increase efficiency or go out of business. Under this regime, the most efficient and profitable companies – the ones that could afford to pay high wages despite high profit taxes – survived, not hand-picked and government-protected 'national champions'.

State intervention was extensive, however, in the labour market, where active labour market policies were used in order to compensate workers displaced by market-driven restructuring and get them back to work quickly. Similarly, a generous universal welfare state compensated workers for the negative consequences of a very liquid and flexible labour market that was mainly governed by collective agreements not legal job protection. The state invested also in public education, providing general and portable skills to workers that made them fit for fluid labour markets. Table 1 summarizes these features and shows how the Swedish model has changed since the 1970s across these institutional domains.

Overall, the Swedish brand of co-ordinated capitalism relied not so much on complementarities narrowly defined as different spheres following similar 'logics' (markets versus extra-market strategic co-ordination). Rather, complementarities took the form of what Deeg (2007) calls 'supplementary complementarity' whereby one institution compensates for the downsides of another. This implies that certain spheres of the Swedish model were remarkably 'liberal', i.e., based on market mechanisms not state intervention or private co-ordination.

From a VoC perspective, such a (supplementary) complementary system can be expected to promote stability, because of the comparative advantage with which it provides firms (Hall and Soskice 2001). Why, then, did the Swedish model undergo such extensive changes since the 1970s?

The answer has to do with the fact that the VoC argument about complementarities as stabilizing force refers to a very specific situation where companies are exposed to *exogenous* competitive pressures (internationalization of markets) and react by exploiting specific competitive advantages provided by the domestic institutional setting (Hall and Soskice 2001). The unravelling of the Swedish model, however, started with the defection of domestic actors from the institutional arrangements. Despite the complementary overall set

Table 1 Overview of institutional changes in Sweden across six spheres, 1970s–2000s

Sphere	Typology	Direction and examples of major changes	Timing
Financial markets	Bank-based (indirect owners) but state-dominated (tight regulation, public sector as most important lender)	Marked shift to market-based system 1980s: easier bond issuing for companies, international issuing 1983: banks no longer have to reinvest 50 per cent of assets in government bonds 1985: 'November Revolution': removal of lending ceilings for banks, removal of placement requirements for insurers.	1983–89
Corporate governance	Insider-dominated	Only moderate legal change; increasing 'diversity' of models in practice 1993: adaptation of company law and related laws to EU directives: removal of obstacles for foreign investors to acquire Swedish shares (e.g., abolishing of 'bound shares' and government approval) 1990s: some increases in minority shareholder protection (MSP); legalization of share buybacks 2005: new ABL adopted, but only limited increase in MSP, dual class shares still allowed	1993–2005
Industrial policy	Market-based (indirect IP reinforcing market pressures through corporate taxation and depreciation rules)	Bias against SMEs and knowledge-intensive sectors removed; increasing state intervention Since 1980s: increased public R&D spending 1990/91: tax reform abolishes investment fund system; corporate tax rates cut from 55 per cent to 30 per cent 1990s: new policies aimed at stimulating SMEs	1990s

(Continued)

Table 1 Continued

Sphere	Typology	Direction and examples of major changes	Timing
Industrial relations	Bipartite corporatism	Increasingly interventionist state and confrontational IRs, return to more coordinated WB after 1997 1974: new Employment Security Law (LAS) ends tradition of non-state intervention 1976: act on employee consultation and participation in working life (Medbestämmandelag, MBL) and act on board-level representation for employees gives unions far-reaching rights to influence firm-level decision-making 1983/4–1990: 'exhaustion' of centralized wage bargaining 1997: LAS reform facilitating temporary work in SMEs and signing of 'Industrial Agreement' introducing pattern bargaining	1974–76 1990
Education and skill creation	State-dominated, unions; employer associations largely absent from vocational training system	Towards more market-based education and higher skills 1971: new curriculum for upper secondary school (Lgy 70) abolishes German-style apprenticeship system (new integrated 'Gymnasierskolor'); shift towards more general and transferable skills 1991: new Schooling Law to reform Lgy 70, simplifies programme structure 1990s: reintroduction of apprenticeships, some firm-level schooling: more firm-specific and higher skills	1990s
Welfare state	State-dominated	End of state monopoly on welfare provision, yet still dominant player 1980s: first social policy reforms mark shift towards private welfare provision 1990s: reduction of unemployment benefits, but unions successfully defend union-managed unemployment funds; corporatist negotiations persist 1994/8: major pension reform, From defined benefit to defined contribution system, partial privatization 2006ff: workfare measures (unemployment benefits and sick pay restrictions)	1990s/ 2000s

up of the Swedish model, it led to strong 'normative dissonances'[2] among certain groups of actors, which created, in turn, incentives to defect from the institution. Such a process can be interpreted as an 'institutional exhaustion', whereby an institutional arrangement contains the seed of its own downfall (Trampusch 2005).

More concretely, 'wage solidarity' turned out to be the Achilles heel of the Swedish model. Wage solidarity – the idea that workers should be paid according to their skills not according to the productivity of the company/industry they work for – created strong normative dissonances, because the most productive workers were required to sacrifice a part of the wage increases they could legitimately ask for in the name of solidarity with less productive workers. Hence, this institution appealed to norms of 'solidarity', 'justice' and 'fairness', which made actors attentive to such issues when they were frustrated (Swenson 1989).

The particular union structure in Sweden, which organizes workers following skill levels, contributed to these frustrations. The increasingly important white collar unions *Tjänstemännens Centralorganisation* (TCO) and *Sveriges Akademikers Centralorganisation* (SACO)[3] were less exposed to international competition than blue collar unions and were therefore less supportive of wage restraint (Steinmo 2010). Consequently, the highest-skilled blue collar workers felt increasingly frustrated about wage restraint imposed by their unions (Oliver 2011).

These increasing tensions culminated on 23 November 1969, when a spontaneous strike took place among workers in the Leveäniemi iron mine near Kiruna in Northern Sweden. From Kiruna, the strikes spread to other parts of Sweden and flared up repeatedly during 1970. Swenson (1989: 84ff) interprets these wildcat strikes as a spontaneous rank-and-file revolt against a perceived discrepancy of the LO's radical egalitarian rhetoric and the miners declining working conditions relative to white collar workers. This 'normative dissonance' created by inbuilt contradictions in the institutional set up better explains why the Swedish model of wage solidarity ran out of steam during the late 1960s than vague references to the fact that the social democratic and trade union leaderships 'had somehow gotten out of touch [with their bases]' as Steinmo (2010: 60) puts it.

The Kiruna strikes had a dramatic impact on the Swedish model and can be considered as the critical juncture, which marked the 'beginning of the end' of the Swedish post-war model (Steinmo 2010: 60). Most importantly, they upset the macro-level political compromise[4] on which the Swedish model was built and thus spilled over into other spheres of the model. Forced into a strong political reaction, the social democratic *Sveriges Socialdemokratiska Arbetareparti* (SAP) made concessions to the radical wing within the trade union movement and adopted for the first time since the 1930s plainly socialist policies, which increased state regulation of industrial relations dramatically in order to improve working conditions and promote 'economic democracy'. Besides a short-lived attempt to adopt more '*dirigiste*' industrial policies (Pontusson 1992) and a programme aiming at the collectivization of ownership through the establishment of wage-earner funds (Högfeldt 2005), laws on employment protection (the *Lag om*

Anställningsskydd, LAS, of 1974), the introduction of board-level codetermination (*Lag om styrelserepresentation* of 1976) and an increase in co-decision rights at the shop-floor level (the *Medbestämmandelag,* MBL, of 1976) were adopted. This change in the SAP's policy undermined the 'historic compromise' with employers by interfering with the corporatist arrangements and led the SAF to declare in 1976 the death of the 'Saltsjöbad spirit' and to adopt, in return, more confrontational strategies (Belfrage 2008).

The radicalization did not serve the SAP well, however, as they were voted out of power for the first time in over 40 years in the 1976 election. As a result, the SAP's return to power in 1982 was marked by another radical programmatic change, with the social democrats reverting this time to a more pro-market strategy with clear neo-liberal elements. Indirectly, the micro-level exhaustion of arrangements in the sphere of industrial relations thus spilled over into other spheres through changes in the SAP's strategy and their impact on the existing socio-political compromise.

The 'Third Way' adopted during the 1980s under the leadership of Finance Minister Kjell-Olof Feldt included market-oriented reforms which were not 'bottom–up' and incremental, as was the defection of actors 'governed' by the institutions of wage solidarity, but 'top–down' through political choices and rather radical at that.

Certainly the most radical institutional change that resulted from this right-ward shift concerned financial markets regulation. The formerly very restrictive financial regime, which imposed lending ceilings on banks and restrained cross-border capital flows, was liberalized by the early 1990s (see Reiter 2003). As a result, formerly virtually non-existent capital markets were 'reactivated' and started to boom from the late 1980s onwards (Högfeldt 2005).

In parallel, the SAP also abandoned two crucial goals of the Swedish model. The principle of 'equal pay for equal work' was replaced by more flexible wage structures even within the public sector (Pontusson 1992: 119). Full employ-ment was abandoned as a policy objective in 1990. The SAP government signalled, hence, that it was no longer willing to address the 'generic problem of full-employment capitalism' (Pontusson 1992: 119), i.e., squaring wage soli-darity, full employment, private sector profitability and low inflation. The two remaining goals – international competitiveness through productivity increases and inflation control – now took centre-stage.

The social democrats' neo-liberal strategies during the 1980s were relatively successful in stimulating growth and reducing the budget deficit. Yet, a severe financial and economic crisis between 1990 and 1994, which was arguably a direct result of the quick financial liberalization, put a definitive halt to this recovery strategy and the SAP lost governmental power again in 1991.

3. LIKE A PHOENIX FROM THE ASHES? CRISIS, REFORM AND RECOVERY

The crisis can be seen as another 'critical juncture', which marks the ultimate breakdown of the traditional model, but also ushered in a new era of reform and growth. Indeed, the SAP's 'Third Way' policies were strongly and openly contested by the trade unions during the 1980s and some of the welfare reforms, aimed at reducing public deficits, were blocked. The massive increase in public spending owing to soaring unemployment (from 1.7 per cent in 1990 to 8.2 per cent in 1993) and a shrinking gross domestic product (GDP) (by 12 per cent between 1990 and 1993), put enormous strain on the public budget (reaching a deficit of 12 per cent of GDP in 1993) (Anderson 2001) and created – together with EU membership in 1995 – a new sense of urgency that led to a cross-party understanding that reform was unavoidable.

Sweden's recovery after 1995 was impressive and many authors consider that it is now once again a model. By the year 2000 the Swedish economy produced sustained growth rates, high levels of investment and the public budget ran a surplus (Steinmo 2010: 69). By May 2011 Sweden's finance minister, Anders Borg, was confident enough to announce that the unemployment rate would be brought down from 7.8 per cent today to 5 per cent by 2014, reflecting the fact that Sweden emerged virtually unscathed from the global financial crisis. *The Economist* (2011) vaunted Sweden as the 'North Star' and some academics even talk about the 'Nordic miracle' (Kristensen 2011a: 5). A growing number of authors therefore see the period since the mid-1990s in Sweden as one of a return to a functioning institutional arrangement, which manages to reconcile some of the traditionally social-democratic features with new growth patterns (Kristensen and Lilja 2011; Steinmo 2010; Pontusson 2011).

The most common explanation of this remarkable 'revival' of the Swedish economy refers to Sweden's successful strategy to restructure its economy away from Fordist mass production towards more knowledge-intensive sectors including biotech and information and communication technology (ICT) services and equipment. Over the period 1980 to 2007, the share of high-tech manufacturing in total manufacturing value added increased from 10.16 per cent to 16.46 per cent, while the share of low-tech manufacturing declined from 33.59 per cent to 23.10 per cent over the same period (author's own calculations based on OECD 2011). This evolution had as a corollary a relative shift in the 'growth motor' from the large, established companies towards mushrooming clusters of small- and medium-sized enterprises (SME) active in the ICT and life science sectors (see, for example, for the highly successful Uppsala biotech cluster, Waxell and Malmberg 2007; for the ICT sector, Parker 2006).

The successful shift in the industrial structure is usually attributed to public investment in basic and adult education, policies promoting higher skill levels and public spending on research and development (R&D) (Kristensen and Lilja 2011; Pontusson 2011). Yet, these accounts are too narrow in that they neglect other, complementary changes that were necessary to make the shift possible. Above all, the growth of SMEs is remarkable, because Sweden was a particularly hostile environment for SMEs and start-up ventures, both in terms of taxes and corporate finance. The following sub-sections discuss the changes in the different spheres which made the most recent 'Swedish miracle' possible.

3.1. Skills, education and the knowledge economy

Investment in skills and education indeed played an important role in shifting Sweden towards a knowledge-intensive economy. In 1990, Sweden spent 5.3 per cent of its GDP on education. This ratio increased to 7.4 per cent by 2000. The expansion was particularly important in higher education, where the same ratio doubled between 1990 and 2000 from 1 per cent of GDP to 2 per cent (Steinmo 2010: 70, table 2.11).

Also, reforms of the vocational training system were implemented with the intent of providing higher-level skills that would better satisfy the needs of the business community than the school-based system introduced in 1971. Among the reforms was the attempt to reactivate a modernized apprenticeship system that would provide more firm-specific skills (Gibbons-Wood and Lange 2000: 29).

Further adult education complemented this training system. One major initiative was the 'Knowledge Lift' of 1997 to 2002, which was aimed at raising the skills of the lowest skilled strata of the workforce to a medium skill level and involved a staggering 10 per cent of Sweden's total workforce (Albrecht *et al.* 2004). Such investments in supply-side labour market policies have led over the last years to high-quality skills even at the bottom of the skill pyramid and to low skill differentials within the work force (Andersson 2003).

3.2. 'Enabling welfare services' and the new economy

In a recent edited volume, Kristensen and Lilja (2011) argue that welfare reforms contributed in a crucial way to the recent success of Sweden and other Nordic countries. Thus, Kristensen (2011a, 2011b) sees in the enabling welfare state, which is defined by the provision of services enabling individuals (in particular women, parents, elderly people and people with disability) to participate in the labour market rather than by cash transfers (similarly, Leira 2006 speaks of a 'caring-state'), a necessary complement to a labour market that is increasingly characterized by a need to show flexibility and accept non-standard forms of employment.

Yet, contrary to what Kristensen (2011b) and Peterson (2011) suggest, the 'enabling' nature of the welfare state in Sweden is not a recent invention but goes back to the 1950s, when the social democrats attempted to promote female participation in the workforce instead of relying on immigrant workers as did many other European countries (Steinmo 2010). Since then, welfare institutions promoting 'defamilization' (Esping-Andersen 1999) have expanded in Sweden (Jordan 2006; Leira 2006). The establishment of enabling welfare services was, hence, not a direct reaction to the crisis but at best a coincidental match with the new environment.[5] On the contrary, the crisis of the 1990s and the consequent welfare reforms led to some cutbacks in enabling welfare services, which increased the demand for (informally provided) private domestic services (Gavanas 2010).[6]

Thus, unemployment benefits were reduced during the 1990s (from 90 per cent to 75 per cent and then to 80 per cent of last salary), which introduced elements of 'workfare' into the Swedish system (Kildal 2001). Also, in many cases state monopolies were broken up (e.g., in primary education) and 'consumer' choice was enhanced through new private providers (e.g., in childcare, eldercare and healthcare). Some observers consider that these reforms add up to a fundamental qualitative transformation of the Swedish welfare system (Bergh and Erlingsson 2009; Blomqvist 2004). Yet, the overall level of welfare spending did not significantly decrease and Sweden has maintained much of the universal character of its welfare system (Pontusson 2011; Steinmo 2010), which leads other authors to consider that 'retrenchment' was very limited (e.g., Lindbom 2001).

However, since the electoral victory of the centre–right coalition 'Alliance for Sweden' in September 2006, more clearly retrenchment- and workfare-oriented reforms have taken place. Thus, the access to and coverage of the unemployment insurance has been reduced through increasing membership fees, which has led many low-income workers to exit the system (Pejer 2010). Regarding sick leave, 'waiting days' and stricter rules regarding medical certificates have been introduced. These and similar reforms, which contributed to reducing public spending, may move Sweden closer to a less enabling Schumpeterian Workfare State (cf. Jessop 1993).

3.3. A new industrial policy for SMEs: R&D, tax reforms and corporate finance

Beyond investment in skills and education and a welfare system favourable to flexible work and career patterns, the shift towards more knowledge-intensive, high value-added activities also required an active industrial policy stimulating entrepreneurship. Indeed, in an environment that was geared towards favouring very large industrial companies, removing some of the barriers to the establishment of new ventures was essential. Policies with this aim were adopted during the 1990s and included temporary financial aids, administrative support for SMEs and measures to promote management skills (Parker 1999: 75). Moreover, Sweden's gross domestic expenditure on research and development (GERD) increased dramatically from 2.18 per cent in 1981 to 3.75 per cent in 2008, making it – together with Finland, Japan and South Korea – the only OECD countries spending more than 3 per cent of GDP on R&D.[7]

Arguably, these measures constitute the first fully-fledged industrial policy adopted by a Swedish government outside of a brief period of selective interventionism during the 1970s crisis. Hence, it constitutes a remarkable shift in the traditional model, with the state taking on a more interventionist role in promoting structural change.

Yet, Sweden's traditional preference for the concentration of capital in large economic entities was mainly achieved through the corporation tax regime and the bank-loan- and retained-earnings-based financial system, which constituted important hurdles to start-up companies (Henrekson and Jakobsson 2001; Högfeldt 2005).

A reform of the corporation tax system was adopted in 1990 when a 'Reaganite' tax reform reduced corporate tax rates from 55 per cent to 30 per cent. Also, the investment funds system was abolished that had allowed companies to transfer 50 per cent of their pre-tax profits every year into an investment fund, which could then be used for investment projects subject to certain rules and government approval (Davis and Henrekson 1997). This overhaul constituted a decisive break with the RMM and contributed arguably to the expansion of knowledge-intensive SMEs. Under the old system, highly profitable and established companies paid *de facto* less tax than new and small companies that could not yet profit from the investment funds system (Davis and Henrekson 1997).

The tax reform and the growth of the SME sector – in combination with the credit crunch of 1990–1994 – also increased demand for market-based sources of finance (Davis and Henrekson 1997; Månsson and Landström 2006). Here, the changes in the Swedish financial system played a crucial role, which is often not acknowledged in accounts of the recent Swedish recovery that instead focus on the supply of skills and the stimulation of R&D (e.g., Kristensen and Lilja 2011). Peterson (2011), for instance, considers that Sweden lacks a functioning venture capital (VC) market and that successful high-tech clusters like the Örnsköldsvik area relied on traditional sources of finance such as family foundations. Yet, this may be too pessimistic a view of Swedish VC markets. Following the opening up of its financial markets during the 1980s, Sweden has had one of the largest VC markets worldwide in relative terms. Thus, Armour and Cumming's (2006: table 1) figures for the period 1990–2003 place Sweden on an equal footing with the United States (US) in second place in terms of total private equity (PE) – including VC – as a percentage of GDP just behind the United Kingdom (UK) (54.5 per cent for the latter, 29.6 per cent for the US and Sweden). This is far above the average for the 15 countries included in their study (16.8 per cent). Different studies show that the Swedish VC market was at first concentrated in late stages (buyout phase) and did not particularly support high-tech sectors (e.g., Braunerhjelm 2000). Yet, other authors have argued that, as venture capitalists acquire more skills and experience, the high-tech and early-stage investment segments are growing quickly (Karaömerlioglu and Jacobsson 2000). Indeed, even in early stage and expansion stage VC, Sweden had one of the largest markets in Europe (Armour and Cumming 2006, table 1).

The expansion of the PE and VC markets is in part explained by the massive inflow of foreign capital following the liberalization of capital flows during the 1980s. Yet, the Swedish government also played an important role in this process by directly providing public funds to VC firms. Public funds such as the *Industrifonden* and *Innovationsbron AB* were established during the 1970s and 1980s as regional development funds, but were increasingly used as VC providers (Karaömerlioglu and Jacobsson 2000). Also, throughout the 1990s the

Swedish government established different investment vehicles and companies that provide start-ups with capital, counsel and services (Månsson and Landström 2006).

The changing industrial structure, changes in the financial needs of companies and the related rise of a VC market, also changed Sweden's corporate governance landscape. The traditional Swedish model of insider-oriented corporate governance and the close control of large companies by a handful of powerful blockholders through a system of pyramid holdings persist at the core of the Swedish economy (Henrekson and Jakobsson 2011). Also legal change in corporate governance remained limited and legal instruments of insider control were not abolished (Schnyder 2011). However, there is evidence of an increasing diversity of corporate governance regimes within Sweden. Henrekson and Jakobsson (2011) find that, besides the traditional insider–blockholder corporate governance model, increasing numbers of companies in Sweden are either fully owned subsidiaries of foreign MNCs or controlled by PE firms, which increases the heterogeneity of the Swedish corporate governance regime at the aggregate level.

Overall, tax reforms and financial reforms have eliminated the complementarity between high corporate taxation, investment fund finance, scarce credit and Sweden's specialization in Fordist mass production in the manufacturing industry and favoured a more equity-market-based system and a more SME-based industrial structure.

3.4. Wage bargaining, jobless growth and the emerging low-wage sector: new complementarity or Achilles heel?

In terms of industrial relations, after the demise of peak-level wage bargaining in 1990, the late 1990s saw a return to more co-ordinated forms of wage setting. After several years of industry-level bargaining, in 1997 the trade unions and employer associations of the manufacturing industries concluded a collaboration agreement (the *Industriavtal*, Industrial Agreement, IA).[8] This agreement – followed by similar collaboration agreements in other industries – specifies the procedures to be adopted in collective bargaining and gave rise to a pattern bargaining system where the export-oriented manufacturing sector played the role of norm-setter. Thus, the collective bargaining system, while often portrayed as a pure industry-level system since the 1990s (see, for example, Oliver 2011), has been considerably recentralized during the late 1990s. Indeed co-ordinated wage setting across sectors can be seen as a functional equivalent to a centralized system (OECD 1997). While the norm set by the export sector can be renegotiated at the industry level, *de facto* the export sector norm has the effect of a 'floor rate' that is respected by other sectors (Calmfors 2008).

A new labour market authority responsible for the facilitation of collective bargaining and wage formation – the *Medlingsinstitute* (National Mediation Office) – was established in 2000 and charged with making sure that the manufacturing sector would maintain its role as 'pattern-setter' for the rest of the Swedish economy (Calmfors and Larsson 2011). This re-introduction of wage *co-ordination* is a very significant element, indicating that Sweden is far from 'converging' on a pure market-based model.

A more serious problem than wage setting, however, was the question of unemployment. The sustained growth of the period 1995–2008 was more the result of productivity increases than job creation and unemployment rates remained a political liability for the SAP (Pontusson 2011). The inability of the SAP governments in power between 1995 and 2006 to bring down unemployment – despite a booming economy – was arguably the main reasons for their electoral loss during the 2006 election (Agius 2007). The now governing centre-right Alliance for Sweden has learned the lessons from this failure.

The centre-right leader Fredrik Reinfeldt's election campaign largely focused on the issue of unemployment (Agius 2007). Since their coming to power in 2006, the centre-right government has managed to reverse the upward trend of unemployment rates during the first half of the 2000s (from 5.6 per cent in 2000 to 7.7 per cent in 2007, but down to 6.2 per cent in 2008) (OECD 2010). In April 2011, Reinfeldt and the other governing party leaders claimed that – through additional value added tax (VAT) reductions on certain services and additional income tax reductions on 'earned income' – Sweden was moving closer to the 'goal of full employment' (Reinfeldt *et al.* 2011). A goal, it should be noted, that had been abandoned by the SAP in 1990. Arguably, different factors contributed to this trend: macro-economic factors (exports to emerging market economies, competitive exchange rate); 'workfare measures'; relative wage restraint achieved through co-ordinated wage bargaining and tax reforms. Yet another important element was the Alliance's reliance on growth in private service jobs.

Like many 'post-industrial' countries, job growth in manufacturing became increasingly sluggish. Moreover, the strategy of job growth through public sector expansion that prevailed notably during the 1970s, when 90 per cent of job growth was in the public sector (Heclo and Madsen 1987: 165), reached its limits at the very latest with the deep financial crisis of the early 1990s. As a result, since the 1990s experts and politicians alike increasingly played with the idea of stimulating job creation in the private service sector in order to bring down high levels of unemployment. After heated debates during the 1990s, a so-called RUT-deduction (*rut-avdrag*) (RUT is the Swedish acronym for 'cleaning, maintenance and washing') aimed at stimulating job creation in the domestic services sector was finally introduced after the centre-right's electoral victory in 2006 (cf. Bowman and Cole 2009). As of 1 July 2007, households can deduct the equivalent of 50 per cent of the cost of hiring domestic workers from taxes. As a result, the domestic services industry has experience an impressive boom with the value of such services provided in Sweden increasing from SEK 240m in 2007 to SEK 2,678m in 2010 (*Dagens Industri*, 18 May 2011).

At first glance, the low-skill and low-wage private services sector seems to complement well the productivity-based and largely jobless growth in the manufacturing industries. However, it also implies that for the first time in Sweden there is an increasing labour market dualism, which contributes to increasing levels of wage differentials in a previously very egalitarian country. There is a real risk that this low-wage sector may become the Achilles heel of the 'new' Swedish model. One way in which this may happen is through its long-term impact on the skill profile of Swedish workers. Pontusson (2011) suggests that there is a direct link between income equality and equality in education and skill levels. It is too early to tell what effects the institutionalization of a low-wage sector through tax subsidies for domestic services will have not just on the skill levels of the workers in these industries, but also on their children's skill levels and ultimately on social mobility. If a certain group of the labour force (mainly immigrant and female)[9] gets locked into the low wage sector, this would seriously undermine what remains of the social-democratic model.

A second, important question is the impact that such a labour market structure will have on the trade unions' traditional role in promoting wage- and skill-compression rather than sanctioning inequalities (Swenson 1989: 29). If we assume that unionization rates remain high, even within the emerging low-wage sector, the very logic of the private service sector based on low skills and low wages may create strong tensions among union members in different sectors; not because skill-level based wage differentials cannot be justified as such, but because a sector of the economy whose success relies on low wages (rather than productivity increases) reduces very considerably the unions' leeway to enhance union members' working conditions. This in turn undermines the unions' 'membership logic'. The negotiations over the new Industrial Agreement of 2011 hint already at the tensions within the unions that can emerge from the co-existence of low-wage and high-wage sectors. Thus, one local union representative in the fast food sector expressed his sector's dissatisfaction with the proposed agreement, stating: 'What is the point with being member of a union that cannot fight for higher salaries, [because it] is tied to an "industrial agreement" …?' (*LO-Tidningen*, 2 May 2011). The reduced leeway for unions to improve their members' working conditions may prove a very tricky circle to square. As such, one might wonder whether the existence of a low-wage sector and high unionization rates are *per se* incompatible institutional features.

More generally, the existence of a low-wage sector creates a strong potential for 'normative dissonance'. One sign of this potential can be seen in the heated debates around the introduction of the 'RUT deductions' since the early 1990s (the so-called 'maid debate') (see Bowman and Cole 2009). Left and feminist circles were increasingly hostile to the proposals despite potential beneficial effects on employment, on grounds that it simply shifted the exploitation from Swedish middle-class women towards immigrant women. Consequently, the SAP ultimately rejected the idea of subsidizing such tax breaks in the run up to the 2006 elections. This shows that among a part of the Swedish public the normative aversion to the institutionalization of low-wage work is strong, because it clashes with the Swedish model's egalitarian ambitions. This new institution may hence be based on weak normative support.

4. CONCLUSION

I have explained the 'decline' of the traditional Swedish model by the propensity of the institution of 'wage solidarity' to create 'normative dissonances', which triggered a process of defection by the actors governed by the institution (cf. Swenson 1989). This type of change is consistent with recent theories of endogenous and actor-driven institutional change (cf. Jackson 2010). It explains why, contrary to the VoC argument, the Swedish system was destabilized despite strong meso-level linkages between institutional spheres. Indeed, institutions that appeal to actors' self-restraint, not in their own interest but with reference to some 'higher objective' (such as 'equality', 'solidarity' etc.), may be particularly prone to defection (cf. Höpner 2007: 11).

Yet, contrary to recent theories of rule-taker-driven processes of change, the transformation of the Swedish system was not incremental, but radical. The reason for this is that the micro-level defection from the existing institutional arrangement in the area of industrial relations undermined the broader macro-level socio-economic compromise that had been crucial to the model (the so-called 'Saltsjöbad spirit'). It is through this mechanism of increasing contentiousness of relations between different actors that the 'exhaustion' of wage solidarity spilled over into other institutional spheres. Indeed, the SAP's strategic reaction to the radicalization of the labour movement led to far-reaching changes first in the area of labour law (1970s) and then in the area of financial market regulations (1980s) and welfare services (1990s/2000s).

It was only after the profound crisis of 1990–1994 that an industrial policy was adopted, which – through reforms in skill formation, education and training, the welfare regime and the financial system – finally seems to have given rise to a successful new model.

Yet, there are reasons to believe that the emerging new model, like the old one, contains contradictions between the actors' ambitions and expectations and the outcomes that the new institutional arrangements will produce, in turn casting doubt on the long-term viability of the new arrangements. Kristensen (2011b), for instance, underscores that many of the social policies facilitating the new growth regime are not consciously designed to complement the social democratic model, but rely mainly on neoliberal premises of individual responsibility and competition between market participants. This may explain why the new model appears patently insensitive towards striking contradictions between social democratic ambitions and recent reforms such as those regarding the low-wage sector. Therefore, what seems at first glance to arise miraculously like a splendid phoenix from the ashes may ultimately turn out to resemble more a Frankensteinian homunculus composed of incompatible and incoherent parts.

The reason for this 'incompatibility' has little to do with an 'incoherence' of ordering principles across institutional spheres; indeed, the traditional Swedish model was able to deal with the meso-level co-existence of market mechanisms and extra market forms of co-ordination successfully for a long time. The increasing market orientation of the model may hence not be the main problem. The more fundamental challenge to the stability of the new system lies in the great potential of institutions in the sphere of welfare and labour markets to create at the micro-level 'normative dissonances' between the social democratic ideals and the new realities.

Indeed the emerging low-wage sector has the potential to create similar 'normative dissonances' as 'wage solidarity', because it implies that a part of the workforce is subject to relatively harsh working conditions in an institutional setting that still signals to people the importance of social democratic values of 'equality' and 'decent working conditions'. The stability of the new model may hence depend either on a move away from these social-democratic ideals, or – conversely – on finding ways in which low-wage work in private services can at the same time provide decent working conditions and be cheap.

Steinmo (2010) reports survey results that show that Swedish citizens are increasingly reluctant to pay for other people's welfare. Such changes in attitudes of Swedes towards inequalities seem a regrettable but necessary complement to reduce 'normative dissonance' in the new context, but clearly constitute a fundamental challenge to the values that define the Swedish model, old or new.

Biographical note: Gerhard Schnyder is Lecturer in Comparative Management at King's College London, UK.

ACKNOWLEDGEMENTS

I am grateful to Richard Deeg, Tony Edwards, Gregory Jackson and participants in the ICaTSEM project meetings, as well as two anonymous referees, for most helpful comments, and to Philipp Kern for excellent research assistance. The research leading to these results has received funding from the European Community's Seventh Framework Programme (FP7/2007-2011) under grant agreement number 225349 (ICaTSEM project).

NOTES

1 Deeg (2007) defines institutional coherence as different institutional spheres being organized according to similar 'logics' or 'ordering principles' (market-based versus extra-market co-ordination).
2 I use the concept of 'normative dissonance' in order to capture a situation that Peter Swenson described as a 'moral economy'. He defines a moral economy as 'a pattern of exchange relations constrained by values and traditions that societal elites impose in interaction with subordinate groups' (Swenson 1989: 12). Swenson underscores that élites' failure to enforce the norms that they establish often leads to sentiments of

'injustice' among rule- (norm-) takers and provokes 'spontaneous rebellions'. I designate as 'normative dissonance' a situation where rule-takers perceive 'injustice' owing to a (perceived or actual) discrepancy between a given institution's affirmed goals or the norms 'signalled' by it and the impact that the same institution has on the actors governed by it.

3 Steinmo (2010: 62) reports that TCO and SACO organized 18.2 per cent of the workforce in 1950, but 41.7 per cent in 1989.

4 Deeg and Jackson (2007) distinguish the micro level of a national business system (the interaction between institutions and rule-takers) from the meso level (the linkages between institutional domains, e.g., complementarities) and the macro level (the politics, actor coalitions and processes that govern institutional reforms).

5 Kristensen (2011b) seems to acknowledge this when talking about 'experimentalist' reactions to new contexts.

6 Kristensen and Lilja (2011) identify as a second important complementarity in the 'new model' the match between the supposedly 'reflexive' and non-hierarchical way of work organization in Sweden (so called 'learning organizations') and its fit with the New Economy that requires increasing 'reflexivity' and worker involvement. For reasons of space this dimension cannot be discussed here. However, see Thompson and McHugh (2002: ch. 11) for a general criticism of this well-rehearsed argument about the necessary match between more flexible, post-bureaucratic 'learning organizations' and the 'New Economy'.

7 The average GERD for OECD countries in 2007 was 2.3 per cent; see http://stats. oecd.org/OECDStat_Metadata/ShowMetadata.ashx?Dataset=CSP2010&Coords= [SUB].[GERD]&ShowOnWeb = true&Lang = en (accessed 28 July 2012).

8 This agreement was renewed on 1 July 2011.

9 Of the workforce in this emerging domestic services industry, 90 per cent are immigrant women mainly from Poland and Russia (Gavanas 2010: 43).

REFERENCES

Agius, C. (2007) 'Sweden's 2006 parliamentary election and after: contesting or consolidating the Swedish model?', *Parliamentary Affairs* 60(4): 585–600.

Albrecht, J., van den Berg, G. and Vroman, S. (2004) 'The knowledge lift: the Swedish adult education program that aimed to eliminate low worker skill levels', *IFAU Working Paper 17:* 1–43.

Anderson, K. (2001) 'The politics of retrenchment in a social democratic welfare state: reform of Swedish pensions and unemployment insurance', *Comparative Political Studies* 34(9): 1063–91.

Andersson, D. (2003) 'LO-ekonomerna inför verkligheten – 1951 och 2001', in L. Erixon (ed.), *Den svenska modellens ekonomiska politik*, Stockholm: Atlas, pp. 145–63.

Anxo, D. and Niklasson, H. (2008) 'The Swedish model: revival after the turbulent 1990s?', *IILS Discussion Paper 189:* 1–35.

Armour, J. and Cumming, D. (2006) 'The legislative road to Silicon Valley', *Oxford Economic Papers* 58(4): 596–35.

Belfrage, C. (2008) 'Towards "universal financialisation" in Sweden?', *Contemporary Politics* 14(3): 277–96.

Bergh, A. and Erlingsson, G. (2009) 'Liberalization without retrenchment: understanding the consensus on Swedish welfare state reforms', *Scandinavian Political Studies* 32(1): 71–93.

Blomqvist, P. (2004) 'The choice revolution: privatization of Swedish welfare services in the 1990s', *Social Policy & Administration* 38(2): 139–55.

Bowman, J. and Cole, A. (2009) 'Do working mothers oppress other women? The Swedish "maid debate" and the welfare state politics of gender equality', *Signs: Journal of Women in Culture and Society* 35(1): 157–84.

Braunerhjelm, P. (2000) 'Replik till Karaömerlioglu och Jacobsson: Starka slutsatser om venture kapital saknar grund', *Ekonomisk Debatt* 28(4): 368–73.

Calmfors, L. (2008) 'Kris i det svenska avtalssystemet?', *Ekonomisk Debatt* 36(1): 6–19.

Calmfors, L. and Larsson, A. (2011) 'Pattern bargaining and wage leadership in a small open economy', *CESIFO Working Paper 3510:* 1–37.

Davis, S.J. and Henrekson, M. (1997) 'Industrial policy, employer size, and economic performance in Sweden', in R.B. Freeman *et al.* (eds), *The Welfare State in Transition: Reforming the Swedish Model*, Chicago, IL: University of Chicago Press, pp. 353–98.

Deeg, R. (2007) 'Complementarity and institutional change in capitalist systems', *Journal of European Public Policy* 14(4): 611–30.

Deeg, R. and Jackson, G. (2007) 'Towards a more dynamic theory of capitalist variety', *Socio-Economic Review* 5(1): 149–79.

The Economist (2011) 'The Swedish economy: north star', 9 June.

Esping-Andersen, G. (1999) *Social Foundations of Postindustrial Economies*, New York: Oxford University Press.

Gavanas, A. (2010) 'Who cleans the welfare state? Migration, informalization, social exclusion and domestic services in Stockholm', *Institute for Futures Studies Research Report 3:* 1–95.

Gibbons-Wood, D. and Lange, T. (2000) 'Developing core skills – lessons from Germany and Sweden', *Education + Training* 42(1): 24–32.

Hall, P.A. and Soskice, D. (2001) 'An introduction to varieties of capitalism', in P.A. Hall and D. Soskice (eds), *Varieties of Capitalism. The Institutional Foundations of Comparative Advantage*, Oxford: Oxford University Press, pp. 1–68.

Heclo, H. and Madsen, H. (1987) *Policy and Politics in Sweden: Principled Pragmatism*, Philadelphia, PA: Temple University Press.

Henrekson, M. and Jakobsson, U. (2001) 'Where Schumpeter was nearly right – the Swedish model and capitalism, socialism and democracy', *Journal of Evolutionary Economics* 11(3): 331–58.

Henrekson, M. and Jakobsson, U. (2003) 'The transformation of ownership policy and structure in Sweden: convergence towards the Anglo-Saxon model', *New Political Economy* 8(1): 73–102.

Henrekson, M. and Jakobsson, U. (2011) 'The Swedish corporate control model: convergence, persistence or decline?', *IFN Working Paper 857:* 1–40.

Högfeldt, P. (2005) 'The history and politics of corporate ownership in Sweden', in R. Morck (ed.), *A History of Corporate Governance around the World*, Chicago, IL: University of Chicago Press, pp. 517–79.

Höpner, M. (2007) 'Coordination and organization. The two dimensions of nonliberal capitalism', *MPIfG Discussion Paper 07/12:* 1–33.

Jackson, G. (2010) 'Actors and institutions', in G. Morgan *et al.* (eds), *The Oxford Handbook of Comparative Institutional Analysis*, Oxford: Oxford University Press, pp. 63–86.

Jessop, B. (1993) 'Towards a Schumpeterian workfare state? Preliminary remarks on post-Fordist political economy', *Studies in Political Economy* 40: 7–39.

Jordan, J. (2006) 'Mothers, wives, and workers: explaining gendered dimensions of the welfare state', *Comparative Political Studies* 39(9): 1109–32.

Karaömerliougu, D. and Jacobsson, S. (2000) 'Den svenska "venture capital" industrin – en stor, diversifierad men ännu omogen ny bransch', *Ekonomisk Debatt* 28(4): 374–76.

Kenworthy, L. (2006) 'Institutional coherence and macroeconomic performance', *Socio-Economic Review* 4(1): 69–91.

Kildal, N. (2001) *Workfare Tendencies in Scandinavian Welfare Policies*, Geneva: International Labour Office.

Korpi, W. (1982) 'The historical compromise and its dissolution', in B. Rydén and W. Bergström (eds), *Sweden: Choices for Economic and Social Policy in the 1980s*, London: Georg Allen and Unwin, pp. 124–42.

Kristensen, P. (2011a) 'The co-evolution of experimentalist business systems and enabling welfare states: Nordic countries in transition', in P. Kristensen and K. Lilja (eds), *Nordic Capitalisms and Globalization*, Oxford: Oxford University Press, pp. 1–46.

Kristensen, P. (2011b) 'Developing comprehensive, enabling welfare sates for offensive experimentalist business practices', in P. Kristensen and K. Lilja (eds), *Nordic Capitalisms and Globalization*, Oxford: Oxford University Press, pp. 220–58.

Kristensen, P. and Lilja, K (eds) (2011) *Nordic Capitalisms and Globalization. New Forms of Economic Organization and Welfare Institutions*, Oxford: Oxford University Press.

Leira, A. (2006) 'Parenthood change and policy reform in Scandinavia, 1970s–2000s', in A. Ellingsæter and A. Leira (eds), *Politicising Parenthood in Scandinavia*, Bristol: The Policy Press, pp. 27–51.

Lindbeck, A. (1997) *The Swedish Experiment*, Stockholm: SNS.

Lindbom, A. (2001) 'Dismantling the social democratic welfare model? Has the Swedish welfare state lost its defining characteristics?' *Scandinavian Political Studies* 24(3): 171–93.

Meidner, R. (1993) 'Why did the Swedish model fail?' *The Socialist Register* 29: 211–28.

Månsson, N. and Landström, H. (2006) 'Business angels in a changing economy: the case of Sweden', *Venture Capital* 8(4): 281–301.

Oliver, R. (2011) 'Powerful remnants? The politics of egalitarian bargaining institutions in Italy and Sweden', *Socio-Economic Review* 9(3): 533–66.

OECD (1997) 'Economic performance and the structure of collective bargaining', *Employment Outlook:* 63–89.

OECD (2010) *Labour Force Statistics 1989–2009*, available at http://www.oecd.org/document/46/0,3746,en_2649_34251_2023214_1_1_1_1,00.html

OECD (2011) *STAN STructural ANalysis Database*, available at http://www.oecd.org/sti/stan/ (accessed 28 July 2012).

Parker, R. (1999) 'From national champions to small and medium sized enterprises: changing policy emphasis in France, Germany and Sweden', *Journal of Public Policy* 19(1): 63–89.

Parker, R. (2006) 'Small business and entrepreneurship in the knowledge economy : a comparison of Australia and Sweden', *New Political Economy* 11(2): 201–26.

Pejer, M. (2010) 'De fattigaste gick ur a-kassan', *Arbetet*, 12 October 2010, available at http://arbetet.se/2010/10/12/de-fattigaste-gick-ur-a-kassan/ (accessed 28 July 2012).

Peterson, C. (2011) 'Sweden: from large corporations towards a knowledge-intensive economy', in P. Kristensen and K. Lilja (eds), *Nordic Capitalisms and Globalization*, Oxford: Oxford University Press, pp. 183–219.

Pontusson, J. (1992) *The Limits of Social Democracy. Investment Politics in Sweden*, Ithaca, NY: Cornell University Press.

Pontusson, J. (1997) 'Between neo-liberalism and the German model: Swedish capitalism in transition', in C. Crouch and W. Streeck (eds), *The Political Economy of Modern Capitalism*, London: Sage, pp. 55–70.

Pontusson, J. (2011) 'Once again a model: Nordic social democracy in a globalized world', in J. Cronin *et al.* (eds), *What's Left of the Left? Democrats and Social Democrats in Challenging Times.* Durham, NC: Duke University Press, pp. 89–115.

Reinfeldt, F., Björklund, J., Olofsson, M. and Hägglund, G. (2011) 'Nytt jobbskatteavdrag införs redan till årsskiftet', *Dagens Nyheter* (online edition), 13 April, available at http://www.dn.se/debatt/nytt-jobbskatteavdrag-infors-redan-till-arsskiftet (accessed 28 July 2012).

Reiter, J. (2003) 'Financial globalisation, corporate ownership, and the end of Swedish corporatism?', *New Political Economy* 8(1): 103–25.

Schnyder, G. (2011) 'Revisiting the party paradox of finance capitalism: evidence from Switzerland, Sweden and the Netherlands', *Comparative Political Studies* 44(2): 184–210.

Steinmo, S. (2010) *The Evolution of Modern States: Sweden, Japan and the United States*, Cambridge: Cambridge University Press.

Swenson, P. (1989) *Fair Shares: Unions, Pay, and Politics in Sweden and West Germany*, Ithaca, NY: Cornell University Press.

Thompson, P. and McHugh, D. (2002) *Work Organisations*, 3rd edn, Basingstoke: Palgrave.

Trampusch, C. (2005) 'Institutional resettlement. the case of early retirement in Germany', in W. Streeck and K. Thelen (eds), *Beyond Continuity: Institutional Change in Advanced Political Economies*, Oxford: Oxford University Press, pp. 203–28.

Waxell, A. and Malmberg, A. (2007) 'What is global and what is local in knowledge-generating interaction? The case of the biotech cluster in Uppsala, Sweden', *Entrepreneurship & Regional Development* 19(2): 137–59.

The trajectory of institutional change in Germany, 1979–2009

Gregory Jackson and Arndt Sorge

ABSTRACT   Over the last three decades, the German political economy can be characterized by both institutional continuity and change. Understanding the dynamics of institutional change therefore requires an examination of the interplay of changes in formal institutional rules and how organizations respond to these changes by strategic attempts to promote or hinder further change in institutions. The macro-level political story of institutional change shows a number of paradoxes resulting in unexpected and often incomplete forms of market liberalization shaped by continued support for some core features of Germany's social market economy. The resulting erosion of Germany's co-ordinated model of economic organization through networks and business associations has gone hand-in-hand with the attempts to preserve these institutions for core workers and sectors of the economy in the face of changing environments. The result is a more varied institutional landscape characterized by international diffusion of liberal policies and the politics of their variable re-embedding within a long-term path of institutional continuity.

1.   INTRODUCTION

The institutions of the German political economy display both remarkable *continuity* and dramatic *change* over the last thirty years. Germany is often considered to be a "co-ordinated market economy" (CME) (Hall and Soskice 2001). Based on the embeddedness of firms in strong sectoral and corporatist associations, as well as dense inter-firm networks (Yamamura and Streeck 2003), stakeholder co-ordination takes place across different institutional domains of financial markets, corporate governance, employment relations and training. However, these co-ordinating institutions have become less encompassing in scope over time. Associations now play a lesser role in financial markets, collective bargaining and training. Likewise, network-based forms of governance (bank and cross-ownership of shares in joint-stock companies) have also weakened substantially. Thus, one can observe substantial liberalization, but also adjustments of existing co-ordinated institutions to these changing circumstances.

Understanding institutional change requires looking at changes in the formal rules, as well as their social and economic prerequisites. One related historical specificity of the German case is the intense problem situation of German unification starting in 1990 combined with the threats and opportunities presented by internationalization. The extension of the German political and economic institutions to the East not only brought back questions about national identity and policy-making; it also stretched the welfare state and tax system to its limits. A new search began to pursue economic performance in the private sector, while balancing of public and social insurance revenue budgets (Streeck 2009). Meanwhile, the external environment changed rapidly and shaped the renegotiation of socio-political compromises underlying several key institutions. Decision-makers were influenced by neoliberal and shareholder-value concepts that diffused through international business contacts (Fiss and Zajac 2004) and supranational regulation (Callaghan and Höpner 2005). However, business and political élites did not form a unitary coalition behind neo-liberal policies – rather, business supported modification but not dismantling of institutionalized co-ordination, particularly in sectors where these yield strong comparative advantages. Other powerful stakeholders and the consensus-oriented features of German politics meant that liberalization occurred through selective and sometimes piecemeal approach to reforms, alongside a dynamic adaptation of organizations to the new meanings and boundaries of institutions.

This contribution looks at the change of economic institutions in light of changes in domestic policies and politics, as well as international influences. In this way, the German case may be suggestive for unravelling the interplay of international influences and the domestic change of institutions in other countries. Reforms sharpened conflicts between corporate governance and the welfare state institutions, in particular. The particular configuration of liberalization in Germany was therefore paradoxical: whereas business maintained high co-ordination among core employees and suppliers, the parallel retrenchment of the welfare state and deregulation of the atypical labour contracts has created distributional conflicts between corporate insiders and outsiders.

2. CRITICAL JUNCTURES AND INSTITUTIONAL CHANGE IN GERMANY

This section provides an overview of the major institutional changes induced by state policies in Germany over the last three decades, which are also summarized in Table A1 in the Appendix (on data sources, see Jackson and Wylegala 2012). While the broad trend can be described in terms of liberalization, these reforms have occurred at different times across different institutional domains involving different degrees of discontinuity with the past and sometimes moving in different directions.

Regarding *financial markets*, legal reforms aimed at wide ranging liberalization. In the 1980s, domestic banks faced a declining demand for credit and loosening of relationships with large firms. The first reforms in 1986 and 1989 opened up the stock exchange trading system through electronic trading and a futures exchange. The critical juncture was the series of four Financial Market Promotion Acts in 1990, 1994, 1998 and 2002. The 1990 act eliminated various taxes of financial market transactions, and established mutual funds and other investment vehicles. The 1994 act established a single national financial services regulator, which represented a major shift from the tradition of corporatist self-regulation toward an increased the role of the state along the model of the Securities and Exchange Commission (SEC) in the United States (US). New regulations were established regarding disclosure and insider trading. The 1998 reforms promoted the stock market and equity finance through new listing requirements and allowing companies to adopt international accounting standards – giving firms a choice to between domestic creditor-oriented rules or international equity-oriented rules. The 2002 act renewed stock market regulation and restricted share price manipulation. Finally, 2002 reforms allowed the tax-free sale of long-term equity stakes held by banks and corporations.

These reforms shifted Germany away from its bank-based financial system and toward more market-orientated finance. Since 1990, around 20 per cent of shares in Germany are held by foreign investors – usually institutional investors from the US or the United Kingdom (UK). The orientation of these investors toward financial returns and arm's-length approach to investment has become an important force in corporate governance. Meanwhile, German banks and firms now have many financial options that were not previously available. These changes have nonetheless had an uneven or even bifurcating effect (Deeg 2009). Large commercial banks, such as Deutsche Bank, underwent very dramatic shifts away from relationship banking and toward investment banking. Meanwhile, the large savings bank and co-operative banking sector maintained a much more traditional relationship banking model, albeit in an evolving form. Overall, the degree of 'financialization' in Germany remains modest, since the household sector is reluctant to purchase equities and private pensions remain modest. Reforms have operated by institutional layering, whereby new practices are facilitated through incentives and rules placed alongside pre-existing practices.

Regarding *corporate governance*, legal reforms increased the orientation of large, listed corporations toward shareholder value. Corporate law reforms in the mid-1990s were focused on minor aspects of accounting and promoting incorporation of small firms. The 1998 reform (KonTrag) was a critical juncture and mixed different political motivations – the desire by the *Christlich Demokratische Union* (CDU) to increase transparency of capital markets, the aim of the *Sozialdemokratische Partei Deutschlands* (SPD) to limit the power of big banks in Germany, and new US-inspired debates over corporate governance (Ziegler 2000). Key provisions included improving auditor independence, as well as disclosure of multiple supervisory board memberships and ownership stakes exceeding 5 per cent. Shareholder influence increased by eliminating multiple voting rights and voting rights restrictions, barring banks from using proxy votes in conjunction with direct shareholding exceeding 5 per cent, requiring banks to solicit proxy instructions from shareholders, and giving the supervisory board greater duties of financial oversight. Restrictions on share buybacks and stock options were removed.

The fall of Enron and recent emergence of the sub-prime financial crisis refocused attention on corporate governance practices. A German Code of Corporate Governance was issued in 2002, outlining best practices inspired from a largely shareholder-oriented perspective, but without much actual regulatory influence (Luetz *et al.* 2011). The new code is embedded in law via a 'comply or explain' rule in the Transparency and Disclosure law (Transparenz- und Publizitätsgesetz). Subsequent reforms improved the independence of the auditor (2005), streamlined the process of shareholder lawsuits (2005), mandated disclosure of executive pay (2005), and streamlined the process for exercising proxy votes (2009).

Takeover rules remain a critical area of regulation. Germany adopted a voluntary takeover code in 1995 to fill the legal gap regarding takeover bids in the absence of a European directive. After a period of low compliance and the hostile takeover of Mannesmann, a new European Union (EU) takeover directive was proposed but deadlocked in the European Parliament (Callaghan and Höpner 2005). A central issue opposed by German industry was the requirement for board 'neutrality' during hostile bids (Culpepper 2011). Germany then passed a Takeover Act in 2002 replacing board neutrality with an option for defensive actions given prior shareholder approval. Specifically, the shareholders' meeting utilize a 75 per cent majority vote to empower management regarding defensive actions for an 18-month period. In 2004, a European Takeover Directive was passed based on principles of the UK Takeover Code (Goergen *et al.* 2005), but allowing Germany to opt-out of provisions regarding some takeover defences.

On the whole, the scope for defensive actions has become relatively constrained.[1] While some legal uncertainty remains, the board must generally be neutral. Defensive strategies are limited to share buybacks, engaging in alternative acquisitions and searching for a white knight. Legal reforms on takeovers and equity swaps, alongside the changes in corporate ownership, have opened the takeover market substantially. During 1991–1997, Germany averaged 1,479 deals annually worth 1.4 per cent of gross domestic product (GDP) (Jackson and Miyajima 2007). During 1998–2005, this level increased to 1,607 deals annually, with a value equivalent to 7.5 per cent of GDP, three-quarters of which was cross-border. The value of domestic deals was 1.9 per cent of GDP compared to 2.4 per cent of GDP for German firms acquiring foreign targets or 3.4 per cent of GDP for foreign firms acquiring German targets. Nevertheless, the number of hostile takeover bids has remained low. The takeover of Mannesmann by Vodafone in 2000 certainly shifted managers' awareness toward the importance of maintaining share prices to hold off unsolicited bidders (Höpner and Jackson 2006).

Taken together, legal reform has increased the salience of shareholder interests (Klages 2012), while often remaining below the radar screen of public debate (Culpepper 2011). Little stakeholder-focused legislation passed, apart from recent regulation of executive compensation (2009) stressing more caution toward stock options and reasonable levels of total remuneration. Nonetheless, unions have succeeded in stopping reforms that would directly endanger the role of co-determination. Corporate governance reform has thus proceeded largely through institutional layering. The growing influence of shareholders and liberalized use of corporate equity co-exist with a largely unchallenged institution of employee codetermination through the supervisory board and works councils. New rules have thus been layered onto past rules, creating a new combination or hybrid of shareholder and stakeholder corporate governance (Faust 2012; Jackson, 2005).

Regarding *employment and industrial relations*, secure employment has been a major institutional feature that reflected the strength of labour in the post-war period (Emmenegger and Marx 2011). However, Germany has been marked by the after-effects of unification: steeply rising unemployment; rapid assimilation of wages between East and West; and massive social transfers from West to East (c. €150 billion per year). On the whole, the institutional package of industrial relations was absorbed in East Germany. Past traditions of management and severe challenges of transformation from a non-capitalist past often led to tightly integrated workforces in co-managed plants and enterprises. If German industrial relations are often typified as harmonious, East Germany fitted in rapidly by becoming super-harmonious, despite the frenzied and conflictual fight to keep companies alive, or maybe because of it. Meanwhile, trade union membership has faced long-term decline. Owing to increasing unemployment in the East and the perceived inability of the new West German unions satisfactorily to address that problem in collective bargaining, unionization soon sunk below West German levels. Comparing East and West in 2009, collective bargaining coverage is lower (34 per cent versus 52 per cent) and works councils represent fewer employees (38 per cent versus 44 per cent), so that only 18 per cent of the East German workforce are covered by these two key institutions (Hans-Boeckler Foundation 2012).

Meanwhile, long-term employment and co-operative industrial relations have also undergone slow erosion in the core sectors of the economy. Three dynamics help explain this. First, collective bargaining coverage become less centralized owing to the growth of company-level rather than sectoral agreements. Wage restraint did help sustain Germany's export surplus in core manufacturing sectors, including investment goods to newly industrializing countries such as China and Brazil. Membership in employers' associations has nonetheless declined, as employers seek more flexibility and seek to cut labour costs. Second, while co-operative industrial relations and long-term employment has remained an asset for German industry, the coverage of these institutions is slowly shrinking with the gradual shift of employment from manufacturing to services. The number of employees in manufacturing was 7.3 million in 1979 and jumped to 10.6 million after Unification in 1990, before declining to 7.4 million in 2009 (Statistisches Bundesamt various years). While German manufacturing employment remains high relative to many other advanced Organization for Economic Co-operation and Development (OECD) economies, its relative share declined from 31.4 per cent to 18.5 per cent of total employment between 1979 and 2009. Third, labour law reform liberalized new patterns of atypical employment. Restrictions on the use of agency work were loosened in 1997 and abolished in 2003. The duration of fixed-term employment contracts was also extended to 24 months in 1996.

Taken together with welfare state reforms discussed below, these trends point toward a growing dualism in the German labour market (Palier and Thelen 2010). As will be discussed below, these trends were reinforced by reforms in the social insurance system and growth in active labour market policies. But despite liberalization, several reforms have sought to at least partially counterbalance existing erosion of German industrial relations. First, works councils were modernized in 2001 in ways that made their structure less bureaucratic and more adaptable to the diverse needs of small and medium enterprises, complex network forms of organization, and different categories of outsourced or temporary employees. Second, the state sought to support social protection by passing a minimum wage for the construction industry as a way of preventing social dumping, given the vast increase of migrant labour in the industry.

Regarding *training and skill formation*, legal reform has not been a major driver of change. The constellation of interest groups is complex, and the social partners and state often face their own internal conflicts of interest. Still, several trends are important. First, policies have sought to broaden and upgrade skills within the occupational training system. Here, a critical juncture was the new regulation of trades in the metal industry and in electrical engineering within the dual system of training during 1990. Reform moved away from specialized and toward broader occupational profiles (Busemeyer 2009a, 2009b). Four new information technology (IT) related occupational profiles were introduced, and the process to upgrade skill profiles was steamlined. Second, the state invested directly in rather generalist, college-type of education through Berufsakademien and Fachhochschulen. An important concern was to better prepare school leavers with deficiencies for basic apprenticeship training, since increasing numbers failed to get places within the apprenticeship system. A series of measures and programmes aimed to provide either substitute training in public schools/workshops, or to remedy skills and knowledge deficiencies of entrants into the labour market. Other policies aimed to make training by apprenticeships more accessible by (re-)introducing trades with two-year training duration in 2003, a reinvention of an older pattern abandoned after 1969. Such training programmes were meant for less demanding occupations, to at least offer something to school leavers with low achievement. Third, the state also intervened to support social partners in ensuring or increasing the supply of occupational training through new funding schemes in 2004 and 2008.

The dual system of training has thus remained attractive, despite some increasing company specificity of training. But it has also suffered from declining interest of employers in offering training places during times of economic downturn. Moreover, the accessibility of training places to lower secondary school (Hauptschule) leavers, notably youngsters from migrant families, has become a problem. There have been shifting coalitions: the state versus the social partners, and unions/the state versus the employers. This constellation led to piecemeal adaptation of existing arrangements.

In terms of the *welfare state*, economic pressures facing unemployment insurance, social benefits and the pension system have grown. Through the 1990s, the costs of German unification became increasingly apparent and placed pressures on the welfare state through rising unemployment and declining labour force participation. The massive transfer of money into the East was mainly financed on the basis of contributions levied on labour costs, so that employment became disadvantaged. Low labour market participation meant reduced contributions that were acute during cyclical downturns. The German state adopted a speedily organized but ill-crafted retrenchment of welfare payments and unemployment benefits, an operation that became known as the 'Hartz Reforms', in 2003. These moves ushered in a new and far more conflictual era of 'managed austerity' (Vail 2010). Meanwhile, employment growth was pursued through the expansion of poorly paid service work or temporary forms of employment through active labour market policies and retrenchment of benefits – resulting in labour market dualism institutionalized with the support of state action (Palier and Thelen 2010).

Welfare state reforms reduced both taxes and expenditures from around 48 per cent to 43 per cent of GDP between 1999 and 2009. Looking at pensions, the Riester reforms in 2000 reduced state benefits from 70 per cent to 67 per cent of salary, and created new incentives for private pension savings. These reforms have had little influence on the development of private pension funds, whose assets remain low at 5–7 per cent of GDP. Consequently, pension reform had very little spillover effects on the German financial system or corporate governance. Looking at social insurance, retrenchment has been greater and spilled over to a larger extent on other labour market institutions. The Hartz I and II (2003) reforms and Hartz III (2004) deregulated the market for atypical employment by liberalizing temporary work via new 'Staff Services agencies' (PSA), created so-called 'mini-jobs' characterized by lower taxes and insurance payments for casual employees, introducing the 'Ich-AG' (Me, Inc.) to support self-employment, and restructuring public job centres. The more dramatic and contested Hartz IV (2005) reform merged benefits for long-term unemployed ('Arbeitslosenhilfe') and the social welfare scheme ('Sozialhilfe'), and shortened the duration of unemployment benefits from 36 to 18 months. The payment for social welfare was set at low level of €359 per month ('Regelsatz') plus the cost of 'adequate' housing. This retrenchment of benefits was also consolidated by activation policies ('workfare') supporting the expansion of around 300,000 so-called '1 Euro jobs' for the long-term unemployed. Today, two-thirds of unemployed receive these low-level residual benefits. Spending on labour market policy fell from around 4 per cent of GDP during the unification era to just 2 per cent in 2009. Most cuts affected benefits or supported forms of employment and training – whereas administrative costs for these programmes rose and also led to an explosion of court cases related to benefits payments. These reforms were successful in lowering spending and relieving the existing welfare state from mounting cost pressures – including lowering contributions from 6.5 per cent to just 3.3 per cent in 2008 (Palier and Thelen 2010). As such, the reforms have probably helped preserve the system for core workers, but nonetheless led to major voter discontent with the Social Democratic Party and in trade unions, together with the eventual rise of the Left Party (Hassel and Schiller 2010).

3. THE POLITICS OF INSTITUTIONAL CHANGE

3.1. International dynamics

The EU-level influence can be understood as extending domestic politics in a multi-level political setting that makes certain reforms more likely than within the domestic political arena (Callaghan 2010). With the deepening of the European market in the Single Market Programme, qualified majority voting had been introduced in the area of economic integration, while social policies continued to be underpinned by inter-governmental principles – the outcome being an asymmetrical relation between negative and positive integration (Scharpf 2010). Crucially, the penetration of European monetary and economic policies into the domestic context of the member states has not been balanced with strong social policy at the EU level. However, in some cases, segments of German industry or other powerful stakeholders have opposed liberalization or sought to limit its impact on existing institutional arrangements. The effect has often been contradictory, involving both market-liberalizing and market-taming types of reforms across different institutional domains. Whereas the EU played a major role in financial market liberalization and corporate governance reforms, its influence was weaker regarding employment, training or the welfare state. The lack of policy coherence has resulted in new re-combinations of liberal and relational institutions in Germany.

The market-liberalizing influence of the EU is most clear in the case of financial markets. As the interests of German banks shifted, forces for financial liberalization made gains as reformers were able to utilize the European agenda to introduce new equity-oriented and shareholder-oriented reforms. For example, financial market liberalization was closely tied to the Single European Act in 1986 after the 'big bang' deregulation of UK financial markets sparked fears of increased foreign competition. Subsequently, as European monetary union became more certain, Germany played a leading role in the development of EU directives on financial markets.

Meanwhile, market-taming reforms have been fewer and less successful in Europe – for example, Germany has not been able to 'export' its stakeholder model of co-determination. For example, European works councils are one new European form of employee participation, but had only a very limited influence on other national systems. Meanwhile, board-level co-determination has not extended beyond requirements in national legislation. Here, Germany acted only to limit measures that would allow German firms to avoid employee codetermination – thus, European rules on the Societies Europeans (SE) in 2000 opened European incorporation only to multinational firms and required social partners to negotiate over company-specific codetermination rules. The SE form has been adopted mainly from German or Austrian firms, and resulted in less extensive co-determination requirements relative to German law (Keller and Werner 2010). In a paradoxical way, an enterprise form intended to be supranational became an instrument mainly used by enterprises from a specifically German institutional and cultural setting.[2] As discussed above, the EU Takeover Directive similarly promoted a largely liberal, UK-style approach and restricts takeover defences for German firms. Here, Germany opposed the measure, but succeeded only in some opt-out clauses regarding certain aspects of the directive.

Thus, Germany pursued liberalization but also sought to limit the direct impact of Europeanization on its existing stakeholder institutions. However, these compromises have only partially stabilized these institutions in the face of changing international circumstances. For example, European courts have driven further liberalization of company location in the EU in ways that increasingly make it possible to circumvent German regulations by locating, for example, the headquarters of a company in a foreign country that does not have board-level co-determination. This possibility was used in a few prominent cases such as Air Berlin, an airline which has become a major rival of Lufthansa in Germany and Europe and as a new member of the international Oneworld Alliance. Similarly, EU directives opened German labour markets to workers formally employed abroad and working in Germany 'on loan', which also depressed wage rates in related jobs and undercutting collective agreements. Initiatives to introduce national minimum wages by law have not been successful, and led to only few sectoral minimum wage agreements. Outsourcing of work to Eastern or non-EU countries has also occurred with ambiguous effects on domestic employment, since domestic firms were sometimes kept viable this way. A recent counter-tendency is to move work back to Germany, in view of logistic, quality or deadline/delivery problems in foreign subsidiaries, suppliers and subcontracting firms. Taken together, Europeanization has not abolished stakeholder-oriented governance institutions, but opened new social spaces at their margins, leading to more frequent contestation of these institutions in practice.

3.2. Political parties and coalitions

The 1980s were dominated by the conservative CDU coalition with the economically liberal *Freie Demokratische Partei* (FDP). Helmut Kohl presided as German Chancellor from 1982 until 1998. A notable feature of this period was the *absence* of aggressive liberalization relative to Thatcher's Britain or Reagan's US. For example, the government pursued policies supporting the numerical labour market flexibility (e.g., temporary workers), but made no move to dismantle co-determination or undermine the power of unions. Likewise, the government supported financial market liberalization, but did not undermine the special position of Germany's regional and co-operative banks, which have strong relationships with small- and medium-sized enterprises (SMEs).

Why was the government not more radical in pursuing liberalization? At least three factors are important. First, business interests remained fragmented and thus only supported moderate reforms. While private banks redefined themselves as investment banks and shifted preferences toward liberalization, large industrial firms enjoyed a period of strong economic growth based on the success of Germany's export sector during the 1980s. Business sought to reduce costs through liberalization of the labour market and social protection, but also benefitted from protections of core workers and the ability to externalize some adjustments costs on the state (Martin and Swank 2012; Trampusch 2009). The slow exhaustion of state-supported adjustment led to a re-politicization of social welfare in the mid-1990s. Whereas the strong sectoral basis of German business associations meant insufficient support for encompassing redistribution represented by the failed 'Alliance for Jobs' effort of the Schröder government, the fragmentation of political power also impeded more sweeping liberalization. Second, the consensus-driven nature of German electoral politics and decentralization of power under the system of federalism all gravitate against radical reforms driven by top–down policies. The majority in one chamber of parliament has often been the opposite of the majority in the other chamber, owing to intermediate elections in the different states. This has created many 'veto points' in German politics, which constrain the retrenchment of existing social protection because *de facto* only a quasi all-party coalition can rule. This casts light on the importance of 'institutional layering' within Germany, where new rules are created to facilitate changes in practice without directly seeking to abolish past practices. Third, German policy discourse remains bound by a normative notion of social market economy. In particular, the CDU have a socially conservative ideological commitment and have historically supported the welfare state (Lehmbruch 2001). The CDU initiated all the major pieces of post-war social legislation, including coal and steel co-determination. Policies of the CDU/FDP coalition in the 1990s were a mixture of liberalism with strong doses of fiscal transfers from West to East and social policies to maintain employment and social standards in East Germany – leading public budget expenditure to all-time peak levels relative to GDP. This ideological difference in the economic worldview of 'right' parties seems worthy of further comparison. The Liberals (FDP) had centred their most recent election campaign with the CDU/CSU being 'enough social-democratic already'.

After Unification in 1990, the political focus was on transferring existing institutions to the East. However, this extension led to many complex changes in the practice of institutions on the ground. No major reforms were undertaken to the main features of the German model as it existed in the West. But by the mid-1990s, the costs of German unification were becoming apparent and created a variety of new pressures on the existing German model. Many of these problems related to the high costs of the welfare state, including the rising levels of unemployment. The massive transfer of money into the East had mainly been financed on the basis of contributions levied on labour costs, so that employment became disadvantaged through rising labour costs and created acute pressures during the cyclical downturn after 2001.

During the period of the left SPD and Green coalition government (1998–2005), liberalization was more far-reaching (see Amable 2011 on the neo-liberalism of the left). The SPD took active measures to dismantle 'Germany Inc.' – the dense network of relationships among large banks and industrial companies, either by cross-holdings of shares or non-bank shares held by banks. The 'power of banks' and 'failure over control and oversight' debates have a long history; they resurfaced amidst public outcry over scandals at Metallgesellschaft, Klöckner–Humboldt–Deutz, and Schneider real estate in the mid-1990s. These debates turned disaffection with control and oversight failures, ascribed to uncritical and cosy personal networks, into an interest in Anglo-American corporate governance through stock markets, dispersed ownership, influence of network outsiders and concern with unambiguous profitability. The IT-related stock market bubble was an important factor influencing the left-coalition to support a more active role for the stock market. This 'party paradox' saw the left party SPD seek to tame big business by encouraging the dissolution of inter-corporate linkages, as well as align themselves with players in financial markets who stood to gain from more market competition, and garner an image of being a modern and economics-focused party (Cioffi and Höpner 2006). But as banks already underwent strategic re-orientation toward international financial markets, politics may have speeded institutional change rather than causing it. Ironically, an SPD chancellor placed his faith in the capacity of shareholder value capitalism to generate increasing public revenue, just at the moment before the first major bubble, in dotcom enterprises, burst in 2002.

Meanwhile, the SPD–Green coalition aggressively cut welfare state supports in 2002 as a way of tackling unemployment and preventing a financial collapse of the public sector. The manner of these reforms and parallel tax cuts for corporations and high-income earners led to massive voter disaffection and abstention on the left, and a fall from grace of the SPD which has still not been reversed. To some extent this evolution was particular to Germany, involving unification problems and specific challenges of the national/Länder competencies mix. The more general international conundrum relates to placing hopes on government revenue and employment from sources exposed to the volatility of financial markets – such as dotcom industries, shareholder value policies and international financial markets. As in some Southern European countries, major instigators of neoliberal reforms were social democratic governments

The subsequent 'grand' coalition of CDU and SPD (2006–2009) was characterized by more modest reforms. The advent of the 2008 financial crisis led to renewed interest in regulation and new rules of executive pay, which if anything suggest some swing back toward a more stakeholder-oriented model. The subsequent CDU and FDP coalition (from 2009) consolidated a path of relative stability in the core features of the German model, albeit along a path of public austerity. No major liberalization of labour markets has occurred, even despite an initiative by the Liberals (FDP) to throw out parity representation in large corporations, as something that was internationally not the state of the art.

In sum, party politics has mattered for the dynamics of institutional reform in Germany, but not in the expected division between centre-left and centre-right. Germany has lacked radical forms of neoliberal policies on the right coalition, whereas the 'new left' has promoted market liberalization not unlike New Labour in the UK. The political institutions of federalism and consensus-driven coalition governments have played an important role in slowing reform, whereas the EU-level directives have speeded liberalization. Similarly, large firms and banks have different preferences regarding liberalization, leading to a push–pull of varied policy preferences.

3.3. Institutional complementarities

Legal reforms to financial system and corporate governance were more far-reaching than in training or employment relations. Financial market liberalization started in the early 1990s, but culminated at a critical juncture around 1998. Thus, an important aspect of understanding the micro level of institutional change in Germany concerns the dynamics of how changes toward market-oriented finance and shareholder-value corporate governance influenced the dynamics of employment and skill formation. Theories of complementarities posit that 'patient capital' provided by German banks and concentrated shareholding played a key role in stabilizing the long-term commitments to employees and co-ordination with other stakeholders.

Indeed, changes in corporate finance have influenced employment or industrial relations institutions. First, dispersed ownership by foreign and institutional investors is associated with higher dividend ratios, and lower levels of employment (Beyer and Hassel 2002). Stock options for top managers have also become widespread and led to increasing inequality in terms of salaries, despite stakeholder opposition or recent attempts to link these incentives to sustainable business practices (Chizema 2010, Sanders and Tuschke 2006). Second, large firms have engaged in corporate downsizing since the 1990s, achieved largely through welfare state supported 'benevolent' methods such as early retirement, rather than lay-offs (Jackson 2005). Liberalization supported the creation of complex subsidiary structures, allowing firms to strategically place work outside of core workplaces governed by social partnership (Casey *et al.* 2012). An excellent example is the field of telecommunications, where corporate restructuring has led to low collective bargaining coverage and the creation of low-paid call centre work (Doellgast 2012, Sako and Jackson 2006). Third, shareholder-value management is strongly associated with adoption of performance-based pay schemes linking salaries to business and/or individual performance (Jackson 2005). The new layer of pay schemes represents a controlled but *de facto* decentralization of collective bargaining. Last, works councils have continued to exercise voice in restructuring decisions, but also lead participation to be closer to 'co-management' that emphasizes the co-operative character of German co-determination (Höpner 2001). Taken together, these changes show the problem of a shrinking core of employees enjoying strong employment security and participation. But these changes are also shaped by a longer-term institutional continuity – the basic normative basic consensus among top managers regarding employee co-determination and legitimate role of labour in having a voice over these changes (Höpner and Waclawczyk 2012).

Labour market and welfare state reforms also had interdependent effects. Union density declined from near 35 per cent after unification to around 18 per cent in 2008. Meanwhile, inequality increased dramatically among low wage earners. The 1980s saw a compression between low-income households and the median. However, this trend reversed with the ratio of median earnings to the bottom 10 per cent increasing from 1.71 in 1996 to 1.92 in 2008 – thus putting Germany in between the UK (1.82 ratio) and the United States of America (USA) (2.11 ratio). Real wage growth has been zero or negative over the last decade, and wages in the growing service sector lag far behind manufacturing. Consequently, the labour share of national income has fallen from around 75 per cent in 1980 to around 65 per cent in 2008, which is similar to the USA. Welfare state retrenchment and emphasis on activation policies has reinforced these trends by pushing people off social insurance benefits into atypical forms of employment. Part-time employment increased from around 11 per cent in the early 1990s to 22 per cent in 2008. Between 1998 and 2008, the growth of regular employment has been negative, whereas atypical employment including fixed-term, part-time and mini-jobs increased by 46 per cent to around 7.7 million persons. Perhaps paradoxically, these changes have kept wage and non-wage labour costs low in German manufacturing, while increasing flexibility for firms. The result of liberalization has not been to undermine co-ordination in core manufacturing sectors, so much as promoting growing fragmentation of conditions between different categories of workers, as well as across sectors and types of firms.

3.4. Diffusion, adaptation and avoidance

At the micro-level, firms have faced a number of new and sometimes contradictory pressures. Newer institutional logics of shareholder-value were layered onto older logics, such as employee codetermination in decision-making. Many new practices and institutional rules have spread through the diffusion of such concepts through EU regulation, private governance codes, or through the internationalization of firms themselves. For example, in response to foreign institutional investors, German companies rapidly set up investor relations departments to communicate with investors during the 1990s. The case of Daimler is illustrative. The company was a pioneer in adopting international accounting standards, listing shares on the New York Stock Exchange, and eventually merged with Chrysler. The merger led to the adoption of international or American levels and methods of executive compensation.[3] While other companies did not adopt such high levels of pay, stock options and related pay practices diffused widely in Germany (Chizema 2010). These practices have remained controversial, and undergone reform toward more transparent and sustainability-focused criteria following legal reforms in 2009 – a prime example of how institutional innovations become adapted to local settings, embodying both change and continuity to a certain degree.

Another firm-level dynamic concerns the avoidance of institutions. The possibilities of moving production abroad and declining coverage of industrial relations institutions in Germany have opened up new social spaces for firms to avoid certain types of institutions. While labour law and welfare state reforms were not intended to dismantle existing institutions, some firms have used newfound flexibility in a strategic way for institutional avoidance (Oliver 1991). For example, before their 2012 bankruptcy, the drugstore chain Schlecker had founded their own temporary work agency, laying off workers and rehiring them at substantially reduced levels of wages and benefits – prompting a major scandal in 2010. Temporary and agency labour are less likely to be covered by collective agreements or often have agreements with substantially lower wages. Likewise, subcontracting methods are widely used to circumvent these wage agreements.[4] This trend toward institutional avoidance has prompted a widespread debate over a statutory minimum wage in Germany. A second and very different example of institutional erosion relates to vocational training. Here the problem of increasing youth unemployment is related to school education deficiencies, notably for youths from migrant backgrounds and the declining capacity of the system to smooth the progression from secondary education to apprenticeship. A distinctive set of challenges arise relative to underdeveloped human resources and underutilized apprenticeship training capacities. As might be expected in a system with a high amount of statutory and collective bargaining regulation and price-setting, the segmentation of labour market situations continues to be strong and it has been fuelled by internationalization.

4. CONCLUSIONS

Comparative studies of capitalism all imply a specific institutional logic of action inherent to a type of national system. This logic is constituted by complementarities or elective affinities, where a characteristic along one dimension (such as industrial relations) will be interdependent with a set of characteristics along other societal domains, such as company finance. On the one hand, complementarities suggest that a major change, such as the international diffusion of shareholder value orientations, will change other institutions in a similar direction along other dimensions. In cases where change amounts to market liberalization of corporate governance and finance, shifts towards corresponding features along other dimensions would in effect boil down to convergence. On the other hand, institutional complementarities have been used to argue that institutional systems are path dependent and characterized by strong inertia (Hall and Soskice 2001). Path dependency thus argues against institutional convergence.

Institutional scholars have not been united or consistent in their stance *vis-à-vis* convergence or divergence (Hall and Thelen 2009). Many cross-sectional comparative studies suggest persistent differences and more-or-less stable clustering of countries over time (Jackson and Deeg 2012). Inter-temporal studies, such as this one, show a more complex picture of both continuity and change. In Germany, changes in finance, the emergence of shareholder-value management styles, declining coverage of collective bargaining and certain educational reforms all point towards a type of convergence. But within this broad trend toward more liberal and market-oriented institutions we observe substantial continuities and thus also divergence across countries. While shareholder-value capitalism has made major inroads into publicly quoted enterprises, the climate of industrial relations has retained strong element of co-operation. Employee representatives on supervisory boards have smoothed this development, rather than being crushed by it. Employers and politicians have moved to scale down co-determination in large enterprises, but have not succeeded despite the governing CDU/FDP coalition. A new exchange for small joint-stock companies (Neuer Markt) was established but subsequently crumbled again. Industry-level collective bargaining has very much come under pressure, but nevertheless the co-ordination and solidarity in wage negotiations helped maintain unit labour productivity and the competitiveness of enterprises.

Much political economy literature on institutions has been side-tracked by this half-full or half-empty debate about change, rather than developing historical analysis of how continuity and change condition one another (Streeck 2010). To this aim, we note that Whitley (2007) distinguishes 'proximate institutions' as specific, normative and tangible norms governing economic action in a particular domain and 'background institutions' as more fundamental and less specific and formalized (e.g., general assumptions about trust or distrust, co-operation or competition, as applying to roughly circumscribed situations). A similar distinction can be made between the 'ostensive' and the 'performative' aspects of behavioural routines, or between the 'etic' and the 'emic' aspects of institutions. Such concepts distinguish between tangible norms and regularities taken at 'face value', i.e., what norms literally say or are taken to mean in a decontextualized understanding, and the meaning implied in specific societal contexts, wherein deeper levels of knowledge, understanding and shared values operate.

This distinction helps view institutional continuity as subject to the dialectics between concrete, specific and tangible 'proximate institutions' at the surface of the institutional landscape, and 'background institutions' at deeper levels. Although tangible institutions are continuously remodelled, the bedrock of more inert institutional continuity shapes the direction and precise content of institutional change. In this sense, a 'metatradition' (Sorge 2005) of institutional continuity exists that in no way contradicts the observation of substantial institutional change. As Stark and Bruszt (1998) argue, even radical institutional change always involves a recombination of the 'new' with the 'old' institutions in creative, original and often surprising ways. We add to this that 'new' proximate institutions tend to be complemented by and amalgamated with a different kind of institutional innovation that draws on resources and capacities embodied by 'old' institutions. For example, the German code of corporate governance promoted a new view of governance in line with the UK approach, OECD recommendations and EU regulation through new norms based in soft law ('comply or explain'), but simultaneously sought to explain the difference between unassailable obligations found in German legal norms and more optional recommendations to an audience of foreign investors. That is, new institutional rules are interpreted within a collective memory of background institutions and bear regard to specific contingencies in economic, political and social opportunities and constraints. Whereas path dependency combines those specific contingencies with background institutions, institutional change is built on institutional imports, institutional avoidance and addressing acute deficiencies of the time, in proximate institutions.

A more fine-grained analysis of institutional change mainly points to three dynamics having different effects with regard to institutional convergence and divergence across countries or between diffusing global practices and local institutions:

(1) Some international trends stemming from supranational government (such as the EU) or quasi-government (such as the normative importance of US stock exchanges, the OECD or the International Accounting Standards organization) clearly produce a certain amount of convergence. In their content, these institutional rules are mostly of a market-liberalizing variety most visible in new codes of practice and international regulation coming out of supranational bodies or transnational associations.

(2) The socio-political situation of each country creates differentiated contingencies and temporalities that shape institutional change. This effect works towards divergence-within-convergence. The German case suggests that political contingencies cannot be read directly off the dominance of left or right political parties, or formal rules of the political system. Which formal rules are adopted and how these are enacted requires looking at historically processes.

(3) Inertial bedrock of background institutions (i.e., basic structures, beliefs and habitualized dispositions) is often invoked by collective actors as a resource and applied to deal with change coming from the international scene and affecting significant change in proximate institutions. This dynamic asserts the specificity, or divergence, of proximate institutions.

It is now possible to differentiate examples for such effects, depending on the relative strength of international regulation or other standards, specific contingencies and temporalities governing the 'import' of standards, and the meta-tradition of background institutions that shape the interpretation and application of new standards.

Corporate governance probably shows the clearest convergence effects in Germany, notably in financial and accounting standards, in the dissolving of share cross-ownership, and in the taking-on-board of EU directives or other international rules on takeovers, financial markets and corporate governance. Here, international laws and standards had the most direct impact. On the other hand, existing institutions of co-determination have also proved to be resilient and strongly shaped how these imported practices are framed and understood in practice.

The second effect, of divergence within convergence, is exemplified by the increase in enterprise-level bargaining and declining union strength, together with the renewed harnessing of collective bargaining in the interest of both enterprise competitiveness and socio-political aspirations. Distinctive contingencies for Germany are visible: Unification led to problems of industrial wage bargaining and competitiveness in view of rapidly rising wage and non-wage labour costs; the subsequent effect of this crisis was to alert the social partners and governments to non-wage labour costs and bring back wage restraint in ways that adhered to past, tacitly observed standards.

The third effect, the assertion of institutional continuities, is visible, for example, in adherence to co-determination despite political pressures and reduced union strength, in the disappearance of the Neuer Markt after its initial success, and in the renaissance of wage restraint in aid of competitiveness, export performance and limiting the public sector financial burden.

Biographical notes: Gregory Jackson is Professor of Human Resource Management and Labour Politics at the Free University of Berlin, Germany. Arndt Sorge is an honorary professor in the Faculty of Economic and Social Sciences, University of Potsdam, Germany.

ACKNOWLEDGEMENTS

The research leading to these results has received funding from the European Community's Seventh Framework Programme (FP7/2007-2011) under grant agreement number 225349 (ICaTSEM project). The authors would like to thank Tim Müllenborn, Nikolas Rathert, and Jasmin Zazei for research assistance on this project. They also thank the *Journal of European Public Policy* referees for their constructive comments.

NOTES

1 For example, US-style 'poison pills' found under Delaware law are impossible in Germany, since issuing discounted shares is incompatible with the equal treatment of shareholders under the EU directive and pre-emptive rights under German law. The board may issue authorized share capital to existing shareholders up to a maximum 50 per cent of capital. Similarly, court decisions (the Holzmüller doctrine) have led to requiring shareholder approval for substantial (>80 per cent) acquisitions or asset disposals.
2 One might speculate that the ingrained propensity to use robust statutory tools for the functional and social integration of larger enterprises made German enterprises go for the SE option, whereas owners and management from other countries feel more comfortable in the 'cash nexus' and the arms'-length relations, by way of capital share ownership, that govern relations between enterprises even when they belong to the same group.
3 The Daimler–Chrysler merger ultimately failed, and Daimler management moved away from their strong shareholder-value focus following the departure of CEO Jürgen Schrempp in 2005.
4 *Die Zeit* online, available at http://www.zeit.de/politik/deutschland/2011-08/lohndumping-leiharbeit (accessed 14 Jun 2012).

REFERENCES

Amable, B. (2011) 'Morals and politics in the ideology of neo-liberalism' *Socio-Economic Review* 9(1): 3–30.

Beyer, J. and Hassel, A. (2002) 'The effects of convergence: internationalisation and the changing distribution of net value added in large German firms', *Economy and Society* 31(3): 309–32.

Busemeyer, M.R. (2009a) 'Asset specificity, institutional complementarities and the variety of skill regimes in coordinated market economies', *Socio-Economic Review* 7(3): 375–406.

Busemeyer, M.R. (2009b). *Wandel trotz Reformstau: Die Politik der beruflichen Bildung seit 1970*, Frankfurt a.M: Campus.

Callaghan, H. (2010) 'Beyond methodological nationalism: how multilevel governance affects the clash of capitalisms', *Journal of European Public Policy* 17(4): 564–80.

Callaghan, H. and Höpner, M. (2005) 'European integration and the clash of capitalisms. Political cleavages over takeover liberalization', *Comparative European Politics* 3(3): 307–32.

Casey, C., Fiedler, A. and Erakovic, L. (2012) 'Liberalising the German model: institutional change, organisational restructuring and workplace effects', *Industrial Relations Journal* 43(1): 53–69.

Chizema, A. (2010) 'Early and late adoption of American-style executive pay in Germany: governance and institutions', *Journal of World Business* 45(1): 9–18.

Cioffi, J.W. and Höpner, M. (2006) 'The political paradox of finance capitalism: interests, preferences, and center-left party politics in corporate governance reform', *Politics and Society* 34(4): 463–502.

Culpepper, P.D. (2011) *Quiet Politics and Business Power: Corporate Control in Europe and Japan*, New York: Cambridge University Press.

Deeg, R. (2009) 'The rise of internal capitalist diversity? Changing patterns of finance and corporate governance in Europe', *Economy and Society* 38(4): 552–79.

Doellgast, V.L. (2012) *Disintegrating Democracy at Work: Labor Unions and the Future of Good Jobs in the Service Economy*, Ithaca, NY: ILR Press.

Emmenegger, P. and Marx, P. (2011) 'Business and the development of job security regulations: the case of Germany', *Socio-Economic Review* 9(4): 729–56.

Faust, M. (2012) 'The shareholder value concept of the corporation and co-determination in Germany: unresolved contradictions or reconciliation of institutional logics?' in C. Lane and G. Wood (eds), *Capitalist Diversity and Diversity Within Capitalism*, London: Routledge, pp. 150–88.

Fiss, P.C. and Zajac, E. (2004) 'The diffusion of ideas over contested terrain: the (non)-adoption of a shareholder value orientation among German firms', *Administrative Science Quarterly* 49(December): 501–34.

Goergen, M., Martynova, M. and Renneboog, L. (2005) 'Corporate governance convergence: evidence from takeover regulation reforms in Europe', *Oxford Review of Economic Policy* 21(2): 243–68.

Hall, P.A. and Soskice, D. (eds) (2001) *Varieties of Capitalism: The Institutional Foundations of Comparative Advantage*, Oxford: Oxford University Press.

Hall, P.A. and Thelen, K. (2009) 'Institutional change in varieties of capitalism', *Socio-Economic Review* 7(1): 7–34.

Hans-Boeckler Foundation (2012) *Vertretung auf Branchen- und Betriebsebene; Reichweite stabilisiert.*

Hassel, A. and Schiller, C. (2010) 'Fiscal federalism and social policy in Germany', *Politische Vierteljahresschrift* 51(1): 95–117.

Höpner, M. (2001) 'Corporate governance in transition: ten empirical findings on shareholder value and industrial relations in Germany', *MPIfG Discussion Paper 01 / 5*, Cologne: Max Planck Institut für Gesellschaftsforschung.

Höpner, M. and Jackson, G. (2006) 'Revisiting the Mannesmann takeover: how markets for corporate control emerge', *European Management Review* 3: 142–55.

Höpner, M. and Waclawczyk, M. (2012) 'Opportunismus oder Ungewissheit? Mitbestimmte Unternehmen zwischen Klassenkampf und Produktionsregime', *MPIfG Discussion Paper, 12(1)*, Cologne: Max Planck Institut für Gesellschaftsforschung.

Jackson, G. (2005) 'Stakeholders under pressure: corporate governance and labour management in Germany and Japan', *Corporate Governance: An International Review* 13(3): 419–28.

Jackson, G. and Deeg, R. (2012) 'The long-term trajectories of institutional change in European and US capitalism', *Journal of European Public Policy* 19(8), doi: 10.1080/13501763.2012.709001

Jackson, G. and Miyajima, H. (2007) 'Varieties of takeover markets: comparing mergers and acquisitions in Japan with Europe and the USA', *RIETI Discussion Paper Series, 07-E-054*

Jackson, G. and Wylegala, J. (2012) *ICaTSEM reform database 1979–2009, European Commission FP7 Project no. 225349, Institutional Changes and Trajectories of Socio-Economic Development Models (ICaTSEM)*, available at http://icatsem.u-bordeaux4.fr/ (accessed 30 March 2012).

Keller, B. and Werner, F. (2010) 'Industrial democracy from a European perspective: the example of SEs', *Economic & Industrial Democracy* 31(4): 40–54.

Klages, P. (2012) 'The contractual turn: how legal experts shaped corporate governance reforms in Germany', *Socio-Economic Review*, doi: 10.1093/ser/mws006

Lehmbruch, G. (2001) 'The institutional embedding of market economics: the German "model" and its impact on Japan', in W. Streeck and K. Yamamura (eds), *The Origins of Nonliberal Capitalism: Germany and Japan in Comparison*, Ithaca, NY: Cornell University Press, pp. 39–93.

Luetz, S., Eberle, D. and Lauter, D. (2011) 'Varieties of private self-regulation in European capitalism: corporate governance codes in the UK and Germany', *Socio-Economic Review* 9(2): 315–38.

Martin, C.J. and Swank, D. (2012) *The Political Construction of Business Interests: Coordination, Growth, and Equality*, Cambridge: Cambridge University Press.

Oliver, C. (1991) 'Strategic responses to institutional processes', *Academy of Management Review* 16: 145–79.

Palier, B. and Thelen, K. (2010) 'Institutionalizing dualism: complementarities and change in France and Germany', *Politics & Society* 38(1): 119–48.

Sako, M. and Jackson, G. (2006) 'Strategy meets institutions: the transformation of management–labor relations at Deutsche Telekom and NTT', *Industrial and Labor Relations Review* 59(3): 347–66.

Sanders, W.M.G. and Tuschke, A.C. (2006) 'The adoption of institutionally contested organizational practices: the emergence of stock option pay in Germany', *Academy of Management Journal* 50(1): 33–56.

Scharpf, F.W. (2010) 'The asymmetry of European integration, or why the EU cannot be a "social market economy"', *Socio-Economic Review* 8(2): 211–50.

Sorge, A. (2005) *The Global and the Local: Understanding the Dialectics of Business Systems*, Oxford: Oxford University Press.

Stark, D. and Bruszt, L. (1998) *Postsocialist Pathways. Transforming Politics and Property in East Central Europe*, Cambridge: Cambridge University Press.

Statistisches Bundesamt (various years) *Statistisches Jahrbuch für die Bundesrepublik Deutschland*, Wiesbaden: Statistisches Bundesamt.

Streeck, W. (2009) *Re-Forming Capitalism: Institutional Change in the German Political Economy*, Oxford: Oxford University Press.

Streeck, W. (2010) 'Institutions in history: bringing capitalism back in', in G. Morgan, J.L. Campbell, C. Crouch, O.K. Pedersen and R. Whitley (eds), *The Oxford Handbook of Comparative Institutional Analysis*, Oxford: Oxford University Press, pp. 659–86.

Trampusch, C. (2009) *Der erschöpfte Sozialstaat : Transformation eines Politikfeldes*. Frankfurt am Main: Campus.

Vail, M. (2010) *Recasting Welfare Capitalism: Economic Adjustment in Contemporary France and Germany*, Philadelphia, PA: Temple University Press.

Whitley, R. (2007) *Business Systems and Organizational Capabilities: The Institutional Structuring of Competitive Competences*, Oxford: Oxford University Press.

Yamamura, K. and Streeck, W. (eds) (2003) *The End of Diversity? Prospects of German and Japanese Capitalism*, Ithaca, NY: Cornell University Press.

Ziegler, J.N. (2000) 'Corporate governance and the politics of property rights in Germany', *Politics and Society* 28(2): 195–221.

APPENDIX

(See over)

Table A1 The trajectory of institutional change in Germany, selected domains

Institutional domain	Typology	Direction of change and examples of major reforms	Timing of major reforms
Financial systems	Bank-oriented → both banks and markets	Shift toward market finance • Deregulation of equity markets • Implementation of EU directives on transparency, etc.	1990s
Corporate governance	Stakeholder-oriented → some elements of shareholder value	Shift toward outsider, shareholder-oriented model • Liberalizing stock options • Voting rights reform • Change in takeover rules 'Hybrid model' – two-tier board and employee codetermination remain	1998–2002
Industrial relations	Corporatism → increasing segmentation	Some flexibilization of labour market for small firms and lower skill employees, but some element of social protection • Liberalization of employment protection in SMEs (although partially reversed in 1998) • Minimum wage in construction industry (1996) • Works Constitution Act modernizes works council procedures for SMEs and non-standard work arrangements (2001) • 'Job centres' introduced (2003)	2001, 2003

Education and skill creation	Associational governance of apprenticeship	Some greater role of the state • Greater public role in apprenticeship system • Policies for low skill workers	1990, 2000
Welfare state	Conservative → limited introduction of market elements, some retrenchment	• Hartz Reforms (shortening length of unemployment benefits) • More employment activation policies • Limited and incremental expansion of private pensions But limited influence on pension system, health system	2002–2003 unemployment, 2000 and 2006 pensions;, 2003 health

Changing French capitalism: political and systemic crises in France

Bruno Amable, Elvire Guillaud and Stefano Palombarini

ABSTRACT   France's model of capitalism experiences a crisis with multiple aspects. First, the French model of capitalism has undergone deep reforms since the 1980s. Second, the French political life is characterized by a political crisis: the vanishing of the space for mediation between the divergent expectations of the social groups composing the dominant social bloc. These crises are linked. First, because the institutional reforms undertaken since the 1980s have changed French capitalism, its institutional complementarities, the profile of socio-political groups, and have contributed to destabilizing social alliances. Second, because the political crisis has pushed policy-makers to turn to institutional change as a necessary condition for opening up new spaces of mediation. This contribution surveys the main changes experienced by the French model over the past 30 years, analyses the break-up of the traditional social alliances and presents the elements of the political crisis in relation to neoliberal structural reforms.

1.   INTRODUCTION

The perception of French capitalism briefly changed immediately after the onset of the Great Recession. Whereas it had been commonplace to mention its difficulties and its 'Thatcher moment' (*The Economist*, 15 November 2007), the Great Recession led to the proclamation of a new European hierarchy (*The Economist*, 9 May 2009), with the French model first, then *Modell Deutschland* and lastly a sinking Anglo-Saxon model. It would nevertheless be erroneous to stop at this spectacular and temporary reversal of appreciation, neglecting the elements that testify to the existence of a crisis with multiple aspects. This contribution will focus on two of them.

The first crisis affects the French model of capitalism, which has undergone deep reforms since the 1980s. The reforms in the financial system, product and labour markets, education and social protection have changed the institutional complementarities at work in the French model of capitalism (Table 2 below).

The second crisis concerns the instability of the socio-political blocs that have structured the French political life. Many symptoms testify of what can be

Table 1 Successive governments and attempted economic policies over the period 1974–2007

Period	President/government	Economic policies' orientation
1974–1981	Giscard d'Estaing (Right)/Chirac–Barre (Right)	Slow transition from Fordism to neoliberalism
1981–1983	Mitterrand (Left)/ Mauroy (Left)	Significant transformations of the economic institutions in a social-democratic way (labour laws, social protection); nationalizations; expansionary macroeconomic policy
1983–1986	Mitterrand (Left)/ Mauroy–Fabius (Left)	Deflationary policy; prominence of the European integration constraints; financial liberalization
1986–1988	Mitterrand (Left)/Chirac (Right)	Attempt at a 'conservative revolution'; neoliberal reforms in employment legislation, social protection and education; privatizations
1988–1993	Mitterrand (Left)/ Rocard–Cresson– Bérégovoy (Left)	'ni-ni' policy (neither nationalization, nor privatization); European integration; competitive disinflation
1993–1995	Mitterrand (Left)/ Balladur (Right)	Privatizations; pension reform
1995–1997	Chirac (Right)/Juppé (Right)	Privatizations; attempts at welfare state retrenchment
1997–2002	Chirac (Right)/Jospin (Left)	35-hours work week; welfare state extensions; privatizations; financial liberalization
2002–2007	Chirac (Right)/Raffarin– Villepin (Right)	Privatizations; tentative labour market flexibilization; slow welfare state retrenchment (health expenditure)

qualified as a *political crisis*: for instance, since 1981 no government has ever been re-elected.[1]

From the viewpoint of the political economy of institutions, the stability of a model of capitalism depends on the stability of the social alliances that support the fundamental compromises on which the model rests. We define the Dominant Social Bloc (DSB) as the social alliance whose interests are protected by the public policy and which is sufficiently strong to politically validate such a policy. In our approach, the stability of an institutional configuration is linked to the presence of a DSB; a situation of *political crisis* corresponds to the vanishing of the space for mediation between the divergent expectations of the various social groups that compose the DSB.[2]

The fundamental pillars of the French model result from the post-war political equilibrium: a set of more or less implicit compromises between a republican

Table 2 The main reforms that transformed the French model of capitalism

Domain	Key reform	Implied change
Financial system	1978: Law on the orientation of savings	Creation of investment companies issuing public shares
	1984: Banking Act	Put an end to administrative control of credit
	1985–1986: Financial Markets Acts	Increased competition among financial intermediaries by abolishing banks' exclusive access to the money market; futures and options market created
	1988: Free mobility of capital (European Directive)	Greater importance of financial markets
	1998: Law of 2nd July	Companies allowed to buy back shares
	2001: Law on new economic regulation and employee saving plans	Changed competition law, corporate governance and merger procedures to adopt 'Anglo-Saxon' standards; lowered taxation on stock options
	2004: The 'Copé' fiscal law on capital gains from equity sales	Exemption from corporate tax of capital gains linked to the sale of a subsidiary owned for at least two years
Product market	1981: Nationalizations	Major industrial firms, banks and insurance companies
	1986–1988, 1993–2005: Privatizations	Major industrial firms, banks and insurance companies
Labour market	1986: Law on dismissal for economic reasons	Abolished the administrative authorization necessary in case of individual dismissal for economic reasons
	1986: Creation of the intermittent work contracts	Reinforced income protection for workers who face temporary interruptions of their work activity
	1995: Law on collective layoffs	Reinforces job protection by introducing statutory requirements concerning the contents of social plans
	2000: Law on the reduction of the working time	Statutory working time reduction from 39 to 35 hours a week; possibility for small firms to use overtime work

(Continued)

Table 2 Continued

Domain	Key reform	Implied change
	2004: Law on vocational training and social dialogue	Possibility to adapt or waive sector agreements on working hours to the specific needs of each business
	2005: Reform of the organization of working time in companies	Extension in time and scope of the derogations to the 35-hours working week (overtime work)
	2005: *Contrat Nouvelle Embauche*	Enabled small firms to hire with a two-year probation period (no entitlement to severance payment)
	2007: Tax law on overtime work	Specific favourable tax regime on overtime earnings
	2008: Law on the modernization of the labour market	Enabled labour contracts to be terminated by mutual agreement; lowers separation costs
Education	1983: Law No. 83-8	Regions can organize professional training
	1987: The 'Seguin' law	Access to all diplomas through apprenticeship and qualification schemes
	2002: Education reform	Adapted the tertiary education system to European standards (the Bologna Process)
	2007: Autonomy of universities	Increased competition in the higher education system
Welfare state	1982: Law on pensions	Legal retirement age is reduced from 65 to 60; minimum contribution period of 37.5 years to obtain a full pension
	1988: Law on the assistance scheme	Created a means-tested minimum allowance for adults over 25: *Revenu Minimum d'Insertion* (RMI)
	1992: Law on unemployment insurance (UI) benefits	Created a unified benefit scheme decreasing over time and expiring after 30 months
	1993: Law on pensions	Minimum contribution period rose to 40 years (private sector); pensions indexed on prices instead of wages

(Continued)

Table 2 Continued

Domain	Key reform	Implied change
	2000: Health care scheme reform	Created a universalist scheme: every individual living in France has access to the national health service
	2001: Tax law on low-wage workers	Created a negative tax subsiding low-wage workers: *Prime pour l'emploi*
	2002: Reform of the UI scheme	Reduced the benefit period to 23 months (maximum)
	2003: Law on in-work benefit	Created an in-work benefit for those having received the RMI for 2 years: *Revenu Minimum d'Activité* (RMA)
	2003: Law on pensions	Extension of the 1993 law to the public sector
	2003–2004: Law on pension schemes	Creation of a 'third pillar' scheme (personal insurance contract, and employee pensions savings schemes)
	2004: Health care reform	Move toward a direct management of the health care system by the state at the expense of social partners; increased control over patients
	2009: Assistance scheme reform	Replaced the RMI and the RMA, and acts as a minimal income for the unemployed whose rights to benefits have expired, and as an income complement for the working poor: *Revenu de Solidarité Active* (RSA)
	2010: Pension reform	Extension of the legal retirement age from 60 to 62, and from 65 to 67 to receive a full pension

Right bloc and a Left bloc over the establishment of social protection and strong state interventionism in the economy.

From the 1970s on, the social compromises that supported the French model went into crisis because of the economic slowdown and the surge of mass unemployment on the one hand and the consequences of European economic integration on the other hand (see Section 3 below). Consequently, public policies have followed strategies either to renew the old social alliances, or to build new ones. In a context of a significant break-up in the existing social alliances, strategies aiming at securing a stable DSB require a change in the (economic) institutions. The modalities of this institutional change (when and how to implement it) depend on which DSB is aimed by the dominant political coalition.

This contribution is organized as follows. The next section surveys the main changes experienced by the French model over the past 30 years. Section 3 analyses the break-up of the social bases of both the Left and the Right and presents the elements of the political crisis. Section 4 analyses the different ways out of the political crisis in relation to neoliberal structural reforms. Section 5 assesses the difficulties associated with the neoliberal strategy. A brief conclusion follows.

2. NEOLIBERAL REFORMS AND FRENCH CAPITALISM

The 'French model' can be associated with the *ideal-typical* Continental European model of capitalism (Amable 2003): a relatively high level of legal employment protection; a certain degree of centralization of wage bargaining; relatively generous social protection financed by social contributions; a certain degree of product market regulation and a sizeable public sector; an insider- rather than outsider-controlled financial system; a public education system, etc. An insider-controlled financial system facilitates long-term strategies and does not compel firms to respect short-term profit constraints. Centralized/co-ordinated wage bargaining favours a solidaristic wage system, while social inequalities are reduced through a redistributive social protection. With respect to this ideal-type, French specificities relate to the prominent role of the State, which compensates for the weaknesses of the traditional actors of a corporatist model of social relationships (Schmitter 1974) in the bargaining between employers and wage-earners, or in defining long-term industrial strategies and monitoring their development (Schmidt 2002).

These characteristics were, up to the recent economic crisis at least, considered as responsible for a certain sclerosis of the model: employment protection supposedly discouraging firms from hiring and so leading to mass unemployment; a bankrupt social protection system failing to 'activate' the unemployed; product market regulation accused of restricting competition and consequently constraining innovation and growth; a financial system lending insufficiently to small and medium enterprises (SMEs), slowing down investment and consumption; an education system failing to provide adequate services both to a majority of young people and to an élite. The large role of the French state was also held to be an additional failure, as a plethoric public sector encouraged inconsistent interventionism, etc.

The Great Recession led to a toning down of these negative appreciations. The weight of public intervention in the economy, in particular income redistribution, allowed effective demand to be stabilized and limited the impact of the recession. Employment protection contributed to slowing down the rise of unemployment. Public universities did not freeze hiring or even fire personnel, as occurred at certain prestigious American universities. Since French households were not as indebted as their American or British counterparts, the impact of the recession on consumption was limited. Generally speaking, the automatic stabilizers of the French model proved to be relatively effective (OECD 2010).

But the French model itself has experienced substantial transformations over the past three decades (see Tables 1 and 2).

The financial system profoundly changed since the deregulation laws of the 1980s (see Table 2). The move towards market-based finance affected cross-shareholding among large industrial firms, banks and insurance companies. This mode of control, intended to protect the stability of capital property and the capacity to implement industrial long-term strategies, had survived the waves of privatization until the early 1990s under the guise of the 'hard cores'. These devices discouraging foreign investors and constituting an obstacle to the development of financial markets were dismantled after the merger between the two insurance companies AXA and UAP in 1996 (Morin 1998). The model of stable financial relations, with its 'patient' capital and long-run manufacturing strategies, was therefore considerably weakened. As in many other continental countries, France gradually adopted the rules of financialized capitalism.

As in most of the other countries of the OECD, the 'flexibilization' of the labour market mostly took the form of the development of atypical contracts, or contracts targeting particular categories of the labour force. A substitution was made to the detriment of permanent employment contracts in favour of flexible (interim, fixed-term contracts, part-time) or helped contracts, fuelling a segmentation of the wage-earner groups which by itself is a factor of decline of the pseudo-corporatist model of the French wage bargaining system, if only because of the disparities of income and status to which it leads.

The reforms of social protection, presented as a way to ensure the sustainability of the system, in fact tighten the links between contributions and benefits and involve the development of new benefits that do not belong to the Bismarkian logic. The degree of social protection ensured by the mandatory public schemes tends to diminish, increasing the dependence on the complementary schemes. The increasing weight of these complements is a factor of social differentiation. The share of the population dependent on means-tested benefits, a characteristic element of the neoliberal social protection regime, is now over 10 per cent (Palier 2008).

Changes on the financing side have had no less impact on the stability of the system. The trend for the past years was to decrease the contributions at the lower end of the wage distribution in order to decrease labour costs and boost the demand for low-skilled workers (eight reforms between 1993 and 2007). These reforms of the financing mode could have significant long-term consequences for the future of the social protection system. The pattern of social contribution by becoming more progressive tends to make more evident the split between clear net contributors (the highly skilled workers) and the beneficiaries of the system (Zemmour 2009), putting the socio-political stability of the system at risk.

To sum up, various changes strengthening each other in their destabilizing effects have changed the French model: privatizations have been instrumental in 'deepening' the financial markets and lowered job security in the firms concerned; financial liberalization has favoured the dissemination of the 'Anglo-Saxon' type of corporate governance; increased competition in product markets has subjected firms to pressures which in turn have made them press harder for labour market liberalization; the decentralization of bargaining has led to an increase in wage inequalities and an increasing differentiation of interests among workers, which has made the social base of a generous system of social protection more unstable; higher education reforms have intensified competition between universities, initiating a transition towards a more private, market-based system (Amable 2009a).

Despite these changes, French capitalism cannot be classified as a market-based model. The main constitutive elements of the Continental model of capitalism have been weakened, sometimes very seriously, as in the case of the financial system, but not erased altogether: there is still a high level of employment protection for regular jobs, and the social protection system is not dismantled. Institutional complementarities characteristic of the Continental model are therefore still existent but operate less strongly than before (Amable 2009b).[3]

From a political economy viewpoint, these changes raise two important issues. The first concerns the motives behind these changes. Pressures from internationalization played a role in the transformation of the financial system and the rules of corporate governance. European integration has also been a factor of homogenization around a neoliberal model (Amable *et al.* 2009). But the idea that the transformations of the French model would come from the outside and be imposed on French political and economic actors is misleading.[4] Behind the structural reforms that most changed the French model is the deliberate action of French political actors who contributed to determining the modalities of the opening of the French economy to foreign competition, European integration and financial deregulation.[5] A substantial literature has emphasized the role of specific agents, in particular firms, in the process of institutional change in France (e.g., Culpepper *et al.* 2006). Two points must be mentioned in this respect. First, the definition of institutions adopted in most of this literature is exceedingly lax; what is labelled 'institutional change' should be in fact considered as change in agents' *strategies*. Second, Culpepper (2006), for instance, considers that 'institutional change' results from firms' actions in reaction to the reforms initiated by political actors, but fails to analyse the reasons why such structural reforms were implemented in the first place.

Our thesis is that these reforms were political answers to the break-up of the social alliances that had been the foundations of the French model. This break-up started in the 1970s with the economic crisis and mass unemployment, and intensified in the following decades. It became blatant in the early 2000s with two significant political events: the presence of the *Front National* candidate in the second round of the presidential elections in 2002 and the rejection of the European Constitutional Treaty in 2005.

The second issue concerns the consequences of institutional change on the structure of socio-economic interests and the profile of socio-political groups. Structural reforms result from political strategies to rebuild a dominant social bloc and have been designed to answer certain political demands. But they have also led to a significant transformation of the social structure and partly accelerated the breakup of the old social alliances: the relative weight of social groups has been altered and new interests and related social demands have appeared. This implies that the content and weight of social demands that public policies should satisfy have evolved, along with French capitalism.

These two issues underline the central role played by the link between changes affecting French capitalism and the crisis that characterizes the system of political representation. Structural changes find their origins for the most part in the attempt to rebuild a stable dominant social alliance and get out of the political crisis. At the same time, these changes alter the profile of social expectations and political demands, and thus alter the chances of success of the political projects aiming to rebuild a dominant social bloc.

It is therefore necessary to turn to the analysis of the political crisis to understand the evolution of French capitalism.

3. THE POLITICAL CRISIS AND THE BREAK-UP OF SOCIAL ALLIANCES

Guillaud and Palombarini (2006)[6] analysed the destabilization of the social alliances in France from the 1970s to the 2000s. The socio-political landscape of France of the 1970s was, compared with that of today, relatively simple: there were two distinct social alliances expressing differentiated demands and represented by well-identified political organizations. The Left bloc, which gathered a majority of the employees of the public sector and workers, was represented by the French Socialist Party and its allies on the left, in particular the Communist Party, in the perspective of forming a left-wing coalition government. The expectations of this bloc were for stronger state intervention in the economy, the regulation of the employment relationship in favour of workers and an increase in the standard of living of the poorest wage-earners. The Right alliance gathered the mean and superior income classes of the private sector, self-employed professionals, self-employed workers (shopkeepers and craftsmen), as well as a majority of farmers. It was represented by the Gaullist party and its liberal allies. The expectations focused on state intervention as an economic strategy protecting 'national interests', i.e., large French firms. This bloc was opposed to (further) nationalizations, which represented an essential point for the government programme of the Left. The differentiation of the Right bloc from the Left alliance also concerned the redistributive action of the state; the Left alliance sought to decrease incomes disparities by increasing taxes, the Right alliance preferred a decrease in taxes, even if it meant an increase in inequality.

The economic crisis of the 1970s, slow growth, high unemployment and the evolutions of the French model in the 1980s slowly modified this socio-political landscape.

The fracture in the Right bloc emerged in the 1980s concerning a possible neoliberal turn in economic policy, and in particular labour market flexibility. The demand from the self-employed for a Thatcherite policy was not shared by private sector employees. In 1988, craftsmen and shopkeepers were more in favour of privatization than the population average (53 per cent against 43.5 per cent), while the reverse was true for private sector employees (40.6 per cent). Therefore, two reference groups for the right-wing government coalition found themselves on opposite sides on a possible neoliberal turning point in institutional change.

The split within the electoral base of the Left appeared during the 1990s around the issue of European integration. Europe was the second factor in the differentiation of social expectations in 1995 (the first one being government intervention in the economy), and the first factor in 1997.[7] For instance, the answers to a specific question by two social groups that traditionally supported the Left can be mentioned. In 1995, 46.2 per cent of the voters considered that France had 'many' or 'sufficiently many' common interests with other countries in Europe. This percentage was 52 per cent among managers and employees of public sector, but only 38 per cent among workers. The fracture in the Left bloc deepened over the next decade: the *Parti Socialiste* officially decided in favour of the European Constitutional Treaty in the 2005 referendum, following a relatively narrow victory in favour of the Treaty in an internal referendum; however, according to an IPSOS poll, workers voted 'no' by an overwhelming majority of 79 per cent.

This twin fracture favoured the rise of political 'extremes', especially the *Front National* which, until 2011, proposed a particular mix of radical neoliberalism domestically and protectionism in trade policy. It captured voters disappointed by the Right for being too cautious on labour market and social protection reforms, and those disillusioned by a Left considered too favourable to a neoliberal Europe.

The European dimension led to a difference of appreciation across the two blocs. Right-wing voters who most opposed European integration were those who expressed most strongly demands for domestic liberalization (no public jobs creation or minimum wage hike, more privatizations). On the left, the voters wanting the strongest form of state intervention were also those expressing the most negative judgments on European integration.

This evolution was confirmed during the 2000s and peaked during the referendum of 2005 on the European Constitutional Treaty. 'No' votes outnumbered 'Yes' votes among voters in the Left bloc which had a negative appreciation of globalization and the single currency, and also in the fraction of the Right bloc which expected a more free-market policy domestically while seeking a certain degree of protection against foreign competition.

Positive judgments on European integration can thus be found among voters of the traditional parties, gathering the superior and average income categories of the private sector (foremen, employees, junior and senior executives), self-employed professionals and farmers for the Right, the superior and average income classes of the public sector for the Left. All the categories with low-income, and/or which felt threatened in their status, drifted away from traditional parties: shopkeepers and craftsmen to the right; workers to the left.

The social alliances that had structured the French political life thus gradually decomposed during the 1990s. The internal contradictions on both sides of the political spectrum can be summed up as follows: on the right, a divergence emerged between the expectations of further liberalization held by self-employed persons and private sector employees who feared that this would lead to increased insecurity in their jobs; and on the left a cleavage emerged between public sector employees and workers, with the former supporting European integration and the latter strongly opposing it, perceiving it as a Trojan horse for neoliberal policies.

4. NEOLIBERAL REFORM AS A STRATEGY TO EXIT THE CRISIS

The political crisis and the uncertainties of France's model of capitalism are related. If the drive to neoliberal reform was simply an attempt to emulate the supposedly superior economic performance of the Anglo-Saxon model of capitalism, one would expect a course reversal after the Great Recession. However, neoliberal reforms are designed as a possible strategy out of the political crisis. The prominence of the question of the French model and its reform is the consequence of a state of systemic crisis (Amable and Palombarini 2009; Palombarini 2009): within the broad existing institutional framework, no strategy is able to generate the support necessary for its political validation.

Political crisis (the absence of a dominant social bloc) and demand for institutional change are related. In a political crisis, a change in institutions is necessary to open a new mediation space between social expectations and to contribute to building a dominant social bloc. However, the absence of a dominant bloc implies that political projects for institutional change will meet strong opposition. The political crisis may then lead to a systemic crisis, characterized by the existence of numerous and contradictory projects for institutional change, none of which are able to prevail over the others. Political circumstances and the capacity of political leadership to grasp opportunities and form varied and specific alliances will determine which political/institutional project will prevail. It is only through the actual implementation of a project of institutional change that the political crisis will end. The winning strategy will determine the profile of the new dominant bloc, and the separation between dominant and dominated interests.

Strategies out of the political crisis must therefore correspond to an exit from the systemic crisis too. Considering the current state of the political forces, one may envisage four possible social alliances and their related economic models.

4.1. Reorganization of the Right bloc supporting a neoliberal model

This option was successfully taken up by Sarkozy during the presidential election campaign of 2007. The main contradiction within the Right bloc was to reconcile expectations of liberalization of the labour market expressed by the self-employed, shopkeepers and craftsmen with the demands of protection expressed by employees in the private sector. The refusal of a radical neoliberal policy by the French Right during the Chirac presidencies had driven the self-employed, craftsmen and shopkeepers away from traditional parties. By showing a determination to implement a *'rupture tranquille'* with the immobility allegedly characterizing previous governments, Sarkozy was able to reunite the Right bloc. Two areas were exploited to reassure private sector employees. The first one was the promise of a possible rise in household disposable income by an increase in the supply of labour. This took the form of an easing of regulations on overtime work and a cut in taxes on related earnings. This was also part of the strategy to empty the 35-hour week regulations of their contents without incurring the political cost of abolishing them, while at the same time keeping and even extending the labour force flexibility measures which had been part of the *quid pro quo* between government and trade unions when the 35-hour law was passed. The second area was the assurance that labour market flexibilization would be based on French-style flexicurity (i.e., flexibility combined with income security) and not purely and simply 'Anglo-Saxon' flexibility.

Sarkozy has encountered difficulties in both areas since the space of mediation between neoliberal expectations and demands for protection seems to have shrunk. The programme implemented by Sarkozy fell short of satisfying the Right's neoliberal wing, which wanted drastic labour market deregulation. Neither the cuts of taxes on extra hours worked nor the pseudo-flexicurity seemed to please neo-liberal economists such as Pierre Cahuc and André Zylberberg, who for instance noted that: 'Far from establishing a culture of work, the cuts in taxes on overtime work facilitate tax opportunism, because everyone has the possibility of paying less taxes by exploiting the flaws of badly designed regulations' (Cahuc and Zylberberg 2009: 164). Regarding employment legislation, the neoliberal ideal appears to be a single labour contract abolishing the distinction between regular and unconventional work contracts. Here, too, Sarkozy has been criticized by Cahuc and Zylberberg:

the law on the modernization of the labour market . . . is not the proof of the success of Sarkozy's method, but well and truly that of its failure. Left free to negotiate without precise directives, labour unions obtained a minimal agreement reflecting the interests of those they represent above all, namely skilled workers and senior employees, as well as the companies that employ them. (Cahuc and Zylberberg 2009: 29–30)

The attempt to reconcile the contradictory expectations of the self-employed and private-sector employees explains the seemingly schizophrenic character of Sarkozy's political discourse. Getting out of this contradiction to satisfy conflicting expectations would require implementing reforms promoting flexicurity. But two major obstacles stand in the way of such a strategy and hint at its likely failure. First, the high level of unemployment and the rising weight of the public debt make a system guaranteeing generous benefits to the unemployed and a strong public financial support for their retraining difficult to sustain. Second, a flexicurity system demands the presence of strong and cooperative labour unions, particularly in the private sector, a condition that is far from being fulfilled in France.

4.2. Reorganization of a Left bloc for a Continental/social-democratic model

The ambiguities of the traditional left parties regarding the type of socio-economic model they want to promote – either a consolidation of the Continental/social-democratic model with regulated markets or the transition toward a Lisbon-strategy-type of capitalism with deregulated markets – are a reflection of the split of the Left bloc, which separates the higher and middle classes of the public sector from workers and employees on the issue of European integration and the limits to impose on the neoliberal path followed by the French model.

A stable Left bloc requires reducing the social rift on European integration, which has led to the drift of a large part of the popular classes away from 'government parties' towards abstention or 'extremes' on the left or on the right. This implies that European integration should no longer be perceived as a Trojan horse for neoliberalism by this part of the electorate. It is partly the consequence of French political leaders' linking neoliberal reforms to the need to respect the 'European constraints' (e.g., the failed 1995 pension reform) but far more significantly a rejection of actual European policies, particularly integration being driven forward at the initiative of the European Commission.

Two types of problems appear to make reunification of the Left bloc difficult. First, if the fracture of the Left bloc stems from the excessively neoliberal orientation of European integration, only a significant reorientation of European policies could be a solution.[8] Yet this is difficult to imagine without a substantial altering of the rules of European integration: the prevalence of the 'fundamental freedoms' (the free movement of goods, capital, services, and people) over social objectives, the statutes of the European Central Bank (ECB), the unanimity rule in tax matters, etc. French Prime Minister Jospin paid the price of the break-up of the Left bloc during the 2002 presidential elections. He was conscious of the difficulties that the European Union implied for the definition of a left-wing policy:

for twenty years, Europe has been a zone of low growth, it was not able to prevent the rise of unemployment, it encouraged little social progress, it was passive in the face of the disorders of globalization. ... Without questioning the European project, which would be madness, there is a very serious need to revise its contents. (Jospin 2010: 255)

In the current configuration of the 27-country Union, this seems difficult. 'As Prime Minister, I did not question the principle of the independence of the European Central Bank. *I could not do it.*' (Jospin 2010: 254, emphasis added). What remains for the traditional left parties is merely to regret the state of things:

the assertiveness of Europe as an economic and political community is for me one of the most innovative and the most fertile facts of the 20th century. Naturally, I regretted the excessively [neo]liberal course of the European construction, but I did not use it as a pretext to turn my back to the project itself. (Jospin 2010: 253)

Second, the divisions of the Left bloc have had consequences on the relative situation between parties. The uncertainty on the reality of the balance of power within the Left makes it difficult to develop a coalition strategy.

4.3. Emergence of a pro-European centrist bloc for a social-liberal model

The third strategy is attempted by the centre-right party (MODEM), parts of the right party *Union pour un mouvement populaire* (UMP) and the Green party and the right wing of the Socialist party. It is a question of re-articulating the French political 'supply' around the support for European integration, acknowledging the split of the Left bloc and betting on the instability of the Right bloc. The new alliance would gather average- and high-income categories of the public and private sectors and exclude the lower classes and a large share of the self-employed. Theoretically possible, this *bourgeois* alliance faces two types of problems. First, the presidential and majoritarian electoral system with two ballots does not facilitate a reorganization of alliances, whereas a proportional system and a new balance of power in favour of the parliament would facilitate it. Such an institutional reform would face the opposition of established politicians. Second, political competition is organized around a right–left axis opposing widely defined in reference to the state intervention in the economy: markets' regulation and income redistribution. The construction of a *bourgeois* bloc demands that this cleavage disappear and that the new dominant cleavage should be the support for European integration. .

The model of capitalism corresponding to this political strategy would be a liberal version of the Lisbon strategy: product and financial market deregulation; labour market flexibility; an 'active' welfare state; and investment in education and high technologies. Such a project is ridden with internal contradictions and is based on incomplete institutional complementarities, being an unstable hybrid of the neoliberal and social-democratic models (Amable *et al.* 2009).

4.4. Emergence of an outsider bloc for a social/neoliberal/protectionist model

This is the follow-up of the traditional outsider strategy of the *Front National* (FN), but pursued with a new ambition by Jean-Marie Le Pen's daughter, Marine. Whereas the economic programme of J.M. Le Pen's party included some extreme neoliberalism (a limit on public spending to 25 per cent of the GDP, a 20 per cent flat income tax, etc.) mixed with protectionism, the 2011 programme incorporates some disparate social elements and focuses on a critique of the traditional Right's neoliberal leanings. The economic strategy of the *Front National* now revolves around the defence of the welfare state and the exit from the European constraints on economic policy, and first of all the euro. This strategy seeks to go beyond the hard core of the FN's electorate (mostly the self-employed and shopkeepers) and to cross over to a working-class electorate disappointed by the Left parties.[9] This corresponds to the symmetrical centrist pro-European strategy mentioned above and would gather the social groups neglected by the *bourgeois* bloc. But the symmetry is incomplete since, unlike the *bourgeois* bloc, the social groups targeted by the FN's new strategy are radically opposed on key economic issues such as the level of taxation, income redistribution or the legislation protecting employment. It could be a successful electoral tactic as long as the vote is an expression of protest against the dominant socio-political alliances, but it can hardly be conceived of as a coherent and sustainable political or economic strategy. The model of capitalism implicitly defined is a hybrid of the social-democratic (welfare state), neoliberal (labour market) and Mediterranean models (product market regulation) with extra nationalist elements added (some welfare state benefits would be limited to French nationals). Notwithstanding the economic and political incoherence of such a model, it is clearly incompatible with the participation of France in the European Union (EU).

5. THE CONSEQUENCES OF THE GREAT RECESSION

The Great Recession implies additional difficulties for each of the strategies presented above. Low growth and enduring public finance problems directly contribute to making political mediation more difficult by reducing available resources. The strategy of unification of the Right bloc rests on the possibility of reconciling the aspiration for a drastic deregulation in the labour market coming from self-employed persons with the request for economic security expressed by wage-earners. The flexicurity formula can only apply under certain conditions, which are at least partly lacking in France: for example, a system of vocational training permitting effective retraining of the workforce;

or powerful labour unions to ensure that flexicurity does not turn into mere flexibility.

But the most serious problem results from the consequences of the crisis in terms of unemployment and public finance. The long-term stability of a system of flexicurity requires that time spent in unemployment be short, given generous compensation and effective (and hence costly) training for the unemployed. The Great Recession makes unemployment spells more frequent and longer than before, increasing the cost of unemployment compensation. The ensuing problems for public finances could lead to limitations in benefit generosity. Only a drastic decrease of other types of public spending could allow for a way out of this difficulty, but this remains quite unlikely both for economic and political reasons. Besides the fact that it may not produce the miraculous economic effects that everyone seems to expect (Amable 2009a), flexicurity may thus be only an illusion, leaving a choice between pure and simple flexibility on the one hand, at the risk of losing support from part of the employees of the private sector, or security on the other hand, at the risk of alienating craftsmen and shopkeepers.

These contradictions are echoed in Sarkozy's hesitations about the right model to follow. He took pride in being nicknamed *Sarkozy l'américain*, and wanted to generalize asset-based mortgages for home acquisition[10] and was generally favourable to the Anglo-Saxon model as late as December 2007.[11] He then veered toward the German model in March 2008 ('we are going to do everything the way [Germany] did it'),[12] before reverting to Great Britain later the same month ('the UK has shown that there was a way in the global economy to attain strong growth, full employment and solidarity ... What is at stake for us is to take inspiration from the lessons of a successful experience, your experience').[13] Six months later, a world had crumbled: 'Self-regulation to solve all problems, this is over. *Laissez-faire*, this is over. The almighty market which is always right, this is over'.[14]

The results of the 2010 regional and 2011 local elections (respectively 35 per cent and 32 per cent of votes went to Sarkozy's UMP) confirmed the difficulties of the president's strategy. The recession has drastically restrained the already narrow space for mediation between the different interests within the Right bloc. So far, Sarkozy has disappointed both sides of his 2007 electorate by not deciding between a 'genuine' neoliberal policy and one that would protect employees against the risks and consequences of unemployment. The first disappointment explains the largely unanticipated revival on the *Front National*, the second the success of 'government parties' on the Left, while both probably explain the record levels of abstention. In such a context, the strategic space of Sarkozy appears drastically reduced. Maintaining a schizophrenic stance on neoliberal reforms would probably fuel the desertion of his electorate in the direction of the far right and the left. The choice is then between a more radical policy, which would keep groups tempted by the *Front National* within the Right bloc, but would lead to a drift of the private sector wage-earners towards the Left (or to abstention), or a rejection of such a policy, which would open an important space for the *Front National*, hoping to capture the vote of the self-employed.

The Great Recession is also a threat for the strategy of the Left bloc because it could strengthen the dualism among wage-earners and thus lead to a divergence between the expectations of groups constituting the traditional social base of the Left. Public finance problems aggravate the tensions between the groups affected by the crisis and those who are net contributors to the system of social protection.

The Left clearly came out of the regional and local elections of 2010 and 2011 as victorious, but this does not imply that it is united around a defined political project. The contradiction between two different political options can be read in the post-election comments of the Left leaders: those who aim at reconstructing the Left bloc, hoping to change the content of European-level macroeconomic policy and Treaty-based constraints on public debt and deficits; and those who accept the European constraints and stress the 'necessity of reforms', rejecting only the 'brutality' of Sarkozy's methods and the social injustice of his fiscal policy.

The Left bloc strategy is made difficult by the crisis and the consequences it has had on the conduct of macroeconomic policy at the EU level. Far from adopting a growth-enhancing stance, the authorities in Brussels and Frankfurt have acted as if the crisis were an opportunity to push for neoliberal reforms. The ECB, after having, albeit more slowly than its United States (US) counterpart, relaxed its monetary policy after the financial crisis, has reverted to a strong anti-inflationary stance in spite of a high level of unemployment in the euro area. Also, the 'pact for the euro' adopted in March 2011 reinforces this conservative trend by putting national budget policies under surveillance and more generally promoting a neoliberal agenda: monitoring of labour costs; deregulating the services sector; promoting labour market flexibility; lowering taxes on labour; etc. The evolution of the EU is therefore contradictory with the implementation of a Left bloc strategy for France.

As mentioned before, the building of the *bourgeois* bloc demands that the traditional left–right cleavage be overcome, i.e., the construction of a new cleavage, pro- versus anti-European integration in lieu of pro- versus anti-state intervention/redistribution. However, the economic crisis has had the opposite effect. It has strengthened the polarization on public intervention in the economy. On the one hand, wage-earners demand stronger protection against the risks of unemployment; on the other hand, the self-employed and small firms tend to consider that taxes, the size of the public sector and labour market regulation are increasingly strong obstacles given the uncertain outlook generated by the crisis. Thus, the crisis has reinvigorated the political cleavage around the mode of intervention of the state in the economy and destabilizes the 'centrist' project. But this does not mean that the project of a *bourgeois* bloc has no future. First, the above-mentioned contradiction within the Left bloc could intensify after the Left's victory at the 2012 presidential elections. Second, a more favourable economic context could lessen the political problems mentioned above. An essential role will be played by the strategy chosen by the Right: the choice of a radical neoliberal transformation of the

French social model will open a space in the centre (appealing mainly to private sector wage-earners) that the Left will be in a position to take over, on the condition of renouncing the support of a share of its social base, mainly the working class. The project of a *bourgeois* bloc could therefore be a possibility, directly supported by a so-called 'modern' Left, rather than by a centre party whose emergence is made difficult by the existing political institutions.

6. CONCLUSION

French capitalism has experienced continuous institutional change over the last three decades. The two attempts at a radical change of model were both short-lived. The Thatcherite shift of the traditional Right in the mid-1980s met strong social and political opposition and led to an electoral defeat that made Right coalitions favour an incremental approach to structural reforms during the following 20 years. The second attempt, with Sarkozy's victory in 2007, started vigorously but the most important economic crisis since the Great Depression quickly made the flexicurity approach to labour market deregulation unsustainable. This explains why the French model of capitalism, although substantially altered in certain domains, can still be considered as a Continental European model of capitalism. Whether the incremental structural transformation approach will be followed until hybridization finally produces drastic effects, or the Great Recession is used as an opportunity to push for more rapid neoliberal reforms, taking advantage of the EU-level instruments such as the pact for the euro, will depend on which socio-political alliance can succeed over the others.

Biographical notes: Bruno Amable is Professor of Economics at the University of Paris I Panthéon-Sorbonne, France, research fellow at CEPREMAP and member of the Institut Universitaire de France. Elvire Guillaud is Assistant Professor of Economics at the University of Paris I Panthéon-Sorbonne, France. Stefano Palombarini is Assistant Professor of Economics at the University of Paris 8, France.

ACKNOWLEDGEMENTS

We thank the editors of this collection and the two *Journal of European Public Policy* referees. This contribution is part of the ICATSEM project. We gratefully acknowledge support from EU and University of Paris 1 Panthéon-Sorbonne.

NOTES

1 The two cases where one right-wing government followed another were clear manifestations of a craving for change: an almost centre-left Chirac protecting the welfare state against the conservative Balladur and his neoliberal policy in 1995; Sarkozy's programme of *rupture* with the alleged immobility of Chirac's presidency in 2007.

2 The existence of a DSB implies neither that the compromise is based on the homogeneity of demands stemming from the social groups belonging to the dominant bloc, nor that the resulting model of capitalism is institutionally isomorphic. The DSB is based on a compromise that steers public policies; from the point of view of their genesis, institutions may stem from various and diverse compromises (Amable and Palombarini 2009).

3 An abundant literature considers this phenomenon as the 'hybridization' of models; see Deeg and Jackson (2007).

4 The existence of multilevel governance may sometimes destabilize a dominant social bloc (Callaghan 2010), but it may also open a new space for political mediation, change the relative bargaining positions of groups within or outside of the dominant social bloc, and facilitate the emergence of a new compromise in case of political crisis.

5 Abdelal (2007); Tiberghien (2007).

6 In their analysis, Guillaud and Palombarini (2006) use data from French post-electoral surveys conducted for five elections over the period 1978–2002 (data available at http://cdsp.sciences-po.fr). In the following, we reproduce part of their results.

7 For a similar analysis about the role of the European integration process becoming an important factor on the voters' space, see Grunberg and Schweisguth (1997).

8 This is the solution envisaged in the *project for 2012* of the socialist party.

9 The core of the *Front National*'s electorate is still composed of groups that expect some radical change of economic model, less taxes and a decrease in employment protection legislation. In the 2011 local elections, 43 per cent of the craftsmen and self-employed voted for the FN, but only 20 per cent of the employed workers.

10 French President Nicolas Sarkozy, speech delivered at *Convention pour la France d'après*, Paris, 14 September 2006.

11 'But one must note that some governments succeed in obtaining a higher growth in the long run for their country … What [the UK] has done, why should we not do it? What the English socialists understood, the French right could implement it' (Sarkozy, 'Discours aux PME', speech delivered at the Centre des Congrès, Lyon, 7 December 2007).

12 Sarkozy, speech given at the *CeBIT 2008*, Hannover, 3 March.

13 Sarkozy, speech before the two houses of the Parliament of the United Kingdom, Palace of Westminster, London, 26 March 2008.

14 Sarkozy, 'Discours de Toulon', speech delivered at the Zenith, Toulon, 25 September 2008.

REFERENCES

Abdelal, R. (2007) *Capital Rules: The Construction of Global Finance*, Cambridge, MA: Harvard University Press.

Amable, B. (2003) *The Diversity of Modern Capitalism*, Oxford: Oxford University Press.

Amable, B. (2009a) 'Structural reforms in Europe and the (in)coherence of institutions', *Oxford Review of Economic Policy* 25(1): 17–39.

Amable, B. (2009b) 'Capitalisme et mondialisation : une convergence des modèles', *Cahiers Français* 349: 57–62.

Amable, B., Demmou, L. and Ledezma, I. (2009) 'The Lisbon strategy and structural reforms in Europe', *Transfer: European Review of Labour and Research* 15(1): 33–52.

Amable, B. and Palombarini, S. (2009) 'A neorealist approach to institutional change and the diversity of capitalism', *Socio Economic Review* 7(1): 123–43.

Cahuc, P. and Zylberberg, A. (2009) *Les réformes ratées du Président Sarkozy*, Paris: Flammarion.

Callaghan, H. (2010) 'Beyond methodological nationalism: how multilevel governance affects the clash of capitalisms', *Journal of European Public Policy* 17(4): 564–80.

Culpepper, P.D. (2006) 'Capitalism, coordination, and economic change: the French political economy since 1985', in P.D. Culpepper, P.A. Hall and B. Palier (eds) *Changing France: The Politics that Markets Make*, Basingstoke: MacMillan Palgrave, pp. 29–49.

Culpepper, P.D., Hall, P.A. and Palier, B (eds) (2006) *Changing France: The Politics that Markets Make*, Basingstoke: MacMillan Palgrave.

Deeg, R. and Jackson, G. (2007) 'Towards a more dynamic theory of capitalist variety', *Socio Economic Review* 5(1): 149–79.

The Economist (2007) 'France: Sarkozy's Thatcher moment. Why Nicolas Sarkozy cannot afford to yield to French strikers', 15 November, available at http://www.economist.com/node/10134061

The Economist (2009) 'A new pecking order: there has been a change in Europe's balance of economic power; but don't expect it to last for long', 9 May 2009.

Grunberg, G. and Schweisguth, E. (1997) 'Vers une tripartition de l'espace politique', in D. Boy and N. Mayer (eds), *L'électeur a ses raisons*, Paris: Presses de Sciences-Po, pp. 179–218.

Guillaud, E. and Palombarini, S. (2006) 'Evolution des attentes sociales et comportement électoral: France, 1978–2002', *Working Paper PSE n° 2006-37*, Paris: Paris School of Economics.

Jospin, L. (2010) *Lionel raconte Jospin*, Paris: Seuil.

Morin, F. (1998) 'La Rupture du modèle français de détention et de gestion des capitaux', *Revue d'Economie Financière* 50: 111–32.

OECD (2010) *Employment Outlook*, Paris: OECD.

Palier, B. (2008) 'Les transformations du modèle social français hérité de l'après-guerre', *Modern & Contemporary France* 16(4): 437–50.

Palombarini, S. (2009) 'La France et l'Italie dans la tempête', *Projet n° 309*.

Schmidt, V. (2002) *The Futures of European Capitalism*, Oxford: Oxford University Press.

Schmitter, P. (1974) 'Still the century of corporatism', *Review of Politics* 36: 85–131.

Tiberghien, Y. (2007) *Entrepreneurial States: Reforming Corporate Governance? in France, Japan, and Korea*, Ithaca, NY: Cornell University Press.

Zemmour, M. (2009). 'The cuts of employer contribution in France: a discrete reform of social security?', Paper presented at the general conference of the *European Consortium for Political Research*, Potsdam, 10–12 September.

From the Southern-European model to nowhere: the evolution of Italian capitalism, 1976–2011

Marco Rangone and Stefano Solari

ABSTRACT   Before the 1980s Italy had the typical institutional configuration of Southern European capitalism: an important role for the state in controlling production activities and markets; limited social security; and high employment protection. In the last 30 years, Italian capitalism underwent a process of institutional change moving away from this configuration. The deepest reforms occurred in the 1990s and aimed to achieve a more market-oriented economy to cope with European market integration. Reforms, however, did not succeed in moving the economy towards a 'liberal market economy': they simply increased *laissez-faire* without achieving better co-ordination through markets, leaving Italy with an inefficient model.

1. INTRODUCTION: SOUTHERN EUROPEAN CAPITALISM REFORMED

Post-war Italian capitalism is included in the 'Southern European' (Sapelli 1995) or 'Mediterranean' (Amable 2003) model. This model has been shaped by the problem of backwardness relative to industrialization, which created difficulties in developing the institutions typical of Continental European co-ordinated market economies (CMEs) (Fuà 1980). That weakness was compensated for by deep structural regulation and massive state intervention to achieve some viable economic co-ordination. In recognition of this, Italy was included in the category of *mixed economies* with the deepest state intervention (Shonfield 1965) and later in *state-enhanced* capitalism (Schmidt 2008). For a long time this state-dominated model assured at least a moderate level of economic efficacy despite its weaknesses.

Industrial relations represented a weakness in this model, as they did not achieve solid and unitary interest representation or some enduring social pact throughout the economy. Nonetheless, for a long time in the core economic sectors the interests of large companies – either state-controlled or private family-owned – and those of trade unions were effectively balanced. In other words, despite labour market fragmentation and often harsh social conflict (Molina and Rhodes 2007a), those interests found some sort of compromise overall (also thanks to government intervention), leading to a distribution of income that was able to drive growth (Belloc and Pagano 2010).

This model underwent a deep process of reform inspired by a liberal view of the economy, which started with some sporadic changes in the 1980s and then ended abruptly in the 1990s. However, the main argument of this contribution is that these reforms only seemingly brought Italy closer to a liberal market economy (LME). Many institutional changes did not deliver the expected results; for example, while the market and institutional power of labour has been weakened dramatically, the entrenched power of family capitalism was not jeopardized, which led to an unbalanced distribution of income and slow growth (Bull and Rhodes 2007). As argued by De Cecco (2007) and Della Sala (2004), Italy became a dysfunctional political economy, with persisting harsh conflicts over the 'rules of the game' and a high exposure to international competition.

The aim of this contribution is to discuss the nexus between evolving political demands and institutional change over the last 30 years, with a specific focus on labour market reforms and the changing role of the state in these reforms. The theoretical framework adopted here considers institutional change as driven by the combination of various socio-economic groups' political demands – often shaped by international constraints. Institutional change produces a more or less coherent (non-conflicting) institutional arrangement, either helping or hindering economic investment and growth (Soskice 2007). A successful model of capitalism is marked by a capacity to grow, reproduce and expand production processes in the interest of the groups that support the government, but without creating macroeconomic and social unbalances (which slow down growth). Institutional change in Italy has made its model even less coherent.

Like Ferrera and Gulamini (2004), we will argue that while the most important changes have been constrained by external ties (Europe), the junctures and the direction of the institutional transformation have been settled by the internal and evolving relative power of domestic economic interests. The most intense changes of the 1990s were helped by entering European Monetary Union (EMU) which induced some collaboration between the social partners (Molina and Rhodes 2007b). However, after an initial benefit from 'liberal-market-oriented' reforms (mainly for financial reasons), the difficulties of the 'renewed' Italian model of capitalism may have worsened.

Three periods of reform are distinguishable and these roughly correspond to each of the three decades examined in this contribution. In the second section, we illustrate the institutional arrangements in Italy in the late 1970s, before the period of reversal in the direction of reforms. This reversal will be discussed in the third section, together with the first set of reforms from the 1980s. The fourth section will focus on the most intense reforms in the 1990s that were motivated by the desire to join EMU. The 'Berlusconi decade' (2000s) will be analysed in the fifth section. The causes, timing and consequences of institutional changes will be discussed in the sixth section, together with in-depth reflections on the viability of the resulting model according to the framework of institutional complementarity and path dependency (Deeg 2007; Deeg and Jackson 2007).

2. ITALIAN CAPITALISM IN THE LATE 1970S

The Italian institutional configuration at the end of the 1970s can be reasonably summarized in a few points.

Italy had a bank-centred financial system shaped by the 1936 banking law (similar to the contemporary *Glass Steagall*), separating short-term from medium-term lending and banks from industrial ownership. One peculiarity was that, as a result of widespread bank rescue programmes in the 1930s, large banks were publicly owned by the Institute for the Industrial Reconstruction (IRI), a state holding company, while local savings banks were in the hands of local government.

Moreover, Italy had a corporate governance system dominated by insiders (Deeg 2005a). This insider–outsider model of company governance (Aguilera and Jackson 2003) has been labelled *family capitalism*, as large non-state companies remained under the control of the entrepreneurs' families. In fact, *Mediobanca* organized a 'trust' of intertwined shareholdings to protect the power position of a number of important families. The reduced transparency of the stock exchange made the position of minority shareholders quite weak. Consequently, domestic savers preferred to invest in treasury bonds (until the middle of 1990s), thereby facilitating the growth of government debt.

On the industrial side, state-controlled companies operated in many manufacturing and service sectors; they invested directly in high-tech production processes, public utilities and industrial activities in less developed areas to reduce the regional gap created by private business. This reinforced the role of a small number of large companies as powerful forces of economic growth from the 1950s to the 1970s. They also spearheaded the export-led growth trajectory that the government chose at the start of post-war development period (Fuà 1980; Graziani 1998). Large companies (private or state-owned) prevailed in the core oligopolistic sectors where trade unions were also strong.

The largest unions were linked to the major political parties, while a large number of small unions thrived in the public sector, and governing parties used them as a means of political control. This fragmentation of unions, and the propensity for conflict that stemmed from it, required the state to play an extensive role in managing industrial conflict. Though the government often involved industry associations and trade unions in the regulative processes of the economy, a neo-corporatist industrial relations system was never achieved, as attempts were inconsistent and weakly institutionalized (Ferrera and Gualmini 2004). Moreover, powerful trade unions ensured that relatively high wages were granted to unionized workers (also in real terms owing to the centrally agreed automatic adjustments to inflation), which induced large firms to adopt capital-intensive techniques. This created economies of scale and mono-polistic positions for large firms which could also enjoy lower interest rates when borrowing from the banking system. A sort of 'institutional equilibrium' between high labour protection of medium- and large-firm employees and strong paternal management and concentrated ownership was therefore achieved (Belloc and Pagano 2010). This pulled the system towards a distri-bution of value added that was relatively favourable to labour (more than 80 per cent of gross domestic product [GDP] in the middle of the 1970s).

The employment relations emerging from the institutional setting of the early 1970s was centred on the long-term relationship between the male breadwinner and the firm. Very low female labour force participation rates, as well as negligible part-time or temporary work contracts, were the norm. The 1970 labour statute provided workplace stability and labour protection to workers in firms with more than 15 employees. Strong labour protection—formalized in the 1970 labour statute – was also consistent with the family-based social security system (Ferrera 1996). In contrast to the conditions for workers in larger firms, very little protection against employers' anti-worker behaviour was granted in small firms. This dualistic approach to the regulation of the productive system made the whole industrial system more flexible (Graziani 1998).

The state assumed a central role in assuring compatibility between family capitalism and high labour protection in the core of the economy by ensuring at least acceptable profitability to business through product market regulation and direct industrial intervention (including favourable credit policies). Although this model of growth was inflationary, it made higher labour costs affordable to companies because of the currency depreciations that were possible (until 1995). Yet, the economic and political compromise described above was difficult to sustain, as it also required growing public deficits. Moreover, it tried to address, though somehow inconsistently, the political and budgetary demands of the increasingly important part of the economy based on small firms and self-employment. In fact, the challenge was to balance such diverse interests as those of 'family capitalism', small entrepreneurship, class-conscious labour and entrenched bureaucracy. This compromise was also challenged by the different needs and demands between regions, not only the traditional North–South divide, but also the emerging Centre–East, the so-called 'Third Italy'.[1]

In the latter region, a huge number of micro firms, specializing in highly prof-itable niches, and small and medium enterprises (SMEs), created a very dynamic and expanding economy, and they typically engaged in cost-driven activities based on incremental process and product innovations. This sector was barely unionized and was marginalized in the centralized bargaining process. However, they could gain from the regulatory role of the state that, with a 'tight' system of permissions and authorizations, fostered high profitability in many sectors. Moreover, by exerting a lax control on business practice, the state contributed to the growth of an unregulated market.

3. POLITICAL INSTABILITY AND THE U-TURN IN THE CONCEPTION OF REFORMS

The 1970s were characterized by progressive reforms orientated to increasing social expenditure (a 'universalist' system of healthcare was introduced and pension entitlements were expanded), on the one hand, and widening the fiscal base of the progressive tax to finance such expenditure (a reform which failed, thus giving birth to huge deficits) on the other. Moreover, the reaction to the oil crisis was based on an expansionary fiscal policy, which helped the continuity of industry (particularly SMEs). This progressive project was possible owing to the rising left-leaning political consensus that put growing pressure on centre-left governing coalitions, both from within – thanks to the Socialist Party – and from outside (the Communist party was the largest party but could not enter governing coalitions for international political reasons). In 1976, the Communist Party opened a new political era by externally supporting the centre-left government (in what has been called the 'historical compromise'), while Bettino Craxi was elected leader of the Socialist party.[2]

This was arguably the period in which Italy was closest to adopting a neo-corporatist framework. Government and industry associations were relatively weak, while the trade unions were at their maximum strength and unity and were ready to move away from conflictual toward participatory relations. Even the Italian General Confederation of Labour (CGIL), in a famous conference in Rome in February 1978, stated that wages could no longer be used as an 'independent variable' in macroeconomic conditions. However, this situation did not last long because of ideological shifts within the ruling coalition: in mid-1976 Bettino Craxi became leader of the Socialist Party and translated the rising political demands of the urban middle class into an alliance with the right-wing sectors of Christian Democrats – rather than the left-wing currents – in order to support his mix of liberal and nationalistic instances.[3] That was an undisputed rightward shift within the coalition. The right turn was also reinforced when the Christian Democrat's left-wing leader, Aldo Moro (he was major supporter of the historical compromise), was kidnapped and then killed by Red Brigades in March 1978.[4] The neo-corporatist solution was thus eventually dumped, only to be occasionally restored in times of difficulty. Subsequently, social pacts have been proposed in cases when a weak, moderate government faced some external challenge, but they were supported by employers for a short time and only when it was economically advantageous (Baccaro and Lee 2007).

The industrial restructuring that followed the second oil crisis spread an insider–outsider dualism even in the core sectors and jeopardized the unions' power. A point of rupture, symbolically and factually, was the long and painful strike at Fiat against planned permanent and temporary layoffs (*Cassa Integrazione Speciale* [CIGS]) of more than 23,000 manual workers. This ended in October 1980 with the defeat of the blue-collar workers after a march organized by clerks and mid-level managers (shopkeepers also supported them) who opposed the strike and called for the 'right to work'. This happened only eight years after the unions obtained a unitary bargaining framework for white and blue collars (1973). The Fiat strike can be assumed to be a symbolic turning point for economic policy; the main problem was no longer macroeconomic regulation, but a loss of competitiveness due to increased labour costs. On several occasions since then, trade unions have found themselves on opposing sides of this issue.

The first consequential institutional change was the labour market reform of 1984 (see Table 1) which had a clear goal of controlling inflation. It was implemented for the first time without the support of the largest trade union. Soon after the liberalization of capital movements in 1986, and with the adoption of a narrower oscillation band of the lira in the European Monetary System, short-term employment was redefined in a more permissive way in order to provide firms with an opportunity to increase their cost-competitiveness and to compensate them for the export sector difficulties caused by the real appreciation of the lira. However, even when the policy framework changed, the weaknesses of the political coalition did not allow the achievement of other relevant reforms (Amable and Palombarini 2009). Some institutional change was undertaken to ensure Italian institutions conformed to European directives, or to ensure they could cope with the constraints of the European Monetary System (see Table 1). For example, major steps were the recognition of the National Commission for Corporations and Stock Exchange (CONSOB) as an independent authority that ruled over the stock exchange, and above all, the liberalization of capital movements in 1986. At the same time, the various governments in that decade were unable to introduce sound measures to reduce fiscal deficits. Distributional tensions between the contrasting interests in the governing coalition prevented both the reduction in expenditure and the raising of taxes (Palombarini 2003).

4. THE AGE OF EMU-INSPIRED REFORMS

The birth of the Single Market and the Maastricht Treaty put the Italian model under renewed stress, and in 1992 the so-called *Tangentopoli* (Bribe-city) induced a marked political discontinuity. The crisis of 1992 represents a further critical juncture as it brought a deep delegitimization of the government coalition and the demise of Christian Democracy. In the political vacuum that arose, a series of governments based on so-called 'technicians' and supported by centre-left coalitions proposed a series of reforms to change the institutional configuration radically and reduce the role of the state in the economy. Progressive-liberal political leaders with strong external legitimization such as Giulino Amato, Carlo Azeglio Ciampi, Lamberto Dini and Romano Prodi took the lead in ensuring a viable programme of institutional change to radically reform the economic system, cut deficits and break the regime of corruption and modern clientelism. Additionally, political institutions were changed so that a roughly majoritarian or 'bipolar' electoral system was introduced (a

Table 1 Institutional change in Italy, a selection of relevant reforms

Institutional domain	Typology	Direction of change and examples of major reforms	Timing of major reforms
Financial system	Bank based: state-owned specialized banks	Incentives to development of stock exchange, introduction of universal banks and privatization	1986
		• Liberalization of capital movements and exchange controls	1990–1996
		• Privatization of state-owned banks	1993
		• Universal banking and de-specialization of credit institutions is reintroduced	
		• Increase of bank transparency relatively to clients	1992; 1999
		• Regulation of public take-over bids and investment funds	1992–1993
		• New framework for financial markets	1998
Corporate governance	Insider dominated: relevance of non-quoted companies	Increased transparency and accountability	1991–1998
		• Increased transparency and accountability; protection of minority shareholders	
		• Reform of the *trade code*, increased statutory autonomy and transparency	2003–2006
Industrial relations	Conflict-ridden: fragmented	De-institutionalization and flexibilization of labour market rules; weakening of trade unions	
		• Cut (1984) and abolished wage indexation mechanism	1984; 1992
		• Fixed-term employment contracts in permanent jobs	1987
		• Intermediate labour, flexible contracts, staff leasing allowed, incentives to part-time; interim employment agencies become employment agencies	1992–2002
		• Employment central agency reformed; redefined unemployment status, removed compulsory quotas for long-term unemployed	1997
Education and skills	Mixed	Orientation to on-job apprenticeship	
		• New regulation of apprenticeship	1997

Welfare state	Conservative-South European: pension-based; universalist health care	Retrenchment and pension rules based on notional defined contribution	
		• INPS is reformed, budgetary principles; previdence and assistance are separated	1989
		• Pension reform, Notional Defined Contribution regime, incentives to pension funds	1992–1997
		• Extends unemployment benefits to 'project workers' as an experimental measure (three years, reduced amount)	2009
Industrial policy	State entrepreneur and regulator	End of structural policies, privatization, deregulation and liberalization	
		• Initiatives for company restructuring and to develop the South	1979–1986
		• Anti-trust law, includes approval of mergers	1990
		• Privatization of state holding	1992–1997
		• Independent authorities for the regulation of public interest services	1993–1994
		• Liberalization of energy market and postal services; deregulation of many small activities; reduction of consumers' exit costs in public utilities contracts	1999; 2006–2007

system that, according to Soskice [2007] favours a liberal market model of capitalism).

Such a profound political crisis opened the doors to a 'liberal-progressive' view of the economy aimed at increasing the role of markets and competition in the economy in line with the logic of the Single Act and the Maastricht Treaty. We may interpret this change as a case of 'crisis exploitation' (Boin *et al.* 2009) where multilevel governance resulting from the European Union (Callaghan 2010) acted as the external constraint, which simultaneously brought forth the unsustainability of previous deficit spending (through high interest rates) and legitimized the direction of reforms.

The main reforms of the period (see Table 1) were the privatization of state-owned companies and the banking law (reintroducing universal banking).[5] Reforms of the pension system were introduced to curb the rising social expenditure that resulted from generous early retirement entitlements, as well as to gain some credibility with international financial investors and thereby reduce borrowing costs (pension system reform is appreciated by both financial markets and European institutions). In this case, the *notional defined benefit* scheme was introduced and some incentives in favour of private pension funds were created to achieve greater solidity of the 'third pillar' of the pension system. On the other hand, labour market reforms progressively increased the flexibility of this market.

Law 359/1992 concerned the general privatization of state holdings. Privatization of these companies occurred primarily from 1993 to 1997 and contributed significantly to controlling the government deficit. On the other hand, law 218/1990 allowed the privatization of state-owned banks (both large banks owned by the state holding IRI and local savings banks owned by local public institutions). This opportunity was exploited over the next few years. The capital deriving from the privatization of local savings banks was invested in local foundations (non-profit institutions) with a cultural promotion mandate. In addition to these reforms, a wide set of changes in the rules governing financial markets and corporate governance was implemented beginning in 1992 until the end of the decade. These aimed to radically change opaque family capitalism (Deeg 2005b, 2009).

Following these reforms, a massive programme of bank concentration that was driven by the Bank of Italy through mergers and acquisitions followed. Such concentration led to a verticalization of power relations in the market and a re-orientation of credit in favour of medium and large firms. Moreover, the new financial structure was able to reorganize the élite of *family capitalism* thanks to a new net of intertwined shareholdings between banks, financial companies and large enterprises (Culpepper 2007).

Labour reforms were conceived to allow the structural (both sectoral and regional) and the macroeconomic adjustment necessary in an open economy. A first big step was the elimination of wage indexation in 1992 by Amato. In addition to taking the first steps toward pension reform, his coalition was able to stipulate an agreement with *Confindustria* and the trade unions to introduce two-level collective bargaining and a framework for subsequent labour market reforms (Agreement, 23 July 1993). In a similar vein to what has been found in other countries, these governments pursued a tentative 'incomes policy' that required the collaboration of trade unions (Hanké and Rhodes 2005). To entice them to participate, a new function in assisting employees in their fiscal duties (such as compilation of income tax statements) was conceived. The leftist government from 1996 to 2000, led by Prodi and eventually by D'Alema, was again concerned with structural reforms of the labour market, both on the welfare side and the labour market *strictu sensu*. In 1997, the Labour Minister Treu reformed many institutions, including apprenticeship and training. Above all, Treu permitted private employment agencies to intermediate labour (interim work), which was previously illegal. However, as the previous law was not abolished, the change was less effective than expected.

Reflecting on left-wing 'emergency' government reforms in the 1990s, Ferrera and Gualmini (2004) argued that Italy was saved by Europe, as the latter acted as a reference for reforms to be achieved and legitimized emergency policies (in the absence of sound electoral support). These governments took up the 'liberal-progressive' orientation of the time and based their idea of change on a free-market view of the economy implied in the Maastricht treaty. In this sense Italy conforms to Cioffi and Höpner's (2006) 'left party paradox' – that left parties were responsible for free market policies in many European countries. Besides adhering to the European constraints, this Italian 'New Left' aimed to dismember the political-economic institutions that had been structured in the previous regime, in particular the complementarity between family capital-ism and high labour protection, which saw the state acting both as a structural element and as a compensating factor for the lack of long term social pacts (Molina and Rhodes, 2007b). To dismember family capitalism, financial markets and corporate governance were reformed to increase the contestability of corporate control and transparency for investors. Moreover, privatization increased stock market flotation and eliminated many of the state holdings that had been 'passive' competitors of private industries (which had assured a quasi-oligopolistic structure and rents). To dismantle high labour protection, reforms were enacted that reduced formal labour protection and entitlements (such as pensions) and stimulated social mobility. The reformation of the train-ing system also confirms the tendency to move away from passive measures towards more active policies that promoted flexibility and on-the-job training. Accordingly, labour market reforms may be read as a programme oriented to introducing more market principles and individual responsibility in this domain. Yet, the result, in the absence of a tangible reduction of family capit-alism, was an asymmetrical change in labour relations through the impairment of workers' contractual positions without a 'reconstruction' of the institutions that could better meet the requirements of a market-based economy.

Flexibility was needed to allow companies to restructure in accordance with the externally-imposed rigidities of the EMU (which was entered at a non-favourable exchange rate). Inflation was lowered by reducing real wages, but it remained higher than in Germany and France by about a one percentage point per year. Therefore, competitiveness was slowly eroded year after year (Graziani 2002). The response of Italian financial élites was to move capital from businesses exposed to global competition towards the newly privatized public utilities (telecoms, motorways, energy production, etc.). Moreover, globalization prompted a further tendency towards de-industrialization as many medium-sized firms moved production outside of Europe. As a consequence, the choice to join the EMU saved Italy from insolvency, but its structural problems were not solved (indeed, perhaps worsened) and the lack of autonomous monetary policy created new difficulties for the economy.

5. THE 2000S: THE 'NEW CONSERVATIVE' MISCARRIAGE AND FRUSTRATION

The centre-right coalition regained control of the political stage in the 2001 election by capitalizing on the popular distress caused by the 'new European arrangements' in many sectors of the economy. Although the vote shares were close to those of the previous elections, the right wing coalition won in almost every district. In fact, the political base of the progressive camp was weakened and disaffected by the 'liberal' policies of previous governments.

The right-wing coalition took the lead, old conservative forces lost importance, and the new right was supported by the interests of SMEs, professionals and finance. While the right governments could have taken advantage of institutional changes achieved by previous reforms and in particular from weakened and divided labour unions, it produced few effective reforms aside from the progressive reduction of labour protections. This ineffectiveness was largely due to the difficulty of building a consensus among the conflicting interests supporting these governments and to the increasingly prominent political role played by the Northern League, which eventually regained support from smaller firms and from part of the northern working class.

The main aim of the right-wing coalition was to erode the independent power of the state bureaucracy, to reduce further 'rigidities' in the labour market and to break down labour associations. The most peculiar aspect of this period is, therefore, the active role of the government in breaking the unions' unity and in the de-legitimization of the largest trade union (CGIL) during the negotiation of labour contracts.

The right-wing government implemented a law that made interim work effective both for permanent and temporary jobs. The aim was to liberalize both firing and hiring procedures. The goal was first achieved in 2003 (*D.Lgs* 276) when many atypical contracts were introduced. In particular, 'project contracts' in the private sector replaced the 'co.co.co' that had designated a form of subordination though formal independent job contracts. Such contracts allowed firms, especially in non-manufacturing sectors, to obtain flexibility and bypass the restrictions of full-time permanent work that were considered too costly by employers. The short-lived (2006–2008) left-wing Prodi government tried to narrow the scope of project contracts, limiting them to temporary jobs (*L.247*/2007). Yet law 133/2008 enacted by the newly elected right-wing government reintroduced and extended to all employers these 'call-up' jobs (*lavoro intermittente* or *a chiamata*) that the *L.247* had limited to a few, well-specified cases. Finally, during the crisis caused by the financial crash, some unemployment benefits were 'experimentally' extended to temporary employees, since employers favoured the extension of this kind of social security.

A further 2003 reform allowed the adoption of a plurality of governance models for companies. Firms could now choose between the traditional Italian model, the 'monistic' (Anglo-Saxon) model, and the 'dualistic' model (German style, but without stakeholder, i.e., labour, representation). Some additional laws increased the transparency of financial markets, clarified the responsibilities of intermediaries (after the Parmalat scandal), enacted the self-discipline of quoted companies and adopted international accounting standards. The Parmalat and many other financial scandals were fundamentally caused by the securitization of banks' bad loans; these were a sign of a growing conflict of interest between universal banks (actually financial conglomerates) after the reforms and the centre of the 1990s. They showed that the idea of a 'free market economy' in a situation of unbalanced power and information asymmetry between the actors led to dysfunctionalities. Subsequent measures to overcome the problem obliged banks to better inform clients, but Italian savers never regained confidence in financial institutions.

The short-lived, left-wing government from 2006 to 2008 adopted a new programme of liberalizations to continue the agenda of the 1990s, starting with product market liberalization and deregulation of free professions. The effort was rather ineffective, as it proved very difficult to undermine the diffuse vested interests since they were not simply rule-based but deeply institutionalized in social habits and consolidated entitlements (as in the patrimonialization of administrative licences).

An example involves taxi drivers who are granted licenses by municipalities on a limited basis. Entry is restricted and licenses are capitalized and traded. Typically, they are used by drivers to finance retirement. Liberalization of licenses would not only mean a fall in prices (owing to increased competition), but also the expropriation of an incumbent's capital. A taxi strike led the government to withdraw the reform proposal. Notaries are another powerful example of an institutionalized rent position. Their functions are crucial in the Italian law system because they must validate many contracts. Moreover, entry into the profession is controlled by their association, which also prescribes fees. The group was able to lobby successfully against both the liberalization of fees and the bureaucratic simplification that eroded their rents.

Although important, this government's effort was badly misdirected inasmuch as inflationary pressures and low productivity arose from the 'privatized and liberalized' sectors more than from small business (Thomasberger and Solari 2007). Additionally, the outcome of the deregulation process was often more a degradation of the conditions of service provision rather than an increase in efficiency. An example is the case of the relaxed controls over the retail sector that had recently gone through a huge crisis. The Chambers of Commerce used to implement spatial planning to uniformly distribute services. However, as this function was eliminated, a harmful 'race to the centre' of towns started, which increased urban rent and left peripheral zones with empty shops and a low supply of good quality services. It appears that an important complementarity exists between the regulation process that is based on legally accorded rent positions of small businesses and the polycentric (and spatially fragmented) nature of Italian economic activities. The demise of such regulatory activity also triggered a deep change in the spatial organization of economic processes, which displayed some undesired and unexpected costs.

6. THE VIABILITY OF LABOUR MARKET ONGOING DEREGULATION

In some respects the Italian process of labour market deregulation resembles the British experience. In the latter case, signs of change were already apparent during the 1970s. In the 1980s a 'muddling through' (Gospel and Edwards 2012) reform process modified irreversibly the institutional framework of the labour market. In Italy the process was similar but took much longer. In three decades, Italy underwent an apparently radical political and institutional change that reversed the priority given in the 1970s to labour stability (Schmidt 2008). In the early 1980s the political environment changed dramatically: Christian Democracy, a truly comprehensive compromise-oriented party, started losing its base of support and gradually gave way to 'new rich' or 'pro-business' specialized parties (these found their apotheosis in *Forza Italia* in the 1990s). Also the PCI (communist party) and its related trade union, CGIL, began to lose a grasp on their social base after a major defeat in the famous 1980 Fiat strike.

Labour reforms thus began as a relatively continuous but fragmented process of incremental changes in the 1980s. Even in the 1990s there was still not a systematic project of institutional reform: in most cases, labour market and industrial relations reforms did not reflect an organic view of how such markets should work in practice and how labour negotiations should take place – they simply reflected the logic of reducing strictures and rigidities for enterprises. Reforms of the 1990s can be seen as an attempt to defeat the consolidated power structure and rent positions that thrived under the previous political compromises. This was sought by introducing 'more market' in every sector of the economic and political system (Cioffi and Höpner 2006).

The economic policy priority of pursing corporate competitiveness eventually became hegemonic and was certainly not discouraged by European institutions. Although the European Union could have provided the opportunity to achieve a legal space of uniform labour protection (as it did for other standards), this was undermined by the Single Act and the Maastricht Treaty that exposed labour legislation to competition. The latter acted as an external constraint limiting the efficacy of previous institutional arrangements, in particular it blocked any 'compensating' role of the state which had been a pillar of the old Italian model. Whereas internal forces settled the junctures and the direction of the process of change, evolving external ties with European institutions deeply affected the relative strength of the negotiating forces and legitimized many specific changes.

However, the interesting fact in the process described above is that when labour reforms assumed a crucial role in the systemic change of the economy, no substantially positive result was actually achieved. Nonetheless, labour institutions were continuously made more flexible according to a generic liberal logic. It is now commonplace to blame the difficulty in achieving coherent reforms on veto players. However, a majoritarian trade union like CGIL cannot be treated as a veto player, which is a term reserved to minority actors in a negotiation. Rather, reform proposals were often unilateral and ignored the unions' different viewpoints. As a consequence, it was difficult to find a general consensus on labour market rules. This is the natural consequence of top–down policy-making.

We argue that, while policy (rule) changes reflect the changing balancing of political forces, the effects of the measures undertaken may also be assessed according to their consistency with the economic and social system as a whole. The two aspects are not necessarily consistent with each other. Let us see why.

Progressive deregulation of labour in Italy has produced a more unbalanced distribution of income between labour and capital than elsewhere. In fact, labour's share of GDP in Italy fell progressively from 79.5 per cent in 1980 to 66.9 per cent in 2007. The Gini index before tax and transfers of working age people rose in Italy from 0.39 in the mid-1980s to 0.49 in the mid-2000s. In contrast, figures in Britain (representing a LME benchmark) remained almost unchanged – labour income share fell from 71.2 per cent to 69.1 per cent, and the Gini index rose from 0.39 to only 0.41. Moreover, exit of discouraged workers from the labour market reached 2.64 per cent of total population in 2008 in Italy but stayed at 0.09 per cent in Britain.

Our explanation of this outcome points to the whole institutional arrangement presently found in Italy and not only on labour market institutions. The specific arrangement of the Southern European model tends to be more exploitative of labour (Rangone and Solari 2012), which needs to be granted solid entitlements to get fair contracts. In other words, we argue that the consolidated power structure was addressed by reforms over the past 30 years but at the cost of disrupting the balance of forces in the economy.

Some elements that have been defined as inefficient and dismantled (e.g., small banks, labour regulation and some state holdings) were important for the co-ordination of economic processes. This caused: (a) severe problems in economic co-ordination, e.g., large banks reduced financing to SMEs, precarious labour spread to advanced services, the fall of R&D expenditure; and (b) stagnation of the economy with related losses in labour productivity (Tronti 2010). At the same time, the EMU blocked any policy measures that could allow Italy to regain competitiveness by macroeconomic adjustments (often a way out in the previous decades). Italian reformers did not sufficiently consider the structural role of crucial institutional complementarities and the bedrock effect of family capitalism.

An equal reduction of power positions of both protected labour and family capitalism can be now recognized as a utopian ambition of reformers (Pagano and Trento 2003). The increased role of the stock exchange and its claimed transparency does not automatically achieve a more competitive corporate sector. Italian entrepreneurs have often used the bull market to increase their leveraged control over companies, and the rebirth of universal banks helped this process.[6] The problems of Italian competitiveness that arose from bad co-ordination strengthened the demand for a progressive flexibilization and pre-carization of the labour force. However, since precariousness increases uncertainty among workers, aggregated demand stagnates and entrepreneurs in turn ask for more labour flexibility to face this uncertainty and flagging demand. Fiat may be taken as a case in point. In a tense industrial dispute over labour conditions in the workplace that carried on into late 2010, the CEO of Fiat threatened to move production out of Italy. He eventually won the dispute on the basis of safeguarding most of the existing jobs while gaining workplace flexibility. Yet, this agreement was reached against the will of the main union (CGIL) that had strong support among the workers.

7. CONCLUSION: 'IF WE WANT THINGS TO STAY AS THEY ARE, THINGS WILL HAVE TO CHANGE'

After reshaping itself within the international context of the 1970s, Italian capitalism was defined as a *dysfunctional system* (Della Sala 2004), which was none-theless made viable through structural state intervention. Such a system had the merit of distributing income in a way that enabled growth via the expansion of consumption.

We have studied institutional change as a result of changing political demand and coalitions. Our analysis began with the change in political demands at the end of the 1970s that caused a 'U-turn' in the direction of institutional change, coinciding with that of many European countries. However, fragmented inter-ests and coalition governments inhibited deep reforms in the 1980s. These could only take place in the emergency situation of the 1990s thanks to a set of progressive governments and the incentives to join the EMU. The 2000s saw an attempt to rebuild a liberal-conservative order or, better, a pro-business regime. However, this too failed to achieve economic growth.

The overall conclusion we draw, given the economic stagnation from 2000 onwards, is that Italy is hampered by 'misguided' rather than 'incomplete' reform. Though we concede that some uncertainty remains as to whether the medicine was wrong or whether we did not take enough of it. This alternative conclusion is the one most commonly advanced by economists (the *Bocconi* orthodoxy), but we think it does not consider the difficulties and unexpected effects of rationalistic top–down reform plans. The only organic institutional change, that of the 1990s, was the result of reforms enacted to comply with external constraints, notably European treaties. The conception of economic institutions expressed in European treaties are apparently at odds with the typical form of Southern European capitalism. They consequently induced an asymmetry between the domestic political forces and weakened the position of labour. The left-wing liberal governments of the 1990s dismantled some funda-mental institutions in the typical Southern European mixed economy, such as state intervention and labour protection. The labour market reforms were along the same lines of those introduced in the UK in the 1980s or in other Euro-pean economies (e.g., Germany), but the impact was different. Above all, they attempted to change the whole balance in society to achieve a more 'market-oriented' system of relationships. While they were able to weaken the position and entitlements of labour, they could not induce effective changes on the finance-corporate side. Family capitalism reorganized in the new context with new financial arrangements. Without the state to compensate and maintain labour's share of national income, and thus aggregate demand, growth suffered. Instead of moving towards a LME, Italy simply fell apart relative to the standards of CMEs.

When the new right came to power in 2001 it took advantage of labour to further deinstitutionalize labour relations to keep profits high – general econ-omic stagnation notwithstanding. The consequence is that any recent effort to increase competitiveness has been made only by the precarization of labour and without serious policies to increase productivity. Therefore, Italy can be said to have enjoyed increased *laissez-faire* rather than better market co-ordina-tion. It is now an even weaker 'Southern Model' with more uncertainty and poor economic performance.

Biographical notes: Stefano Solari is Associate Professor of Political Economy at the University of Padua, Italy. Marco Rangone is Senior Lecturer in Econ-omic Policy at the University of Padua, Italy.

ACKNOWLEDGEMENTS

The study has received funding from the European Community's Seventh Fra-mework Programme FP7-2007-2013 under grant agreement number 225349.

We wish to thank the *Journal of European Public Policy* referees for their constructive criticisms.

NOTES

1 Attention was focused on territorial differences, as problems in the South involved an acute unequal distribution of income, but they were never taken up consistently. This problem of dualism has been a recent subject of a comparative study on capitalism (Gambarotto and Solari 2009) showing that in these regions, the fracture between centre and periphery is still relevant.
2 The idea that the country could be object of a Chile-like 'golpe' was at the origin of the 'historical compromise', a strategy the Communist Party adopted to back their own electorally based stance towards an active role in government.
3 See Ginsborg (2003: ch. V.4).
4 Terrorism heavily affected the labour relations system of the decade, which was already under pressure owing to the oil crises and other inflationary strains. The catchphrase of the 1978 congress of Rome was that wage could no longer be considered an 'independent variable'. This meant the end of an era of conflict, supporting the idea that workers had to accept wage reductions in order to beat inflation and invert economic recession. The newly acquired 'sense of responsibility' of trade unions was stated so markedly that on 24 January 1979 the Red Brigades killed Guido Rossa, a blue-collar worker and CGIL representative at Italsider who reported terrorist activity in his factory. That was a deathblow for the unions, and CGIL in particular, as it found itself in the uncomfortable position of supporting a restructuring policy while defending their battling role on the workplace.
5 The first attempt to reintroduce universal banking dates back to 1986, when mixed banking groups were allowed. However, it failed to deliver results.
6 As an example, thanks to the emission of new capital during the bull market, the owners of Geox S.p.A. can control 71 per cent of a 429 million euro net capital (2010) with a simple initial investment of 18 million euro.

REFERENCES

Aguilera, R.V. and Jackson, G. (2003) 'The cross-national diversity of corporate governance: dimensions and determinants', *Academy of Management Review* 28(3): 447–85.
Amable, B. (2003) *The Diversity of Modern Capitalism*, Oxford: Oxford University Press.
Amable, B. and Palombarini, S. (2009) 'A neorealist approach to institutional change and the diversity of capitalism', *Socio Economic Review* 7(1): 123–43.
Baccaro, L. and Lee, S.H. (2007) 'Social pacts as coalitions of the weak and moderate: Ireland, Italy and South Korea in comparative perspective', *European Journal of Industrial Relations* 13: 27–46.
Belloc, M. and Pagano, U. (2010) 'Co-evolution of politics and corporate governance', *International Review of Law and Economics* 29: 106–14.
Boin, A., Hart, P.'t and McConnell, A. (2009) 'Crisis exploitation: political and policy impacts of framing contexts', *Journal of European Public Policy* 16(1): 81–106.
Bull, M. and Rhodes, M. (2007) 'Introduction – Italy: a contested polity', *West European Politics* 30(4): 657–68.
Callaghan, H. (2010) 'Beyond methodological nationalism: how multilevel governance affects the clash of capitalisms', *Journal of European Public Policy* 17(4): 564–80.

Cioffi, J.W. and Höpner, M. (2006) 'The political paradox of finance capitalism: interests, preferences, and centre-left party politics in corporate governance reform', *Politics and Society* 34(4): 463–502.

Culpepper, P.C. (2007) 'Eppure, non si muove: legal change, institutional stability and Italian corporate governance', *West European Politics* 30(4): 784–802.

De Cecco, M. (2007) 'Italy's dysfunctional political economy', *West European Politics* 30(4): 763–83.

Deeg, R. (2005a) 'Remaking Italian capitalism? The politics of corporate governance reform', *West European Politics* 28(3): 521–48.

Deeg, R. (2005b) 'Change from within: German and Italian finance in the 1990s', in W. Streeck and K. Thelen (eds), *Beyond Continuity: Institutional Change in Advanced Political Economies*, Oxford: Oxford University Press, pp. 169–202.

Deeg, R. (2007) 'Complementarity and institutional change in capitalist systems', *Journal of European Public Policy* 14(4): 611–630.

Deeg, R. (2009) 'The rise of internal capitalist diversity? Changing patterns of finance and corporate governance in Europe', *Economy and Society* 38(4): 552–79.

Deeg, R. and Jackson, G. (2007) 'Towards a more dynamic theory of capitalist variety', *Socio-Economic Review* 5: 149–79.

Della Sala, V. (2004) 'The Italian model of capitalism: on the road between globalization and Europeanization?', *Journal of European Public Policy* 11(6): 1041–57.

Ferrera, M. (1996) 'The southern model of welfare in social Europe', *Journal of European Social Policy* 6(1): 17–37.

Ferrera, M. and Gualmini, E. (2004) *Rescued by Europe? Social and Labour Market Reforms in Italy from Maastricht to Berlusconi*, Amsterdam: Amsterdam University Press.

Fuà, G. (1980) *Problemi dello Sviluppo Tardivo in Europa. Rapporto su Sei Paesi Appartenenti all'OECD*, Bologne: Il Mulino.

Gambarotto, F. and Solari, S. (2009) 'Regional dispersion of economic activities and models of capitalism in Europe', *Economie Appliquée* LXI(1): 5–38.

Ginsborg, P. (2003) *Italy and its Discontents: Family, Civil Society, State, 1980–2001*, New York: Palgrave MacMillan.

Gospel, H. and Edwards, T. (2012) 'Strategic transformation and muddling through: industrial relations and industrial training in the UK', *Journal of European Public Policy*, 19(8), doi: 10.1080/13501763.2012.709023

Graziani, A. (1998) *Lo Sviluppo dell'Economia Italiana: Dalla Ricostruzione alla Moneta Europea*, Turin: Bollati Boringhieri.

Graziani, A. (2002) 'the euro: an Italian perspective', *International Review of Applied Economy* 16(1): 97–105.

Hancké, B. and Rhodes, M. (2005) 'EMU and labour market institutions in Europe', *Work and Occupations* 20(10): 1–33.

Molina, O. and Rhodes, M. (2007a) 'The political economy of adjustment in mixed market economies: a study of Spain and Italy', in B. Hancké, M. Rhodes and M. Thatcher (eds), *Beyond Varieties of Capitalism. Conflict, Contradictions, and Complementarities in the European Economy*, Oxford: Oxford University Press, pp. 223–52.

Molina, O. and Rhodes, M. (2007b) 'Industrial relations and the welfare state in Italy: assessing the potential of negotiated change', *West European Politics* 30(4): 803–29.

Pagano, U. and Trento, S. (2003) 'Continuity and change in Italian corporate governance: the institutional stability of one variety of capitalism', in M. Di Matteo and P. Piacentini (eds), *The Italian Economy at the Dawn of the 21st Century*, London: Ashgate, pp. 177–211.

Palombarini, S. (2003) *Dalla Crisi Politica alla Crisi Sistemica*, Milan: Franco Angeli.

Rangone, M. and Solari, S. (2012) '"Southern European" capitalism and the social costs of business enterprise', *Studi e Note di Economia* XVI(1): 3–28.

Sapelli, G. (1995) *Southern Europe since 1945*, London: Longman.

Schmidt, V.A. (2008) 'European political economy: labour out, state back in, firm to the fore', *West European Politics* 31(1): 302–20.

Shonfield, A. (1965) *Modern Capitalism: The Changing Balance of Public and Private Power*, Oxford: Oxford University Press.

Soskice, D. (2007) 'Macroeconomics and variety of capitalism', in B. Hancké, M. Rhodes and M. Thatcher (eds), *Beyond Varieties of Capitalism. Conflict, Contradictions, and Complementarities in the European Economy*, Oxford: Oxford University Press, pp. 89–121.

Thomasberger, C. and Solari, S. (2007) 'Reforms and continuity in the Italian economy: EMU at risk?', in E. Hein, J. Priewe and A. Truger (eds), *European Integration in Crisis*, Marburg: Metropolis Verlag, pp. 163–93.

Tronti, L. (2010) 'The Italian productivity slow-down: the role of the bargaining model', *International Journal of Manpower* 31(7): 770–92.

The role of state in development of socio-economic models in Hungary and Slovakia: the case of industrial policy

Anil Duman and Lucia Kureková

ABSTRACT This contribution systematically evaluates patterns of change in socio-economic models in Hungary and Slovakia, highlighting the role of the state in the process. While the countries share general similarities in their type of capitalism, a closer overview of institutional domains reveals that important differences exist in the character of change and the role of key actors. In terms of the overall reform paths, Slovakia, especially since the late 1990s, is more coherent and overwhelmingly in a liberal direction, while Hungary appears less radical and encompasses a combination of liberal elements and active state involvement. In this contribution we focus on industrial policy and find that Hungary adopted more comprehensive and vertical industrial support geared towards upgrading, foreign-capital openness throughout the economy, and support of the domestic small and medium enterprise sector. Slovakia developed its industry more through regulation than a direct intervention, opened to foreign capital only in late 1990s, and since then eschewed any attempt to nurture domestic capital.

1. INTRODUCTION

There have been various attempts to apply the Varieties of Capitalism (VoC) concepts to the emerging economies of Central and Eastern Europe (CEE)[1] since the seminal work of Hall and Soskice (2001). While some studies tried to locate the post-socialist countries in the liberal–co-ordinated market economy (LME–CME) continuum (Knell and Srholec 2007; Lane 2005; McMenamin 2004), others highlighted their transitional character (Hancké *et al.* 2007). Another strand emphasized the differences between CEE and the post-Soviet countries (King 2007; Myant and Drahokoupil 2012). Lastly, some scholars found variety within the CEE region, with Slovenia and Estonia as institutional antipodes resembling a CME and LME economy respectively (Buchen 2007; Feldman 2007).

There are also studies pointing out the ineptness of the VoC classification in capturing the characteristics and developments of the socio-economic models of the transition economies: these countries are faced with the paramount influence of transnational factors and their institutional set-up is to a large extent unstable and unconsolidated (Bohle and Greskovits 2009; Nölke and Vliegenthart 2009). Moving beyond the VoC categories, Bohle and Greskovits (2007) propose that there are divergent paths towards neoliberalism – neoliberal (Baltic countries), embedded neoliberal (Visegrad) and neocorporatist (Slovenia) – whereby external influences are shaped by an interplay of structural and institutional factors, past legacies and their perceptions by the political élite. Adopting the VoC's analytical concepts most rigorously, Nölke and Vliegenthart (2009) argue that a distinct capitalist model, namely 'dependent market economy' (DME), has emerged in these countries. This model is particularly characterized by a high degree of reliance on foreign capital and export-led growth. The Visegrad countries that are deemed exemplary cases of DMEs share a 'new' institutional complementarity built on skilled but cheap labour and the provision of technological knowledge and capital via foreign firms. They thus possess a comparative advantage in the assembly and production of complex manufacturing durables.

This contribution illustrates the role of state in shaping socio-economic models in two CEE economies – Hungary and Slovakia – by comparing their development trajectories in the two decades following regime change. Hungary and Slovakia are classified as belonging to a similar variety of capitalism in the more encompassing typologies of post-socialist capitalism (Bohle and Greskovits 2007; Myant and Drahokoupil 2011; Nölke and Vliegenthart 2009;). They both adopted a path of foreign-dependent export-led growth that, in contrast to the Baltic states, was more 'embedded' through the provision of relatively generous incentive packages to foreign investors and social protection to domestic electorate, but unlike Slovenia lacked more genuine co-ordination between social partners. Our motivation for choosing these cases is driven by the goal of highlighting the different paths taken in spite of similar international financial institutions (IFIs) and transnational (private foreign capital) influences. These differences can be attributed to the countries' distinct economic positions at the onset of the transition, especially the external debt and the degree of openness, as well to the process of nation-making in Slovakia.

We complement the existing research by placing greater attention on the role of state in shaping the socio-economic models, providing historically detailed and country-specific accounts in a comparative perspective (cf. Nölke and Vliegenhart 2009: 673). To this end, the contribution provides rich empirical evidence that maps the dynamics of change in the last 20 years along six institutional domains: corporate governance; financial systems; skill formation and vocational training; employment and industrial relations; welfare state; and industrial policy. Through a brief but systematic overview of these domains, the contribution lays out differences in the socio-economic models in the two countries as found in 2010. In order to demonstrate more clearly the details of state activism and relative importance of different actors, we select industrial policy as an exemplary institutional domain and examine the variation across two countries and over time.

In terms of the overall reform paths, Slovakia, especially since its turning point in 1998, embarked on a more coherent and overwhelmingly liberal direction. In contrast, Hungarian reforms appear less radical and encompass a combination of liberal elements and active state involvement in most institutional domains. The differential goals set by the governing parties at the beginning of the transition constrained or enabled by socialist legacies (i.e., market openness, foreign debt, welfare state), political context (i.e., nation-building, minorities) and the role of institutional veto players (i.e., constitutional court) have been important factors that contributed to different paths of change and state activism. Therefore, even if Hungary and Slovakia can still be classified broadly as 'dependent market economies' or 'embedded neoliberals', there are significant differences between them in their adaptation and implementation of industrial policy, which significantly affects their capacity for maintaining their existing socio-economic models.

In the institutional area of industrial policy we find that Hungary adopted a more comprehensive and vertical industrial policy geared towards upgrading, and introduced relatively early schemes aimed at the development of domestic small and medium enterprises (SME) without necessarily disfavouring foreign firms. The Slovakian state was initially more subject to pressures from local business groups and adopted a foreigner-friendly approach only after the turning point in 1998, when the pro-reform coalition replaced illiberal Mečiar government. It developed its industry more through regulation than a direct intervention, abstaining from any attempt to nurture a domestic bourgeoisie. Hungarian governments managed to pursue an outward-looking policy from the start of the transition, unlike Slovakia, which could not resist the domestic business élites and pursued an outward-looking policy only from late 1990s. The initial choices enabled Hungary to enjoy a first-mover advantage, and later on these choices put the countries in significantly different positions with different capacities and possibilities for industrial policy.

Section 2 discusses each institutional domain in conjunction with the main features and broad underlying factors of the socio-economic models in both countries. In Section 3, industrial policy is evaluated by examining the key external and internal actors' impact as well as firm responses to the policy decisions. Section 4 concludes.

2. CHARACTERISTICS OF NATIONAL MODELS AND FIVE INSTITUTIONAL DOMAINS

The institutional starting points of Hungary and Slovakia were very different at the outset of their post-communist transition. Liberalization in Hungary already began at the end of 1960s when the country introduced elements of market competition, and prior to 1989 it established a handful of institutions that allowed it to progress very quickly at initial phases of transition. Greater openness of the Hungarian economy also meant that the country entered transition with high foreign debt. This is one of the key reasons for opening up the banking and manufacturing sectors very early on to foreign investors. Hungary was rewarded for its reform progress and pro-foreign attitudes with record high inflows of foreign direct investment (FDI). However, the country ran into severe fiscal problems and had to implement an austerity package, known as the Bokros package, in the mid-1990s. This is generally viewed as a turning point in the character of its model owing to its major effect on tripartatism and Hungary's welfare state.

Hungarian politics has been characterized by strong polarization of its polity and society, which has affected the depth and stability of the institutional reforms and led to policy oscillations. Contrary to the developments in Hungary, the socialist regime in Czechoslovakia became even more stringent politically after the 1968 Prague Spring, and the economic realm remained oriented towards the Council for Mutual Economic Assistance (COMECON) until the regime's collapse. After the Czechoslovak split in 1993, Slovakia took on a nation-building path under the leadership of Vladimir Mečiar signified by an anti-foreign stance and attempts to build a national business élite. The low initial foreign debt limited foreign influence on the government, and it postponed most of the reforms until after the political power shifted in 1998 to pro-integration and pro-Western government led by Mikulas Dzurinda. While the labour unions were marginalized in Hungary and did not play a significant role in instigating change, the Slovakian turning point was brought about with the support of unions for a mixed broad left–right coalition. Two pro-reform governments that took power from the end of 1990s significantly reshaped the Slovak socio-economic model.

The changes in Hungary and Slovakia over the last two decades were fundamental in both countries but they took a more gradual pace in the former and a much faster and deeper form in the latter. While both systems were fragile and heavily dependent on foreign investments at the end of the last decade, the Hungarian system overall appeared to be relatively solidaristic and characterized by a powerful and active state. The Slovak path was typified by a more dramatic withdrawal of the state, especially from the welfare system where extensive redistributive liberalization took place. There was also a rhetorical and an actual shift towards a regulatory state. The variation in timing as well as the type and extent of changes carried out in different institutional areas are summarized in Tables 1 and 2, and the key changes are discussed in the following sub-sections.[2]

2.1. Financial system and corporate governance

Two important processes marked the development of financial markets in transition economies: development of financial systems through bank restructuring and privatization; and the liberalization of capital accounts. In both countries the financial system is bank-based and investment capital has been generated primarily through the inflow of FDI. The national stock markets were opened up at the beginning of transition but the corporate governance standards in Hungary and Slovakia were formalized only in the early 2000s.

Table 1 Institutional design and change (2009): Hungary

	Typology	Major changes	Timing
Financial systems	Bank-based	Restructuring and privatization of state-owned banks. Several changes to the regulatory and supervisory structures resulting in streamlining and integrating supervisory structures in the National Bank.	1995–1998
Corporate governance	Insider-dominated	Introduction of CG Code which became binding for listed companies in 2004. Monistic company board structure (Anglo Saxon style) allowed since the 2006 Company Law amendment.	2004, 2008
Industrial relations	Conflictarian Dominant bargaining level: company Recognition of unions: Limited role owing to fragmentation which has been used to weaken and play off the unions	Tripartite and Labour Market Law (part of the same Labour Code) 1992 – established dualism; bargaining function to labour unions, consultative function to work councils; weaker position of unions compared to the Code of 1968; 2001 – established greater flexibility and gave more powers to work councils; transposed nine EU directives; 2002 - Labour Code amended after the social–liberal coalition won the elections and repealed several elements, i.e., changing the system of interest reconciliation (New Interest Reconciliation Council), repealing the amendment on work-council powers.	1992 2001 2002

(Continued)

Table 1 Continued

	Typology	Major changes	Timing
Education and skill creation	State-/school-based	Systemic and substantive reforms of vocational education and training very early on in transition and in mid-2000s:	1993 2005–2008 1993, 1996, 2005
		• substantive changes in National Core Curricula on all educational levels; • training levy and Vocational Education Fund; • Regional Training Centres; • National Council for Vocational Education; Progressive methodology introduced to devise study programmes based on labour market needs (2008).	
Welfare: pension system	Weakly privatized	1997–1998 – Major two-pillar pension system introduced 1998–2002 – Gradual implementation that was legislated was slowed down, changes to indexation. 2006–2010 – Reform continued, new measures introduced in the course of the 2009 economic crisis. 1994 – introduction of voluntary pillar.	1997–1998

Welfare: labour market policies	Welfare-workfare welfare system	1992–1993 – First major significant downward adjustment to UB. 2000–2001 – Eligibility eased but lowered duration of benefits, work availability requirement introduced; greater emphasis given to Labour Office tasks (job search assistance, career management, brokerage services). 2005–2006 – Conceptual remodelling of the system, activation logic fully introduced, replacement rates for UB lowered, contribution period requirement increased.	1992–1993 2000–2001 2005–2006
Welfare: healthcare system	State-controlled healthcare	Mid-1990s – privatization of primary care and drug sector, rationalization of in-patient care. 2006–2008 – Reform introduced more competition but preserved the control function of state, greater financial participation of patients while keeping solidarity of the system and universal (but controlled) assess.	1995–1997 2006–2008
Industrial policy	Active state	1988 – Act on the Investment of Foreigners – opening to foreign capital. 1993 – Industrial export processing zones. 2000 – 2003 – Szechenyi Plan and its followers. 2001–2003 – Wage regulation.	1988 1993 2000–2003

Source: Authors.

Table 2 Institutional design and change (2009): Slovakia

	Typology	Major changes	Timing
Financial systems	Bank-based	Restructuring and privatization of state-owned banks. Several changes to the regulatory and supervisory structures resulting in streamlining and integrating supervisory structures in the National Bank.	2000–2002
Corporate governance	Insider-dominated	Introduction of CG Code which became binding for listed companies in 2002–2003.	2002–2003, 2008
Industrial relations	'Corporatist' (relative to Hungary but not Western style corporatism) Dominant bargaining level: Industry and company Recognition of unions: Yes, relevant partners in legislation discussions and in tripartite dialogue.	Tripartite Law and Labour Market Law: 1997 – Repulsion of Tripartite. 1999 – Tripartite re-established. 2001 – Labour Code amendment reduced flexibility and increased power of labour unions. 2003 – Over 200 amendments substantially changed the Labour Code towards more flexibility, unions' role weakened. 2007 – Increased security, power of labour unions and decreased flexibility.	1999–2001 2003–2004 2007
Education and skill creation	State-/school-based	Vocational Education Reform: Transformed curricula in secondary vocational and technical training education.	2007–2009
Welfare: pension system	Strongly privatized	2003–2004 – Parametric reform. 2004–2005 – Second pillar introduced. 2006–2008 – Changes to several rules of the second pillar. 1996 – Third voluntary private pillar introduced.	2004–2005

Welfare: labour market policies	Workfare welfare state	1992 – First major significant downward adjustment to UB. 1992
		1996 – Act on Employment – institutional changes to provision of 1999–2001 services, more emphasis on disadvantaged groups 2003–2003
		1999 – 2001 – further downward adjustment to UB levels and eligibility; the concept of 'subjective' reasons for becoming unemployed introduced.
		2003–2004 – Act on Social Assistance and Subsistence, Act on Social Insurance, Act on Employment Services – major overhaul of the labour market policies set-up.
Welfare: healthcare system	State-regulated healthcare with market elements	Mid-1990s – Privatization of primary care and drug sector. Mid-1990s.
		1999–2002 – Rationalization. 2002–2004
		2002–2004 – Change of legal personalities of healthcare providers 2006–2010 to introduce market and competitive elements, hospital rationalization and restructuring, transformation of legal status of healthcare insurance companies to profit-making institutions. Reform shifted the role of the state to one of regulator, introduced more competition in each healthcare sector market segment.
		2006–2010 – Several elements of the reform reversed or unfinished.
Industrial policy	From protectionist paternalism to regulatory state.	1997–1998 – Beginning of support for the automotive sector. 1999–2001
		1999 – Opening to FDI.
		2000 – SARIO established (Investment agency).
		2001 – Law on Industrial parks, aggressive investment incentive.
		2004 – Flat tax reform.

Source: Authors.

The Hungarian government made a conscious decision to privatize the banks to strategic investors, and in 1995 six large Hungarian banks were sold to foreigners. By the end of 1990s, 70 per cent of the banking system was under foreign ownership, mainly of European Union (EU) origin. Such early privatization to foreigners encouraged further FDI inflows to Hungary, as the investors were able to find branches of domestic banks in the country (Szapary 2001). Hungarian regulation also allowed foreign banks to set up new branches (EBRD 1998). In Slovakia, during most of the 1990s, bank regulation was intertwined closely with state enterprise restructuring and state-owned banks were utilized as tools of support for large state-owned enterprises. Restructuring of the banking sector in Slovakia started only in late 1990s and was Slovakia's first major reform of the Dzurinda government. In the autumn of 1999, the government, being the last among the Visegrad countries, began to recapitalize and restructure the state banking sector in preparation for privatization. By 2007, the Slovak banking system was dominated by private commercial banks, which constituted nearly 88 per cent of the financial sector assets (IMF 2007).

While corporate governance in both countries is insider-dominated, several differences can be observed in the process through which corporate governance (CG) regulations emerged. First, in spite of later privatization and acceptance of foreign ownership, Slovakia adopted formal corporate governance regulation earlier than Hungary. The second round of amendments of the CG Codes took place in 2008 in both countries and it had been explicitly related to the need to respond to new EU regulation. Second, in Hungary the process of corporate governance reform was solely in the hands of Budapest Stock Exchange, while in Slovakia a handful of different actors were involved, including non-governmental actors and associations. Third, while the Hungarian CG rules provide for a one-tier board system, in Slovakia only a two-tier board is allowed. However, the actual governance issues in foreign-controlled companies are decided by headquarters abroad (Nölke and Vliegenhart 2009), which limits the states' capacity to regulate their activities.

2.2. Industrial relations, and vocational education and training

Industrial relations in Central and Eastern Europe can be characterized as acquiescent, employer-oriented and with a strong position for governments. The position of social partners seems to be relatively more established in Slovakia than in Hungary, but the actual powers of unions has been subject to frequent legislative changes at the will of governments in power (Stein 2001). Hungarian industrial relations have suffered from fragmentation owing to its dual system – work councils at the company level and trade unions at the sectoral level. Additionally, there are multiple organizations and representations on both the unions' and the employers' sides. Hence, despite the early legislation on social partnership, the Hungarian tripartite system is practically ineffective. This allowed governments to play the social partners off each other and even take over some of the typical union issues such as minimum wage and public sector salary increases (Fazekas 2004). The weak position of industrial actors in Hungary enabled the state to stand firm against the domestic pressures from the beginning of transition and make more autonomous policy choices.

The Slovak system of industrial relations has been more concentrated with centralized representation, both on the side of the unions and the employers. Although there have been fluctuations in Slovak industrial relations in line with the ideological orientation of the governments in power, the existence of tripartite institutions was largely preserved. The comparatively more institutionalized and effective industrial relations system in Slovakia forced the government to opt for an inward-looking economic policy in the early 1990s, though this was largely abandoned later on, partly owing to the diminishing strength of labour. The most fundamental reform of the labour law, which includes industrial relations legislation, was carried out in 2003. It was heavily opposed by the unions and supported by the employers' associations, as well as the chambers of commerce representing mainly foreign companies. In addition to significantly increasing the flexibility of the labour market, the reform also restricted the coercive character of the labour law and reduced labour union power (Jurajda and Maternova 2004).

In spite of the fragmented industrial relations in Hungary, reforms of vocational education and training were introduced early on in the transition which led to a greater involvement of the social partners in the skill-formation system. The Vocational Training Act of 1993 and the Chamber Act of 1994 provided a legal framework for shifting the responsibility for practical training back to industry and re-introducing apprenticeships. The social partners had an advisory role in the development of vocational training policies and the distribution of funds for practical training (OECD 1999). The first co-ordinated attempt at curricular reform of vocational training in Slovakia came much later in 2009 with the adoption of the Vocational Education Act. Until this reform, employers and unions had limited influence over the development of educational and training curricula, with the exception of the leading sectors – i.e., automotive or financial services (Vantuch 2007). Therefore, the established industrial relations system in Slovakia did not translate into co-ordination and co-operation among the social partners on some of the institutions that can generate benefits in the long run.

2.3. Welfare systems

A big share of the variation among the Visegrad countries comes from their welfare systems which have served as compensating mechanisms, especially during the 1990s. Social policies, together with public education and healthcare, have been used as tools of economic restructuring and to provide a skilled and healthy labour force (Greskovits 2010). Welfare systems carried important legacies from the socialist and pre-socialist periods, but over the last two decades important changes took place in all core policy segments.

Hungary and Slovakia inherited highly redistributive pay-as-you-go pension systems from the socialist regime. Pension privatization was an area where the countries received significant technical help and pressure from the international financial institutions. All countries in CEE gradually introduced parametric or systemic reforms to their pension systems that, however, differed in timing and scope. In 1997–98 Hungary was the first CEE economy to undertake a systemic reform towards a three-pillar pension but opted instead for a weakly privatized system. Slovakia followed suit only in 2005, though it did so with the highest allocation of resources to the second (private) pension pillar among the new accession states (Wagner 2005).

A comprehensive reform of the healthcare system came on the agenda relatively late in the transition. A major restructuring of the system took place in Slovakia between 2002 and 2004 and aimed at changing its incentives and basic functioning principles. While keeping solidarity and universal coverage, the reform introduced more competition into each market segment, as well as greater individual responsibility for health and health expenses (Pazitny *et al.* 2006). In the autumn of 2006, the Hungarian healthcare reform laws were passed, in many aspects modelled according to the Slovak example. The reform turned out to be highly controversial and led to the breakdown of the government in 2008 (Mihalyi *et al.* 2009).

Unemployment and other non-employment benefits – early retirement, disability pensions and social assistance – served as important tools to help the society to adjust to the market transition (Vanhuysse 2006). All the countries in the CEE region adopted comprehensive regulations encompassing the provision of income support for the unemployed almost immediately after the regime change. Both Hungary and Slovakia concentrated on unemployment benefit schemes and their re-calibration for most of the 1990s, while active labour market policies entered the agenda more substantively around the time of their EU accession. They were designed in line with the Western activation principles, emphasizing better institutional quality and improvements to the scope of job search advice and placement (OECD 2007). Over time the unemployment benefit systems in both countries underwent a series of amendments resulting in tightened access or shortened duration. These were decreased most dramatically at the beginning of the transition and then again in the early 2000s. In Slovakia, labour market legislation and the structure of social benefits underwent the most comprehensive changes in the 2002–2006 period and ended up being one of the most restrictive unemployment benefit systems in Organization for Economic Co-operation and Development (OECD). Overall, Slovak social assistance has gone through substantive redistributive liberalization and weakened solidarity, achieved by regulatory tightening (Bodnarova 2006). In Hungary the system remained more generous and family allowance schemes provide an additional sizeable form of income support.

A careful analysis of the successful and failed reforms across the welfare system areas highlights the role of domestic veto players and electoral politics. In Hungary, the Constitutional Court played a crucial intervening role in halting the planned liberalization or increased privatization of education and the healthcare systems (Mihalyi *et al.* 2009). Moreover, party polarization in Hungary resulted in preservation of the system since each succeeding government revoked the previous liberalization attempts. Generally, the Slovak Court has played a less powerful role in shaping policy trajectories and outcomes. Also the reform path initiated by the two liberal governments in Slovakia between 1998 and 2006 was maintained by their socialist successor.

3. INDUSTRIAL POLICY

In this section we focus on industrial policy to demonstrate more clearly the features of state activism and the different choices made in the two countries. We define industrial policy as a set of policies aimed at affecting particular industries to achieve the outcomes which are perceived by the state as efficient for the economy as a whole (Chang 2006). Industrial policy comprises government interventions directed towards enterprises, industries or sectors and aimed at influencing the industrial structure (Budzinki 2004). There is a distinction between general (horizontal) and selective (vertical) industrial policy, as the former targets all sectors and interventions are applied across the board, while the latter is about promoting specific sectors and industries. In practice, the distinction between them becomes much blurred. Some of the policies that are technically horizontal can end up having differential effects across sectors. For instance, energy or training subsidies can be given to all firms, but in fact energy or skill-intensive firms would benefit disproportionately from such support. Nevertheless, the distinction is still useful because the degree of verticalness or horizontalness helps to explain the governments' overall development strategy.

Hungary and Slovakia diverged in both the timing and character of their industrial policies. This occurred despite similar external pressures stemming from the process of EU accession or IFI policy advising in the early period of transition. First, the level of state aid in Hungary was significantly higher than in Slovakia, especially during the 1990s. Budget subsidies as a share of gross domestic product (GDP) declined in Slovakia from 4 per cent to 2 per cent between 1992 and 1998, while in Hungary they remained between 5 per cent and 6 per cent (EBRD 2005). Second, although their subsidy levels converged in the early 2000s, the structure of state aid differed substantially. Hungary targeted its manufacturing industry, while Slovakia preferred regional state aid which has a horizontal character (European Commission 2009a). The third difference exists in the SME sector size – in 2008 over 56,000 enterprises were present in Hungary with less than 249 employees, while only 8,000 existed in Slovakia (European Commission 2009b). In sum, Hungary took a more active and vertically oriented approach to industrial policy. The following sub-sections highlight the underlying political, social and structural reasons for these differences.

3.1. Major external actors

The external actors that were influential over policy-making in the two countries were similar. The International Monetary Fund (IMF) and World Bank had significant leverage at the beginning of the transition period and promoted a mainstream approach to industrial policy. These organizations support only horizontal, generic or sector-neutral industrial policy and adamantly oppose changing relative sectoral prices through vertical intervention. For them, optimum industrial upgrading and development are expected to emerge automatically as the government plays a role in supporting the market by getting the prices right and building the correct institutional set up (Wade 2010). This understanding was supported to differing degrees by domestic policy-makers, as the above-presented data (and the discussion in the next subsection) demonstrate. Although external openness in both trade and capital accounts were seen as the sources of innovation and industrial restructuring, and any form of state interventionism or market protectionism was labelled as unproductive and inefficient, each country intervened actively into the process of restructuring. After a very short initial period following a hands-off approach that conformed to neoliberal expectations, massive efforts to actively soften the adverse effects of the transition were launched, including intervention in firm restructuring and the mode of privatizing large state-owned enterprises which were, in effect, sectorally specific (Török 2007; cf. Hanley *et al.* 2002; King and Sznajder 2006).

The most important external actor in the transition process was the European Union, which implicitly holds a slightly different view on the issue of industrial policy. EU rules bring several tools typically used as industrial policy under its purview. With the aim of securing fair competition across the single market, the EU regulates and controls state aid. While new member states only had to comply with these rules after accession, they were encouraged in the late 1990s to establish state aid-monitoring authorities and adopt EU-compliant state aid legislation (Mogyorosiova 2006). The promotion of agriculture, promotion of backward areas (i.e., regional development) and important projects of common European interest represent exceptions to the state aid surveillance. Hence, while after accession Hungary and Slovakia both became more limited in their options regarding, for example, free economic zones and other FDI incentives, the resources available through EU structural funds and the ability to direct investments into underdeveloped areas offered multiple tools for continued support of selected sectors or regions. In a way, through the need to prepare operational programmes and plans to channel the available funds, industrial policy has become even more formalized.

Recently the EU prescriptions for industrial policy heavily emphasize the importance of innovation, knowledge and research and development (R&D). The R&D focus is an indication of a shift towards horizontal measures, but in practice the member states still support certain sectors, such as manufacturing, more heavily. Indeed, in 2009 over 60 per cent of all state aid accrued to the manufacturing sector, excluding crisis measures (European Commission 2009a). In sum, although there have been external constraints on the extent and form of industrial support since the beginning of the transition, the exact policy was determined by each country's preferences and domestic resources.

3.2. Government policies

Immediately after the regime change, the transition countries maintained a liberal approach to industrial policy since the major structural changes were expected to take place through markets. The governments were initially hesitant to use (or proclaim that they use) vertical interventions, partly owing to the association of the term with the old regime, but nevertheless enacted several specific measures very early on. Both countries allocated sizable resources to support enterprises in the 1990s. These were primarily foreign-owned or domestic firms in preparation for privatization in Hungary and big companies in state controlled sectors in Slovakia. Importantly, both the Hungarian and Slovak governments used privatization decisions as a tool for economic intervention via the allocation of property rights (Hanley *et al.* 2002; Miklos n.d.).

Hungary's industrial policy is characterized by extreme openness towards foreign capital throughout the post-communist period. This is partly owing to the economic reforms preceding the change of the regime. In 1984 it passed a Law on Enterprise Councils which introduced a self-management system in large- and medium-sized enterprises and increased the role of managers rather than state officials. In 1988 it adopted an Act on Investment of Foreigners which set the stage for early FDI entry. Hungary offered considerable incentives to foreign investors and was also the first country to involve foreigners in privatization. Likewise, Hungary very early on allowed Export Processing Zones (EPZs), which offered simplified customs regulations and duty-free imports, investment incentives and government support. These succeeded in attracting a range of green-field investments that fostered modernization of the Hungarian economy. In respect of domestic enterprises, what first appeared as a marked *laissez-faire* approach soon took on a more strategic course of crisis management. Launching the 'Dirty Dozen' consolidation package in 1994, the Hungarian government decided that active involvement was required to prevent the collapse of a handful of manufacturing firms that were crucial for employment generation and exports (Török 2007).

Furthermore, as the efforts to attract FDI continued, in 2000 the conservative Orban government introduced the Szechenyi plan, which was a medium-term development plan for SMEs. The plan, amounting to 3.5 per cent of Hungarian GDP (HUF434 billion), aimed to improve competitiveness by supporting infrastructure, real estate, tourism, R&D and subcontractor networks. Local and regional governments, as well as firms, could participate in projects co-funded by the central government with their own developmental plans (Doliak and Kollarova 2002; Török 2007). The programme had two successors: Szechenyi Programme for Enterprise Development and 'Smart Hungary'.

The former offered preferential credit, mainly to domestic companies, while the latter established tax credits in accordance with the EU rules and gave firms the option of creating tax exempt financial reserves for later investment. The Joint Research Centres schemes offered R&D capacities to companies like Audi and Nokia. Another innovative element of SME support consisted of the 'simplified corporate tax' introduced in 2003, which unified different taxes for companies generating turnover below a certain threshold (Török 2007).

Slovakia entered its transition with a particularly unfavourable industrial structure consisting of armaments production and heavy industry – steel, iron and some chemical production. By the mid-2000s, the industrial profile of the country had changed profoundly, and the country has become one of the leading car producers and exporters in the world (on a per capita basis). The industrial policy of Slovakia can be divided into two distinct phases.

Until 1998 the government's policy concentrated on the preservation of national champions in the energy and steel sectors at the expense of SMEs. While the official rhetoric acknowledged the unfavourable economic structure, there were no moves towards changing it (Beblavy 2000). After the separation of Czechoslovakia the policy was characterized by hold-ups, especially in the large-scale privatization process, increased concentration of government power, and favouring the management of state-owned enterprises (SOEs) or other previously determined interested parties (Miklos n.d.). The decision to support large domestic firms and to close off privatization to foreign investors was related to the nation-building efforts after the separation of Czechoslovakia and the ambition to create and support domestic capital. The implicit industrial policy consisted primarily of subsidized energy prices, since energy sector ownership and distribution were kept in state hands (Doliak and Kollarova 2002). Additionally, cartel regulation and merger control enforcement were applied in a manner supportive of greater domestic market power when it was considered beneficial for the export competitiveness of a Slovak company (Török 2007). Major resources were used to develop the energy infrastructure, such as finishing the Mochovce nuclear power plant and investing in the Gabcikovo damn. State loan guarantees to big enterprises were another tool that was used to sustain big domestic employers (Beblavy 2000). The loan guarantees offered to SOEs, in effect, postponed rather than promoted firm restructuring.

Slovakia offered foreign investment incentives for a very brief period in the early 1990s, attracting investors to automotive industry, but then stopped giving them until the late 1990s. The form of privatization through vouchers, the attitude of Mečiar's government towards foreign investment, and political instability, led to low foreign investment levels. An example of the anti-foreign attitude was the 1995 Act on Ensuring State Interests in Privatizing Strategically Important State-Owned Companies, which excluded monopolies from privatization and implicitly discriminated against foreign participation.

Yet a major shift in the Slovakian industrial policy occurred in the late Mečiar government. As the production and exports of one single company – VW Bratislava – rose to significant levels, there was a swing in its production strategy to which the government responded with its own supportive steps. In 1997, a position of plenipotentiary for the development of automotive sector was established, followed by a governmental decree in 1998 which approved tax incentives to the company (Jakubiak *et al.* 2008). From 1998 onwards, with the change in the governing forces, a further shift in industrial policy ensued. In the early 2000s the country introduced an aggressive investment incentive scheme and opened up privatization to foreigners in order to catch up with its regional neighbours. The 2001 law on industrial parks allowed the government to cover up to 70 per cent of designated investment costs in certain areas (Bohle and Greskovits 2006). Seeking to further distance the country from 'Mečiarism', accelerate the delayed restructuring and the EU accession processes, and to make the country more attractive to foreign investors, the government implemented sweeping reforms across different areas, such as business, environment, labour market, and tax policy. A flat tax rate (19 per cent) was adopted in 2004, which earned the country international attention and became an important element for a positive international image and investor recognition (*ibid.*). While industrial policy became more general in its emphasis on the creation of a favourable business and investment environment, the projects that gained major government support concentrated on the automotive and, later, electronics industries. A policy supporting domestic SMEs or R&D schemes of the sort introduced in Hungary did not surface.

The industrial policy choices of the Hungarian and Slovakian governments might appear similar overall, but, as described above, there are important distinctions between them, especially in the timing, level and type of support provided to foreign and domestic firms. While Hungary combined aggressive incentive schemes to foreign investments with state aid to SMEs at a much earlier stage, Slovakia was not only late in welcoming foreign capital but also did not extend industrial support to domestic capital formation in the later phases. These government choices reflect the power balance between the domestic élite and political actors, and are not fully determined by the structural constraints brought on by their transition experience and status in the world division of labour.

3.3. Responses and actions of multinational corporations (MNCs)

The benefits of industrial policy accruing to domestic and multinational firms in Hungary and Slovakia also differ. Hungary started the transition with large-scale privatizations aimed at decreasing state ownership rapidly. The government gave considerable privileges to foreign investors, including monopoly rights and market protection at the beginning of the transition, and promoted green-field investment projects (Antaloczy and Sass 2001). However, there was no explicit bias toward either domestic or foreign firms, as the investment promotion schemes were based on performance. Any company, domestic or foreign, was eligible to receive tax exemptions and other support. Moreover, while foreign buy-outs were concentrated in certain sectors (i.e., manufacturing and export-oriented sectors), those companies in which foreign interest was low were given out under preferential terms to domestic owners, often outside the management–employee buy-out frameworks (Hanley *et al.* 2002). Thus, foreign investors were favoured at the expense of domestic investors in Hungary only in the first half of the 1990s.

In Slovakia, as part of the attempt to create a domestic business class, competition laws included exemptions for domestic firms that have an existing or potential market power. That said, the government's approach was still in line with horizontal measures and domestic investors were favoured through implicit methods. After the separation of Czechoslovakia, privatization decisions were erratic, but there were attempts to support management–employee buy-outs (Brzica 1998). Owing to the lack of necessary capital for restructuring and technological upgrading, most of the companies had to undergo a second round of ownership change or faced bankruptcy. After 1998, Slovakian industrial policy became much more outward oriented and multinationals started to enjoy tax exemptions and other forms of support.

A combination of the above described policy efforts and favourable skill endowments in the region made Hungary and Slovakia home to important investors in complex manufacturing industries with a measurable rate of upgrading (Pavlinek *et al.* 2009). However, as foreign-owned companies have become the key drivers of export-led economic development and growth, it can be argued that both countries are dependent on the strategic interests of multinational firms. Individual foreign firms control large shares of output, employment and exports in these countries.

Alongside EU accession, the attraction and retention of foreign companies served as important reform anchors for both countries. In this way the MNCs had an indirect effect on the discussed reforms. The period between 2000 and 2004 was characterized by a cut-throat competition to attract green-field investments between Visegrad countries. MNCs responded strongly to the offered investment incentives, since otherwise these countries are similar structurally and skillwise (Greskovits 2010). Transnational firms in CEE generally do not recreate their domestic institutional set-ups (Bluhm 2007). Rather, they use the CEE institutional context to complement what they were missing at home (Bohle and Greskovits 2009). Therefore, MNCs did not try to interfere in the domestic industrial policy-making in either country unless it conflicted with their interests. The state aid to SMEs and other forms of support to domestic capital were not opposed by MNCs as long as the governments did not decrease active or passive assistance to the foreign firms.

4. CONCLUSION

Hungary and Slovakia are widely seen as having a similar type of socio-economic regime with high reliance on foreign capital and a mixed approach to social policy. However, significant differences exist between them, especially in the role of key actors who set the direction and magnitude of change in the main institutional domains. In Hungary, reforms took a more gradual path with heavy involvement of the state, particularly in education and training, the welfare system and industrial policy. In contrast, in Slovakia the governments have taken a liberal stance and assumed a regulatory role in almost all institutional areas, especially since late 1990s. The most similar patterns are observed in finance and corporate governance, as both countries continue to have bank-based and insider-dominated systems.

Given that the transition led to low international competitiveness, booming unemployment and other socioeconomic difficulties, an active industrial policy became essential for recovery and establishing a viable private sector. Although the imperative of industrial restructuring and technological upgrading held for both countries from the outset of the transition, only Hungarian governments managed to pursue an active and comprehensive industrial policy continuously from the beginning. Instead of accepting a minimal state and relying solely on markets, in Hungary the state shaped the socio-economic model into a more mixed type. While early attempts at liberalization and massive privatization allowed foreign capital to become a crucial player, the state continued to hold a strong hand through the incentives and subsidies it provides to large investments. Moreover, it actually put more effort and resources into assisting SMEs in their industrial upgrading. Lastly, the socio-economic consequences of industrial restructuring were partly compensated by the social policies, since Hungary maintained relatively large public programmes in pensions, healthcare, labour market and family policies.

We find that the differences in the role of state and the extent of interventionism in the two countries illuminate our understanding of the developments in their socio-economic models. While the type of change that materialized in the two countries is by all accounts transformative, it was more gradual in Hungary and more radical in Slovakia. The Slovak socio-economic configuration in 2010 also appeared to be more coherent than the Hungarian one, but the long-term sustainability of the models in both countries is questionable. This is partly owing to their heavy reliance on foreign-owned firms and the degree to which foreign influence permeates across institutional areas. However, the analysis also revealed the importance of factors such as pre-1989 legacies (the level of foreign debt and market openness), domestic political context (nation building process, political polarization), and the role of institutional veto players (i.e., Hungarian Constitutional Court) in setting boundaries of the types of change and the resulting socio-economic configurations. Moreover, our account also highlighted that the manner in which Hungary and Slovakia were inserted into the international system was a matter of political choice and active state agency.

Since we emphasize the country specific conditions for industrial policy formation, our results would not necessarily apply to the other CEE transition countries. Similar analysis underlining the interplay of macro, meso and micro factors in shaping socio-economic trajectories of other DMEs could be developed for the remaining Visegrad countries – Poland and the Czech Republic – in future research.

Biographical notes: Anil Duman is Assistant Professor at the Department of Political Science at Central European University in Budapest, Hungary. Lucia Kureková is a Senior Research Fellow at the Slovak Governance Institute in Bratislava, Slovakia.

ACKNOWLEDGEMENTS

Research for this contribution was funded by FP7 Institutional Changes and Trajectories of Socio-Economic development Models (ICaTSEM) project (Project no. 225349). The authors wish to thank the Political Economy Research Group at the Central European University (CEU), the ICATSEM research network and two anonymous reviewers for valuable comments. All errors remain our own.

NOTES

1 Central and Eastern Europe includes the Czech Republic, Estonia, Hungary, Latvia, Lithuania, Poland, Slovakia and Slovenia.
2 A detailed reform database can be downloaded from the ICaTSEM website: http://icatsem.u-bordeaux4.fr/

REFERENCES

Antaloczy, K. and Sass, M. (2001) 'Greenfield investments in Hungary: are they different from privatization FDI?', *Transnational Corporations* 10(3): 39–59.
Beblavy, M. (2000) 'Industrial policy', in A. Marcincin and M. Beblavy (eds), *Economic Policy in Slovakia 1990–1999*, Bratislava: INEKO, pp. 228–63.
Bluhm, K. (2007) 'Dealing with the regulation gap. Labor relations in Polish and Czech subsidiaries of German companies', in A.-M. Legloannec (ed.), *Non-State Actors in International Relations: The Case of Germany*, Manchester: Manchester University Press, pp. 176–94.
Bodnarova, B. (2006) 'Social policy', in M. Bútora, M. Kollár and G. Mesežnikov (eds), *Slovakia 2005. A Global Report on the State of Society*, Bratislava: Institute for Public Affairs, pp. 471–92.
Bohle, D. and Greskovits, B. (2006) 'Capitalism without compromise: strong business and weak labor in Eastern Europe's new transnational industries', *Studies in Comparative International Development* 41(1): 3–25.
Bohle, D. and Greskovits, B. (2007) 'Neoliberalism, embedded neoliberalism and neocorporatism: towards transnational capitalism in Central-Eastern Europe', *West European Politics* 30: 443–66.

Bohle, D. and Greskovits, B. (2009) 'Varieties of capitalism and capitalism *tout court*', *European Journal of Sociology* 50(3): 355–86.

Brzica, D. (1998) 'Privatization in Slovakia: the role of employee and management participation', *Working Paper*, Geneva: ILO.

Buchen, C. (2007) 'Estonia and Slovenia as antipodes', in D. Lane and M. Myant (eds), *Varieties of Capitalism in Post-Communist Countries*, Basingstoke: Palgrave Macmillan, pp. 65–89.

Budzinki, O. (2004). 'A European industrial policy: concepts and consequences', Presentation at Philipps-University of Marburg, Osnabrück, 6 January.

Chang, H.-J. (2006). 'Industrial policy in East Asia – lessons for Europe', Paper prepared for the *EIB Conference in Economics and Finance 'An industrial policy for Europe?'*, Luxembourg, 19 January.

Doliak, M. and Kollarova, M. (2002) 'Hospodarske reformy v krajinach V4' [Economic reforms in V4 countries]', in A. Marcincin (ed.), *Hospodarska politika 2000–2001*, published with the support of the Dutch Embassy in Slovakia, pp. 105–28.

EBRD (1998, 2005) *Transition Report*, London: The European Bank for Reconstruction and Development.

European Commission (2009a) 'State aid scoreboard: winter 2009 update', Brussels: Commission of the European Communities.

European Commission (2009b) *SME Perfomance Review: 2009 Annual Report*, Brussels: Commission of the European Communities.

Fazekas, K. (2004) *The current situation at the labor market and labor market policy in Hungary*, Budapest: Hungarian Academy of Science.

Feldman, M. (2007) 'The origin of varieties of capitalism. Lessons from post-socialist transition in Estonia and Slovenia', in B. Hancké, M. Rhodes and M. Thatcher (eds), *Beyond Varieties of Capitalism: Contradictions, Complementarities and Change*, Oxford: Oxford University Press, pp. 328–51.

Greskovits, B. (2010) 'Central Europe', in K. Dyson and A. Sepos (eds), *Which Europe? The Politics of Differentiated Integration*, Basingstoke: Palgrave Macmillan, pp. 142–55.

Hall, P.A. and Soskice, D. (eds) (2001) *Varieties of Capitalism: Institutional Foundations of Comparative Advantage*, Cambridge: Cambridge University Press.

Hancké, B., Rhodes, M. and Thatcher, M. (2007) 'Introduction: beyond varieties of capitalism', in B. Hancké, M. Rhodes and M. Thatcher (eds), *Beyond Varieties of Capitalism: Contradictions, Complementarities and Change*, Oxford: Oxford University Press, pp. 3–38.

Hanley, E., King, L. and Toth, J.I. (2002) 'The state, international agencies, and property transformation in postcommunist Hungary', *American Journal of Sociology* 108(1): 129–67.

IMF (2007) 'Slovak Republic. Financial system sustainability assessment update', *IMF Country Report No. 07/243*.

Jakubiak, M., Kolesar, P., Izvorski, I. and Kureková, L. (2008) *The Automotive Industry in Slovakia: Recent Developments and the Impact on Growth*, Washington, DC: The World Bank.

Jurajda, S. and Maternova, K. (2004) 'How to overhaul the labor market: political economy of recent Czech and Slovak reforms', Background paper prepared for the *World Development Report 2005*, available at https://openknowledge.worldbank.org/bitstream/handle/10986/9131/WDR2005_0012.pdf?sequence=1 (accessed 11 November 2009).

Knell, M. and Srholec, M. (2007) 'Diverging pathways in Central and Eastern Europe', in D. Lane and M. Myant (eds), *Varieties of Capitalism in Post-Communist Countries*, Basingstoke: Palgrave Macmillan, pp. 40–64.

King, L. (2007) 'Central European capitalism in comparative perspective', in B. Hancké, M. Rhodes and M. Thatcher (eds), *Beyond Varieties of Capitalism: Contradictions, Complementarities and Change*, Oxford: Oxford University Press, pp. 307–27.

King, L. and Sznajder, A. (2006) 'The state-led transition to liberal capitalism: neoliberal, organizational, world-systems, and social structural explanations of Poland's economic success', *American Journal of Sociology* 112(3): 751–801.

Lane, D. (2005) 'Emerging varieties of capitalism in former state socialist societies', *Competition and Change* 9(2): 27–47.

McMenamin, I. (2004) 'Varieties of capitalist democracy. What difference does East-Central Europe make?' *Journal of Public Policy* 3: 259–74.

Mihalyi, P. *et al.* (2009) 'The 2007–2009 reform of the Hungarian health insurance system', Background paper, Ministry of Health of Hungary, available at www.eum.hu/download.php?docID=1318 (accessed 3 December 2009).

Miklos, I. (n.d) Privatization in Slovakia during 1991–1995, MESA 10, available at http://www.internet.sk/mesa10/PRIVAT/GLOB95.HTM (accessed 21 August 2011).

Mogyorosiova, Z. (2006) 'Adaptation of the EU competition policy in Slovakia – selected problems', *Narodohospodarsky obzor* 1: 43–9.

Myant, M. and Drahokoupil, J. (2012) 'International integration, varieties of capitalism, and resilience to crisis in transition economies', *Europe–Asia Studies* 64: 1–33.

Nölke, A. and Vliegenthart, A. (2009) 'Enlarging the varieties of capitalism: the emergence of dependent market economies in East Central Europe', *World Politics* 61(4): 670–702.

OECD (1999) *Thematic Review of the Transition from Initial Education to Working Life. Hungary. Country Note. February*, Paris: Organization for Economic Cooperation and Development.

OECD (2007) *OECD Economic Surveys: Hungary*, Paris: Organization for Economic Cooperation and Development.

Pavlínek, P., Domański, B. and Guzik, R. (2009) 'Industrial upgrading through foreign direct investment in Central European automotive manufacturing', *European Urban and Regional Studies* 16(1): 43–63.

Pazitny, P., Szalay, T., Szalayova, A. and Madarova, H. (2006) 'Health care', in M. Butora, M. Kollar and G. Meseznikov (eds), *Slovakia 2005. A Global Report on the State of Society*, Bratislava: Institute for Public Affairs (IVO), pp. 490–516.

Stein, J. (2001) 'Neocorporatism in Slovakia', in S. Crowley and D. Ost (eds), *Workers after Workers' States. Labor and Politics in Postcommunist Eastern Europe*, Lanham, MD: Rowman and Littlefield, pp. 59–78.

Szapary, G. (2001) 'Banking sector reforms in Hungary: lessons learned, current trends and prospects', *Working Paper 5/2001*, Budapest: National Bank of Hungary.

Török, A. (2007) 'Industrial policy in the new member countries of the European Union: a survey of patterns and initiatives since 1990', *Journal of Industry, Competition and Trade* 7: 255–71.

Vanhuysse, P. (2006) *Divide and Pacify: The Political Economy of Welfare State in Hungary and Poland, 1989–1996*, Budapest: Central European University Press.

Vantuch, J. (2007) *Vocational Education and Training in Slovakia. Thematic Overview*, Bratislava: Third Edition. [Prepared as the background report for CEDEFOP].

Wade, R. (2010) 'After the crisis: industrial policy and developmental state', Unpublished mimeo, London: London School of Economics.

Wagner, H. (2005) 'Pension reform in the new EU member states', *Eastern European Economics* 43(4): 27–51.

Strategic transformation and muddling through: industrial relations and industrial training in the UK

Howard Gospel and Tony Edwards

ABSTRACT   The contribution considers two related institutional domains, industrial relations and industrial training, in the United Kingdom. It analyses the trajectory and magnitude of change, seen in terms of (a) forms of co-ordination/governance and (b) the saliency of these domains. The contribution covers a long time period, pivoting on the years of Conservative government between 1979 and 1997. It argues that trajectories of change in these two domains began earlier than these years and are still not fully unfolded in the industrial training area. Throughout, change involved combinations of both strategic transformation and muddling through by key actors. There are some complementarities between these two domains and with other domains, but there are also significant disjunctures. In explaining change, some emphasis is placed on politics, but also on the 'voluntaristic' nature of labour market institutions in Britain and on employer preferences in labour, product and financial market and in political contexts.

1.   INTRODUCTION

In popular discourse, it is often assumed that the years of Conservative government between 1979 and 1997 marked a significant turning point in the United Kingdom (UK) political economy in general and in labour markets in particular. According to this view, the policies of Margaret Thatcher represented a decisive break in traditional institutions. Her governments had a clear set of objectives, were determined to use all the available resources of the British state to achieve these, and brought about a radical and irreversible set of changes. In academic analysis, the Thatcher years are also seen as ones of 'turmoil' or 'shock', during which the UK took a decidedly 'neoliberal' turn involving extensive liberalization and privatization in product markets, the deregulation of financial markets, and the undermining of collective institutions and flexibilization in labour markets (e.g., Crafts 1991; Crouch 2005; Howell 2007; Millward *et al.* 1992; Pontusson 2005). The UK is consequently now categorized as a prime example of a 'liberal market economy' (Hall and Soskice 2001).

While there were undoubtedly major transformations in the institutional configuration of the country during these 18 years, we argue that in the two areas or domains of industrial relations and industrial training the focus on the period as a turning point is justified, but also needs to be qualified. The trajectory of change goes back beyond this period, the process of change was more incremental and patchy than is often thought, the changes across the two domains and their linkages with other domains were uneven, and some of the changes would probably have occurred regardless of the government in power. We argue that there is a need for a corrective to the view that there was a coherent, politically driven strategic transformation of the institutions which governed the labour market and that the term 'muddling through' has some analytical purchase in explaining this story.

The contribution focuses on the development of industrial relations and industrial training in the UK private sector as examples of institutional change in two labour market domains. These two areas are related but nevertheless distinct, and allow us to examine different trajectories of development and different explanations of change. The contribution is concerned with when, how and to what extent institutions in these areas changed. The time period covered pivots on the years of Conservative government from 1979 to 1997, but this is placed in a context which goes back further in time and comes forward up to the present.

Broadly, the argument is as follows. In terms of industrial relations, in early post-Second World War Britain there was a system of co-ordination or governance which was initially seen by contemporaries, both domestic and foreign, as performing reasonably well. It involved significant co-ordination and attempts at corporatist-type arrangements. In some respects, it resembled a 'co-ordinated market economy' (Hall and Soskice 2001). However, the foundations were weak. Institutions were skeletal, and legal supports were minimal. This weakness became increasingly evident through the 1960s and 1970s, as the salience of the industrial relations 'problem' also rose, and the system began to be slowly transformed, as employers, unions and governments searched for new arrangements. The advent of the Thatcher government accelerated, rather than initiated, the trajectory of change in terms of the levels of co-ordination. By the beginning of the 21st century, British industrial relations had indeed been transformed, and, in the private sector, industrial relations was no longer a salient policy issue. In the area of industrial training, post-war Britain also had a system of co-ordination and governance based around apprenticeships which, if anything, seemed to perform even better than the industrial relations system. But again, contrary to appearances, the foundations were weak and the system became increasingly strained. Here, also, the actions of the Thatcher government accelerated changes which were already underway. In industrial training, it was only in the final years of the Conservative government that attempts were made to build new arrangements. For various reasons, however, the system of industrial training has not been transformed in the way that industrial relations has.

The next section presents some definitions and concepts. The third and fourth sections provide stylized accounts of industrial relations and industrial training. In the final section, an attempt is made to map the trajectory of change more analytically in these two related domains. This section also considers causes, links with other domains, and possible future trajectories.

2. GUIDING DEFINITIONS AND CONCEPTS

A number of concepts are defined. First, the contribution is concerned with the interrelationship between employers, employers' organizations, trade unions, other forms of employee representation, and the state and its agencies. A particular focus of industrial relations is on collective bargaining and other forms of rule-making. The focus in industrial training is on the intermediate level of skills, covering the range from semi-skilled to skilled work, particularly the mix between apprentice-type training, upgrade training within the firm and training via colleges.

Second, we are concerned with co-ordination or governance in terms of how transactions and relations are organized. Co-ordination takes place in various ways: through the market; through the firm; through quasi-market or associational mechanisms such as employers' organizations and trade unions; or through the state and its agencies. The focus is both on the level at which co-ordination takes place, especially whether it is single-employer or multi-employer or both, and on the governance arrangements whereby decisions are made, especially whether they are made unilaterally by employers, bilaterally between employers and employee representatives, or multilaterally involving the state.

Third, we are concerned with salience, which concerns the extent to which issues are perceived as a problem. In political science, this is seen primarily in terms of salience to the public: an issue becomes salient when it grows to be important enough that political parties build electoral strategies around the issue; in other words, salience is high when it is a 'public' rather than a 'private' concern (Culpepper 2010). Salience may be gauged by references by politicians in manifestos, etc., government reports, legal intervention and the creation of special agencies. Salience for politicians is likely to coincide with salience for key actors, such as employers and unions, but this is more difficult to gauge. Here we focus on how industrial relations became salient in the 1960s–1980s and how industrial training later assumed greater salience in the 1990s–2000s.

Fourth, the contribution is concerned with institutional change. Institutions are here seen as the 'rules of the game' which structure the relations between those who largely create such arrangements (rule-makers) and those who largely operate within them (rule-takers). Following Streeck and Thelen (2005), institutional change is about both the processes and outcomes of change. Sometimes change is radical in both process and outcome terms, as at critical conjunctures such as the aftermath of wars and major political upheavals. For the most part, though, Streeck and Thelen (2005) argue that change is incremental and comes about in a number of ways. Traditional institutions may become discredited or marginalized (displacement), layers of new institutions may be added to old ones (layering), old arrangements may atrophy and cease to operate as intended (drift), institutions may be converted into functioning in a different way (conversion), and patterns of behaviour permitted under institutions may eventually undermine these institutions (exhaustion).

Finally, we use the notion of 'muddling through' to describe an important aspect of the processes and outcomes of change. Building on Lindblom's (1959, 1979) classic formulations, muddling through refers to the search for solutions to problems and the gradual and often incoherent change in policy and practice. Lindblom noted the benefits to be gained by making minor, incremental changes in both economic and political spheres and that ultimately such changes can lead to radical change over an extended period, as we will see in the case of industrial relations in Britain. Two dimensions of the concept should be noted. First, actors may have reasonably clear desired objectives, but in practice change is usually more gradual than envisaged because original plans are opposed by groups which have countervailing power. In the business sphere, firms are made up of a plurality of groups which interact in an uncertain environment. In the political sphere, change also tends to be gradual and evolutionary because it is negotiated between competing interest groups. Thus, while changes are sometimes the result of rational, strategic plans, they are also usually the result of compromises and responses to unanticipated events. Second, change is often not 'joined-up' across spheres. While the 'varieties of capitalism' approach emphasizes the importance of 'complementarities' in which practices in one sphere reinforce those in another (Hall and Soskice 2001), muddling through entails changes which are not so related, with the pace, nature and sometimes direction of change differing across domains (Callaghan 2010; Crouch 2005; Howell 2007). In other words, there may be a lack of strong horizontal integration across spheres.

One objection to the concept of muddling through is that it applies to all countries. Nevertheless, we think it appropriate to use it in the case of industrial relations and industrial training in the UK for three reasons. First, as we seek to demonstrate below, the UK has a strong tradition of '*laissez-faire*' and 'voluntarism' in the sense of leaving governance to the voluntary activities of employers and employees and to their organizations. Collective agreements and other institutional arrangements were not deeply embedded in law and were, therefore, vulnerable to the forms of gradual change that Streeck and Thelen (2005) identified, particularly displacement, layering and drift. Second, there is some precedent in both historiography and the social sciences for using the concept of muddling through in Britain. Thus, a leading modern historian uses the term in the title of a well-respected book about the Thatcher years (Hennessy 1996), arguing that even with the first-past-the-post electoral system which allowed the Conservatives large parliamentary majorities, despite having only just over 40 per cent of the popular vote, there were nevertheless obstacles to major reforms of areas such as the welfare state (see also Gamble 1994). Third, in terms of management, the term 'muddling through' is arguably particularly pertinent in the British context where the historical weaknesses and informalities of the management process have been often documented (Gospel 1992), while Hyman (1987: 26) has referred to 'unscientific management' as 'a traditional feature of many areas of employment in Britain' (see also Bach 2002; Edwards *et al.* 1992). In contrast to their American counterparts, for instance, British managers were historically less well equipped to initiate and implement radical changes in business strategy.

3. INDUSTRIAL RELATIONS

In the first two decades after the Second World War, the UK had a system of industrial relations which met with much approval by contemporaries and which was often praised by foreign commentators (Brown 2004). 'Voluntarist' multi-employer bargaining, largely at national level, was a key feature of the system, with the law not having the same role in governance as in many other countries. While there were many high-profile industrial disputes, which were sometimes large in terms of numbers of days lost, they also tended to be rather infrequent.

However, there were weaknesses in the system. In particular, national agreements were skeletal and gaps increasingly opened up between formal national rules and informal workplace practices. The lack of legal supports accentuated these weaknesses. By the mid-1960s, this fragility had become clearer and the saliency of upward wage drift, unauthorized work practices and more frequent small strikes rose. These were notably analysed in a major government report of the Donovan Commission in 1968 (Donovan Royal Commission 1968).

In response to the growing saliency of the 'trade union problem', there were various kinds of government interventions. Under Labour governments, there were some restrictions, such as incomes policies, and some changes in collective and individual employment law, culminating in the so-called Social Contract of 1974 to 1979, the high point of neocorporatism in the UK. At one point, co-determination via employee representation on company boards was on the agenda, but unions were ambivalent and employers strongly opposed to such arrangements (Bullock Royal Commission 1977). Under Conservative governments, there was some attempt to restrict union influence through the law which eroded the voluntarist tradition, though these did not achieve the stated aims, as is illustrated in the collapse of the Industrial Relations Act of 1971 (Weekes *et al.* 1975).

More significantly than government intervention, changes occurred in the rules of the game driven by employers. More so autonomously than at government prompting, employers started to reform their arrangements. They looked less and less to employers' associations or even left them altogether; they developed their own in-house personnel capabilities; and they came increasingly to bargain at establishment and occasionally at enterprise level. While this was overwhelmingly done bilaterally with trade unions, there was also new thinking about direct employee participation and joint consultation which might be layered alongside collective bargaining arrangements (Brown *et al.* 2009; Gospel 1992; Millward *et al.* 2000).

In 1979 began 18 years of Conservative government, comprising four administrations. However, it was a government which was necessarily pragmatic and it had not forgotten the failure of the legal reforms of the early 1970s. Monetarist policies led to the deepest recession up to that point in post-war history and unemployment rose dramatically. The government eschewed incomes policies with employers and unions and instead step-by-step introduced a series of legal reforms (seven in total) progressively curtailing union power. It also gave support to employers in major disputes, in particular the coal miners' strike in 1984. These signalled to employers that they should stand firm against unions and to employees that unions would find it more difficult to win in disputes in the way they had hitherto. In these years, there was also some abolition of auxiliary supports for low wages and some weakening of individual employment rights in areas like dismissals. At the same time, however, because of membership of the European Union (EU), there was also a slow build-up of new employment rights which acted as a countervailing force.

With the advent in 1997 of the New Labour government (under Tony Blair), comprising three administrations up to 2010, there were changes in policy. Gifts were given to unions in the form of new recognition rights and (because of EU obligations) new information and consultation rights for employees. However, neither of these have had much direct effect and only little indirect effect, though the introduction of a national minimum wage was more significant. In the main, the Labour governments of 1997 to 2010 largely accepted the industrial relations path which the Conservatives had charted, with this forming a part of the move to the centre ground that the party leadership saw as crucial to electoral success.

Compared to 1979, the UK system of industrial relations had changed significantly in important respects. Foreign multinationals played a significant part in this, but domestic UK companies paralleled them (Edwards and Walsh 2010). Industrial relations had moved to the single-employer level and had to a large extent ceased to be bilateral with trade unions. As collective bargaining had shrunk, so joint consultation had grown relatively, as had various forms of direct employee involvement at work. Where it survived, as in the private sector, collective bargaining increasingly took the form of consultation rather than negotiations and private sector trade union membership fell sharply (Brown *et al.* 2009; Millward *et al.* 2000). While the speed and magnitude of change in levels of co-ordination and methods of governance undoubtedly owed much to the actions of the Conservative governments, we contend that to a significant extent many of the changes would have happened to a large extent anyway, even in the absence of Conservative governments.

The move to the single-employer level had begun before the Thatcher government and would almost certainly have continued even in the absence of that government. It had begun in the 1960s and accelerated through the 1970s. In the private sector, it was the direction in which most British employers, trade unions and both main political parties wanted to go. While the UK was certainly a leader within Europe in moving in a decentralized, more market direction (Katz and Darbishire 1999), this was a very long-term development rather than one beginning in 1979; it was speeded up by political developments, but not initiated by them.

The decline in union membership did indeed begin in 1979, prompted in part by the high unemployment in the 1980s (created by Thatcher), the labour laws introduced by the Conservative government, and privatization of major industries and union defeats in major disputes. In these ways, the years of Conservative government had an effect. However, again there were other, longer-term factors at work. Crucially, the habitat of private sector trade unions was changing, in particular with the decline of manufacturing and large workplaces and the growth of part-time work. A new generation had entered the labour force which had less experience of unions and the benefits of union membership seemed less obvious. In a more competitive environment, employers had become more ready to bypass and ignore unions. Moreover, the existence of a more supportive Labour government for 13 years from 1997 onwards did little to change things, despite favourable legal changes and a more benign economic environment (Fernie and Metcalf 2005).

Concerning employers, the decline of the collectivist model presented an opportunity to introduce new practices. While there was certainly considerable interest shown in new forms of flexibility and direct employee involvement, both case study and survey data suggest that firms took a highly pragmatic approach and the take-up of new 'human resource management' practices was patchy (Cully *et al.* 1999; Storey 1992). Management's approach to the decline of collectivism was opportunistic with less coherent a sense of what was going to replace it.

In terms of our broad themes, industrial relations in the UK was slowly transformed over a long time period, beginning in the 1960s with employers slowly developing single-employer bargaining. The decline of bilateral regulation also developed gradually through the 1980s and 1990s, and here undoubtedly the actions by the Conservative government of the time played a role, though not as large as is often suggested. By 2010, British industrial relations had undoubtedly been transformed, but it was a transformation based not so much on a decisive politically driven turning point but also on long-term structural changes and pragmatic adaptation by employers.

4. INDUSTRIAL TRAINING

We turn now to industrial training, an obviously related domain, but one where the nature of change in the UK has been significantly different. Immediately after the Second World War, the UK had a system of industrial training based on apprenticeships which again performed reasonably well. Apprenticeship training had increasingly come to be regulated by multi-employer agreements between employers and trade unions. This contrasted with the pre-war situation where employers had not been prepared to enter into agreements about apprenticeship training and where at workplace level unions asserted control only in periods of upswing. In the 1950s and 1960s, there were some reforms to apprenticeship systems, in particular a shortening of time periods served and provision being allowed for college attendance. Through this system, the UK produced apprentices in terms of quantity and quality similar to West Germany, which was to become the main comparator in this area (Broadberry 2004; Gospel 1992). However, again it was a system which was skeletal and lacked legal supports, especially in terms of requirements on employers, regulation of content and enforcement of arrangements.

The saliency of the training issue grew slowly from the early 1960s onwards, though in no way like the industrial relations issue. It was argued that apprenticeships had not been sufficiently updated, standards were variable, skills were produced in relatively narrow ranges, and for the most part apprenticeships excluded females. In 1964, the then Labour government introduced an Industrial Training Act which met with wide support. Under this there existed a government agency to oversee the reform of training, which involved employer, union and government officials. At industry level, a series of Industrial Training Boards were established, again with joint employer and union representation. These had the legal power to impose levies on their industries and to pay grants to firms which trained. They also had a broader remit to update training by reforming apprenticeships in a more inclusive and expansive direction. This represented a clear neocorporatist approach to industrial training.

Some significant reforms were affected under this system in terms of content and delivery, such as the extension of modular training and college attendance. However, some employers, especially smaller ones, found the system irksome, and, in 1975, the then Labour government introduced the right to be exempted and began the process of unwinding the institutions. In 1982, the Thatcher government abolished the Training Boards in all sectors except construction, which was felt to have particular problems. This fitted with the new approach to the economy and the labour market and was also a reversion to a more voluntarist approach. Though the abolition was opposed by the unions, the continuation was not supported by the employers. Overall, the Thatcher government was not supportive of apprenticeship training, seeing it as closely associated with trade unions (Central Policy Review Staff 1980; Finegold and Soskice 1988; Senker 1992).

In the high unemployment of the early 1980s, there were two further developments. First, employers were able to recruit trained staff in the external labour market and chose increasingly to develop them through upgrade training within their own internal labour markets. This meant less reliance on apprenticeship training. Second, government-funded training schemes were expanded to deal with youth unemployment and to offer some skills training. This marked the beginnings of increased government funding for youth training, but a continued neglect of content and standards.

However, by the early 1990s, the saliency of training had re-emerged, among employers, unions, educationalists and the general public. It never rose to the heights of concern about industrial relations, but it became sufficient to prompt new actions. In 1994, the Conservative government (now under John Major) re-launched apprenticeship training under the so-called Modern Apprenticeship, marking some continuity but also change. As they developed, the new arrangements entailed a peak body to guide and to provide government funds, while at industry level sector skills councils were established to draw up standards and to co-ordinate arrangements. However, though these were termed 'employer-led' bodies, active employer participation has been limited and union involvement has been minimal.

Further characteristics of the developing system should be noted. Apprenticeships have come to be significantly based on competency testing via National Vocational Qualifications which, according to many commentators, represent an approach imposed by government on employers and employees. The cost of training for most apprenticeships has come to be mainly paid by the government, while actual training is increasingly carried out by for-profit training providers rather than the actual employer. In these circumstances, both unions *and* employers have become disengaged from the system (Ryan and Unwin 2001; Ryan *et al.* 2007). Meanwhile, college-based vocational education has expanded and is significantly larger in terms of numbers than apprenticeship training.

With the advent of the Blair Labour government in 1997, these arrangements remained. However, by way of small gifts to the unions, the government did introduce the right to appoint so-called union 'learning representatives'. No further legal obligations or supports were added.

Over this long time period what has actually happened to intermediate training in the UK? In 1966, there were approximately 244,000 apprentices in the UK, falling to 115,000 in 1979 and 34,000 in 1990. By 2010, the number had risen to 81,000 higher level and 158,000 lower level apprentices. Positively, apprenticeships have been extended to new sectors such as business administration and IT (though with limited success) and to females (though they tend to be segregated into stereotypical female areas, such as hairdressing and retail). Negatively, apprenticeships in areas such as engineering and construction have struggled to maintain their numbers and many trainees finish their apprenticeship at a low level relative to their counterparts in German-speaking countries (Gospel 1995; Steedman 2010).

In terms of our broad themes, the UK traditionally had a voluntarist system of intermediate level training based on apprenticeship which began to decline in the 1960s. Neocorporatist interventions over a 20-year period had some effect in supporting and modernizing the system, but were dismantled in favour of more market-based approaches in the 1980s. Meanwhile, employers have largely gone their own way, looking to the external labour market for skills or relying on internal labour market upgrade training. Since the early 1990s, governments have sought to build a new system. In this area, more reliance is still based on multi-employer action, though largely without trade unions, reflecting a continuing felt need to use this kind of co-ordination in this area. However, few would say that these have worked, and industrial training remains a salient issue, as governments experiment – 'muddle through', in our terms – in a search for workable arrangements.

5. DISCUSSION AND CONCLUSIONS

Here we summarize the pattern of change in these two domains and consider the main determinants of change. In the conclusion we consider linkages in terms of complementarities with other domains and speculate briefly on likely future directions of change.

5.1. Mapping the trajectory of change

Figure 1 provides a diagrammatic summary of the two narratives outlined above, showing the trajectory of development of industrial relations and industrial training over the period under consideration, in terms of co-ordination/ governance and salience. This is obviously highly stylized and should not be seen as implying a neat transformational trajectory which would certainly not fit with our theme of muddling through.

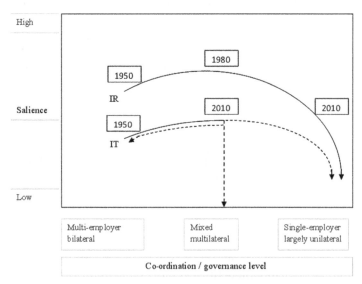

Figure 1 Trajectory of industrial relations (IR) and industrial training (IT), 1950–2010

The horizontal axis shows three broad levels and methods of co-ordination or governance. First, to the left, the main level is seen as multi-employer, at either industry or regional level or both. For the sake of the argument, but also reflecting the actual history, the method of governance is here also seen as bilateral, involving employers and their organizations and trade unions. Conceive of this as the period at the beginning of our analysis, in the 20 years after the Second World War. Second, in the middle, the level of co-ordination is more mixed, involving both multi- and single-employer levels; in other words national, industry, regional, company and establishment levels. The method of governance is also more mixed, involving not only employers and unions but also shop stewards at workplace level and the government at national level. In terms of industrial relations, for example, this is a period roughly around the late 1960s and 1970s. Third, to the right, the main level of co-ordination is the single-employer level, *viz.* it takes place within the individual firm or establishment. The method of governance is also shown as more unilateral; in other words management now decides the rules of the game, within the firm, subject to legal constraints. For industrial relations, again, think of the period from the 1990s/2000s onwards. For industrial training, which we revert to below, we see more uncertain movement, more ongoing experimentation and more mixed co-ordination which continues to exist up to the present date, which we represent towards the middle of our spectrum. For industrial training, also, there is a dotted line which suggests various future possible movements.

The vertical axis shows saliency, defined in Section 2 in terms of the importance of an issue to political parties and governments and as gauged by references in party manifestos, etc., government reports, legal intervention and the creation of special agencies. As already stated, saliency involves real issues of an economic, social and political nature. It also involves the perception of issues. In our usage, high saliency is a stimulus for action by key players, driving the search for solutions to problems, though not determining outcomes. We have suggested that the saliency of private sector industrial relations rose through the 1960s and 1970s, but has declined over the last 20 years. By contrast, the saliency of industrial training was historically lower, but has slowly risen and is now higher than that of industrial relations.

Consider in more detail the industrial relations trajectory in the private sector in the UK. Here we see the unfolding of a relatively 'full' story over the period from circa 1950 to circa 2010. Initially, co-ordination was significantly shaped by multi-employer bargaining between employers' organizations and trade unions. In this respect, the UK was like many other European countries. However, the system had weak foundations and was beginning to change. At that time, industrial relations was a reasonably salient issue, especially significant where there were large national disputes. Over time, moving into the 1960s and 1970s and reflecting multiple pressures, the level of co-ordination became more mixed, taking place at various levels. Governance was also becoming increasingly multilateral, involving shop stewards at the workplace level through shop-floor bargaining and the state at the national level through incomes policies and legislation. Disputes were frequent and the system was seen by many as dysfunctional, a perception that was strengthened by the so-called 'Winter of Discontent' of 1978–9. This is the period when the saliency of industrial relations was highest, and in the early 1980s this manifested itself in markedly different public policies towards unions and collective regulation (Grant 2008). The third phase saw the final stages of an already initiated shift to the single-employer level; in other words, more was done, and done exclusively, at company or establishment level. Moreover, employers came to decide matters unilaterally, with much less or no union involvement in issues and with little direct state involvement in collective issues of pay and conditions, notwithstanding the greater presence of individual employment rights. At this stage, the saliency of industrial relations declined, having become 'privatized' within the human resource management of the firm. In addition, industrial relations ceased to have prominence in political debate, and the Labour governments of 1997–2010 were anxious not to revive its saliency. Of course, contentious issues still remained between employers and employees in the private sector, but these are largely confined within the organization, and attracted less public and political attention.

Consider second the industrial training trajectory. Here the unfolding of the story is less 'full' and the sequencing is also different. As suggested above, industrial training was traditionally a less salient issue through most of the early part of the period, with the exception of the 1964 Industrial Training Act, though we would argue that the exceptional nature of this, its dilution and later repeal supports our contention. Hence, in Figure 1 we begin by drawing the line lower. Towards the beginning of the period, the co-ordination of training also had a significant multi-employer element and unions were involved in governance, although many employers' associations were reluctant to bargain in any detail with unions about apprenticeships which were at the core of the training system. However, over the last 20 years, as 'skills problems' have been increasingly identified in a growing competitive environment, salience has risen and now stands higher than in the industrial relations domain. In the training area, also, the level of co-ordination/governance became and has remained more hybrid, with mixed levels and significant state intervention, though with greatly reduced union intervention. Salience remains high, as evidenced by enquiries, government interventions, the creation of new agencies and public expenditures. This is a classic case of 'still muddling through', with a continuing search for solutions but a lack of coherent change. Hence, in the industrial training domain, there are still significant choices to be made, and the dotted lines in Figure 1 depict possible future trajectories.

One possible trajectory in the training area is to remain at this mixed level, with a degree of multilateral co-ordination. In time, it is conceivable that many of the problems will be resolved, reducing saliency. A second logically conceivable possibility might be to move back to the left and towards multi-employer co-ordination, with bilateral or multilateral governance. However, this is highly unlikely because the relevant institutions of industrial relations no longer exist to support such an option. A third possible development is to move incrementally further along the curve towards decentralized single-employer and unilateral governance; in other words to move in the same direction in which industrial relations has already moved. As in industrial relations, this may concomitantly ease the problems and reduce the saliency of the issue.

5.2. Causes and complementarities

We turn finally to causes of these trajectories of industrial relations and industrial training. In doing so, we revert to the theme of the importance of politics in general and the Thatcher years in particular, relative to other factors, and also consider complementarities with changes in other domains. Table 1 provides a summary of this and possible complementarities with other domains.

As a first explanation, it should be recalled that we have argued that in the early post-war period, though *prima facie* the institutions of industrial relations and industrial training in the UK performed reasonably well and were admired by contemporaries and overseas observers, in practice they had weak foundations. The skeletal and voluntary nature of the arrangements must be a starting point for any explanation of change in the UK system. The arrangements were skeletal because employers had largely wanted them that way and, for the most part, had not wanted to develop detailed bilateral regulation with unions. For their part, unions would have liked the rules to be fuller and the state was largely indifferent on this matter. The arrangements were voluntary because historically all parties preferred to keep them so: unions for the most part preferred to keep the law out of these areas; employers also preferred to exclude the state wherever possible; and governments were quite content not to interfere too much so long as 'private' matters did not overlap into 'public' saliency. When pressures built up from the 1960s onwards, these arrangements were not well equipped to withstand them. In addition, compositional change, in the form of the decline of manufacturing, reduced the traditional private sector habitat of trade unions, collective bargaining and industrial training, arguably earlier than in other countries such as Germany, France and Italy. Equally, the advent of privatization and marketization of the public sector also removed 'supporting institutions' and 'beneficial constraints' (Finegold and Soskice 1988; Martin and Thelen 2007; Streeck 1997)

A second possible explanation for the trajectory of developments in industrial relations and industrial training focuses on trade unions, their members and potential members. Trade unions came out of the war years with considerable commitment on the part of ordinary workers. In years of economic expansion, low unemployment and high price inflation in the 1970s, membership grew and spread to new groups in the labour force. In these circumstances, unions were able to win benefits for their members and played some role in sustaining apprenticeship training and their local shop stewards drove some of the movement towards plant-level bargaining. However, the situation changed from the 1970s, and especially the 1980s, onwards. Unions were pilloried in the media

Table 1 UK: institutional overview at present time

Institutional domain	Type at present	Direction of change/ major reforms	Timing of major reforms
Industrial relations	Liberal	Move to single-employer, decentralized Increasingly unilateral Increasingly flexibility But a number of EU directives	Begins 1960s Accelerates 1980s
Industrial training	Market-based; some industry co-ordination; increasing government intervention	Attempts to revive apprenticeship Move to single-employer, decentralized Some industry co-ordination, but employer-led Increased emphasis on college and university education and training	1960s co-ordination reversed in 1970s and 1980s; 1980s–increased government financial support; 1990s–attempts to revive apprenticeship, but also expansion of college- and school-based system
Industrial policy	Small	Deregulation Privatization	1980s
Financial markets and system	Market – outsider-oriented	Intensification of market finance Deregulation of banking Deregulation of equity markets Increased emphasis on disclosure regulation But a number of EU directives	1980s–1990s–
Corporate governance	Shareholder-oriented	Law and codes Strong market for corporate control	Slow build-up 1980s–

(Continued)

Table 1 Continued

Institutional domain	Type at present	Direction of change/ major reforms	Timing of major reforms
Labour market and welfare state	National welfare state, with means testing	Increasing introduction of market principles Adoption of welfare-to-work On-going reforms of health and benefit systems	1980s–
Product markets	Liberal, open	Open, pro-competition Deregulation Privatization	1950s– 1980s–

and their salience grew in a negative way. In part because they lacked legal supports, in hard times unions were unable to support the system of collective bargaining and industrial training. In general, it might be said that British unions had had significant power, but not of an initiatory kind. Unions were not strong enough to support the traditional arrangements or to create new ones with a role for themselves.

A third explanation is in terms of political influence. As already stated, in the two decades after the Second World War, governments of both main political parties were prepared largely to accept and support the systems of industrial relations and industrial training which had developed. This began to change from the 1960s, before what is often seen as the 'tipping point' of the Thatcher years. Both Labour and the Conservatives became more interventionist, thereby eroding the voluntarist tradition, not only in the collective area but also in terms of individual employment rights. The advent of the Thatcher government in 1979 undoubtedly represented a marked change in the pace and magnitude of change, with the government taking actions which previous administrations had not taken. The Thatcher government had broad long-term aspirations in industrial relations – the reduction of union power and the contraction of the coverage of bargaining – but they had less clear plans as to how to obtain these objectives, and were prepared to operate tactically and opportunistically. The supportive role the government played *vis-à-vis* employers in a number of major disputes which the employers won was important. Undoubtedly, the actions of governments constrained union power, facilitated various employer actions which otherwise would have been less likely, and provided a 'legitimating discourse' which helped bring about change (Béland 2009; Schmidt 2001). However, this is not to say that the Thatcher government had a clear, detailed vision of industrial relations reform and the legal reform programme was highly incremental. The policy of privatization was something which the government also discovered over time and the negative impact this had on trade unions was a largely unanticipated bonus.

For industrial training, governments played a less clear role in changing the system. Labour governments in the 1960s acted to support apprenticeship training, but then backed off from this in the 1970s. The Thatcher government acted to undermine the apprenticeship system as it had operated, representing a departure from a largely cross-party consensus. However, it was from the early 1960s onwards that apprenticeship had really begun its long-term decline. Later, from the early 1990s onwards, both political parties have tried to recreate a new system of apprenticeship training, both building on and subtracting from their predecessor's schemes. Whereas industrial relations has seen a strategic transformation that was caused in significant part by political influence, industrial training has been the subject of muddling through by all governments and other actors, and in particular employer preferences have been more significant in shaping the training system.

Finally, we turn to the behaviour of employers in their market and political contexts. Here we refer to labour, product and financial markets. Taking industrial relations first, British employers had been key players in creating the system of industrial relations which existed after the Second World War. However, their lack of systematic management structures and processes had played an important part in allowing disorderly industrial relations to develop as occurred in the 1960s. Spurred on by product market forces (increasing competition and threats to profits), from the mid-1960s onwards they began incrementally to change the level of co-ordination towards single-employer bargaining (Gospel 1992). Even in the absence of government prompting, it is highly likely that employers, both British companies and foreign multinationals, would have moved in this direction anyway, though perhaps not as far or as fast. From the 1980s onwards, increased product market pressures (Brown 2008) and new financial market pressures (Gospel and Pendleton 2006) meant that employers had further incentives to move towards establishment level bargaining and even more away from bilateral governance with trade unions. Moreover, in the industrial relations area also, the changed political context from 1979 onwards and the reduction of union power had made it easier to move in directions in which market forces were also prompting.

Turning to industrial training, British employers had played their part in the creation of the industrial training system which existed in the two decades after the Second World War. They were happy to see some modernization of apprenticeship training, but they were dissatisfied with the interventionist Training Board system. In the 1970s and 1980s, they were increasingly prepared to rely on slacker external labour markets for recruitment. Despite protests to the contrary, they were also prepared to delegate more: to the state in terms of funding; to the vocational education system; and to intermediaries such as sector skills councils and private training providers. Market pressures on them were contradictory: where labour markets were tight, they favoured training and vice versa; where product markets were competitive, they had to train; and, from the 1990s, increasing financial market pressure was a constraint on committing resources to intangible assets such as skills. These conflicting pressures contributed to the approach that we have characterized as 'muddling through' by both governments and employers.

5.3. Conclusions

We have charted institutional changes in two labour market domains in the UK private sector. In the industrial relations area, the system has moved to one which is solidly single-employer and largely unilateral. In the industrial training area, change has been less clear, with a move to a mixed system of co-ordination, at various levels and with multilateral governance, involving the state and employers, but trade unions only to a limited extent. Both trajectories have been in a broadly liberal market direction, mirroring developments to some extent in other domains over the last three decades and more. Thus, industrial policy has been transformed through the abolition of tripartite structures shaping economic policy and privatization. Financial markets were deregulated, beginning in the 1970s, but then more thoroughly from the 1980s. The financing, ownership and governance of corporations have also developed in a more market-oriented direction (see Table 1). In this way, there are complementarities across various economic and social domains, which in sum constitute a move by the UK in a more liberal market direction over the last 30 years.

There has thus been a transformation, driven in part by government, especially the Thatcher government, in the industrial relations area. However, we have urged caution in placing too much emphasis on political factors in isolation and, to a significant extent, the changes pre-date the purported 'tipping point' of 1979–1997 and occurred in a pragmatic, incremental way. Nor are the institutional configurations in these two domains fixed at a definitive end point. In particular, we have seen that alternative developments are conceivable in relation to the present mixed system of industrial training. However, in industrial relations there is little prospect of a return to collectivist institutions in the private sector, but there is considerable uncertainty over the nature of public sector industrial relations.

While we acknowledge the existence of some complementarities, the links between these trajectories are clearly not tight. When, further, we extend the analysis to other domains, such as the welfare state, we see that despite the Thatcher governments' rhetoric and some substantive changes, the welfare state and public support for social safety nets have been surprisingly resilient (Pontusson 2005). Even if the reforms to the welfare state being implemented by the present Conservative–-Liberal Democrat coalition which took office in 2010 bring about radical changes, it would be difficult to argue that these are linked to the much earlier changes in other domains. As Howell (2007: 259) notes: 'The British case suggests a certain degree of autonomy of institutions in different spheres ... In other words, the narrative of postwar institutional change may be quite different depending upon which institutions one is talking about.'

We conclude by highlighting two implications of our argument. First, a theme of this collection has been to emphasize political developments in accounting for institutional change. The contribution has acknowledged the importance of this in the British case, especially in the long 18 years of Conservative government after 1979, but has also sought to show the limitations of politics as a sole driver of change. We have argued that in industrial relations the transformation of the British system also owes much to the opportunism and pragmatism of British employers. Second, change in the two closely related domains of industrial relations and industrial training has had some similarities, but there are also clear differences, and the two trajectories have followed different paths in a non-sequential way. If this is the case across two such related domains, it is not surprising that we see disjunctures in the form and extent of change to be even greater across less related spheres. Given the extent of change, but also taking the pragmatic and incremental nature of change on the one hand, and the differential and non-sequential trajectories of change across domains on the other, we feel that the British story should be framed in terms of both strategic transformation *and* muddling through.

Biographical notes: Howard Gospel is Professor of Management at King's College London, UK. Tony Edwards is Professor of Comparative Management at King's College London, UK.

ACKNOWLEDGEMENTS

We wish to thank the *Journal of European Public Policy* referees for their comments, and would also like to thank J. Edmonds and P. Kern.

REFERENCES

Bach, S. (2002) 'Public sector employment relations reform under Labour: muddling through on modernization?', *British Journal of Industrial Relations* 40(2): 319–39.
Béland, D. (2009) 'Ideas, institutions and policy change', *Journal of European Public Policy* 16(5): 701–18.
Broadberry, S. (2004) 'Human capital and skills', in R. Floud and P. Johnson (eds), *The Cambridge Economic History of Modern Britain, Volume 2: Economic Maturity, 1860–1939*, Cambridge: Cambridge University Press, pp. 56–73.

Brown, W. (2004) 'Industrial relations and the economy', in *Cambridge Economic History of Modern Britain, Vol. 3: Structural Change and Growth, 1939–2000,* Cambridge: Cambridge University Press.

Brown, W. (2008) 'The influence of product markets on industrial relations', in P. Blyton, J. Fiorito and E. Heery (eds), *Handbook of Industrial Relations,* London Sage, pp. 113–48.

Brown, W., Bryson, A., Forth, J. and Whitfield, K. (2009) *The Evolution of the Modern Workplace,* Cambridge: Cambridge University Press.

Bullock Royal Commission (1977) *Report of the Committee of Inquiry on Industrial Democracy, Cmnd 6706,* London: HMSO.

Callaghan, H. (2010) 'Beyond methodological nationalism: how multilevel governance affects the clash of capitalisms', *Journal of European Public Policy* 17(4): 564–80.

Central Policy Review Staff (1980) *Education, Training, and Industrial Performance,* London: HMSO.

Crafts, N. (1991) 'Reversing relative economic decline? The 1980s in historical perspective', *Oxford Review of Economic Policy* 7(3): 81–98.

Crouch, C. (2005) *Capitalist Diversity and Change,* Oxford: Oxford University Press.

Cully, M., Woodland, S., O'Reilly, A. and Dix, G. (1999) *Britain at Work,* London: Routledge.

Culpepper, P. (2010) *Quiet Politics and Business Power,* Cambridge: Cambridge University Press.

Donovan Royal Commission (1968) *Report of the Royal Commission on Trade Unions and Employers' Associations, Cmnd 3623,* London: HMSO.

Edwards, P. *et al.* (1992) 'Great Britain: still muddling through', in A. Ferner and R. Hyman (eds), *New Frontiers in European Industrial Relations,* Oxford: Blackwell, pp. 1–68.

Edwards, T. and Walsh, J. (2010) 'Foreign ownership and industrial relations', in W. Brown, A. Bryson, J. Forth and K. Whitfield (eds), *The Evolution of the Modern Workplace,* Cambridge: Cambridge University Press, pp. 285–306.

Fernie, S. and Metcalf, D. (eds) (2005) *Unions and Performance,* London: Routledge.

Finegold, D. and Soskice, D. (1988) 'The failure of training in Britain', *Oxford Review of Economic Policy* 4(3): 21–53.

Gamble, A. (1994) *The Free Economy and the Strong State: The Politics of Thatcherism,* 2nd edn, Durham, NC: Duke University Press.

Gospel, H. (1992) *Markets, Firms, and the Management of Labour in Modern Britain,* Cambridge: Cambridge University Press.

Gospel, H. (1995) 'The decline of apprenticeship training in Britain', *Industrial Relations Journal* 26(1): 32–45.

Gospel, H. and Pendleton, A. (2006) *Corporate Governance and Labour Management,* Oxford: Oxford University Press.

Grant, W. (2008) 'The changing patterns of group politics in Britain', *British Politics* 3: 204–22.

Hall, P. and Soskice, D. (2001) *Varieties of Capitalism: The Institutional Foundations of Comparative Advantage,* Oxford: Oxford University Press.

Hennessy, P. (1996) *Muddling Through: Power, Politics, and the Quality of Government in Postwar Britain,* London: Indigo.

Howell, C. (2007) 'The British variety of capitalism: institutional change, industrial relations and British politics', *British Politics* 2: 239–63.

Hyman, R. (1987) 'Strategy or structure: capital, labour and control', *Work, Employment and Society* 1(1): 25–55.

Katz, H. and Darbishire, O. (1999) *Converging Diversities: Worldwide Changes in Employment Systems,* Ithaca, NY: Cornell University Press.

Lindblom, C. (1959) 'The science of "muddling through"', *Public Administration Review* 19: 79–88.

Lindblom, C. (1979) 'Still muddling, not yet through', *Public Administration Review* 39(Nov/Dec): 517–26.

Martin, C. and Thelen, K. (2007) 'the state and coordinated capitalism: contributions of the public sector to social solidarity in postindustrial societies', *World Politics* 60(1): 1–36.

Millward, N., Stevens, M., Smart, D. and Hawes, W. (1992) *Workplace Industrial Relations in Transition*, Aldershot: Dartmouth.

Millward, N., Bryson, A. and Forth, J. (2000) *All Change at Work*, London: Routledge.

Pontusson, J. (2005) *Inequality and Prosperity: Social Europe versus Liberal America*, Ithaca, NY: Cornell University Press.

Ryan, P. and Unwin, L. (2001) 'Apprenticeship in the British training market', *National Institute Economic Review* 178(1): 99–114.

Ryan, P., Gospel, H. and Lewis, P. (2007) 'Large employers and apprenticeship training in Britain', *British Journal of Industrial Relations* 45(1): 127–53.

Senker, P. (1992) *Industrial Training in a Cold Climate*, Aldershot: Avebury.

Schmidt, V. (2001) 'The politics of economic adjustment in France and Britain: does discourse matter?', *Journal of European Public Policy* 9(6): 894–912.

Steedman, H. (2010) *The State of Apprenticeship in 2010*, London: Centre for Economic Performance, London School of Economics.

Storey, J. (1992) *Developments in the Management of Human Resources*, Oxford: Blackwell.

Streeck, W. (1997) 'Beneficial constraints: on the economic limits of rational voluntarism', in J. Hollingsworth, J. Rogers and R. Boyer (eds), *Contemporary Capitalism: The Embeddedness of Institutions*, Cambridge: Cambridge University Press, pp. 197–218.

Streeck, W. and Thelen, K. (2005) *Beyond Continuity: Institutional Change in Advanced Political Economies*, Oxford: Oxford University Press.

Weekes, B., Mellish, M., Dickens, L. and Lloyd, J. (1975) *Industrial Relations and the Limits of the Law: The Industrial Effects of the Industrial Relations Act, 1971*, Oxford: Blackwell.

The limits of liberalization? American capitalism at the crossroads

Richard Deeg

ABSTRACT   From the 1930s to 1970s the United States (US) model of capitalism was based on a Keynesian growth model. Collective bargaining and pro-labour policies were widely accepted. Product market regulation was fairly extensive. Industrial policy in the US was less overt than in other advanced economies, but quite extensive in certain sectors. By the late 1990s the US model had clearly coalesced around a new set of institutions based on a different set of complementarities: deregulated labour markets combined with shareholder-oriented finance and corporate governance to produce a system with highly flexible allocation of productive resources marked by high levels of financialization. This contribution explains this transformation as a combination of three variables: structural features of the US economy; the fragmented institutional character of US policy-making and regulation; and policy convergence between left and right.

1.   INTRODUCTION

For the past 30 years the United States (US) led the world in the uneven but widespread march toward market liberalism. The recent global financial crisis calls this global trend into question, not least because the US, alongside the United Kingdom (UK), suffered the worst in this crisis and struggles to return to steady and sustainable growth. One might be tempted to conclude that the US has begun to recast its model of capitalism, but that would be a rash conclusion. For while the US still struggles to right itself, the basic principles of its finance capitalism were only briefly (and partially) called into serious question among the public and its political leaders. Even though stricter financial regulation has been passed, it appears unlikely to dramatically alter the trajectory of American capitalist development. That said, the present era may yet turn out to be a critical juncture for the US model if its consumption-led growth model cannot be revived in a more sustainable form.

From a theoretical perspective, the evolution of US capitalism over the last three decades accords well with the varieties of capitalism (VoC) prediction that inherently liberal market economies (LMEs) will, under increased competitive pressures, become even more liberal (i.e., market oriented) in their economic governance (Hall and Soskice 2001). Yet, this theory gives us no way to explain or predict the degree to which an LME will liberalize, nor does it help us understand why the US economy became as financialized as it did, i.e., dependent on finance-driven activity for economic growth. It also does not help us understand why the US model came to rely increasingly on excess leverage by banks and especially consumers as its source of growth. There are a variety of structural theories that explain liberalization and financialization in the US, but this contribution will argue that structural factors alone are insufficient. Rather, answering these questions requires a historical examination that also incorporates the role of US-specific institutions and institutional complementarities – especially between finance, corporate governance and labour relations – and the political coalitions that emerged to reshape the rules defining the US model. This contribution summarizes and analyses the institutional evolution of American capitalism since the Reagan era, the critical juncture that marks the beginning of the current liberal model of capitalism. During the Clinton presidency this policy paradigm became dominant on both the mainstream left and right. Thus, by the 1990s, the current trajectory of the US model was firmly ensconced.

In keeping with the objectives of this collection, the next section briefly highlights key institutional changes in five of the six core domains that constitute the political economy. The third section will analyse the politics of this institutional trajectory with a particular focus on developments in the financial domain. Finance is singled out for several reasons: first, it is the domain where we find the greatest institutional change in the US model of capitalism; second, the financial sector has come, in many ways, to define the American model of capitalism; and third, changes in finance are important drivers of change in other institutional domains.

2. INSTITUTIONAL CHANGE IN THE US MODEL OF CAPITALISM

From the late 1930s to 1970s the US model of capitalism was based loosely on a Keynesian growth model. The state pursued policies to simulate and maintain aggregate demand, including the promotion of core sectors of the economy such as housing and infrastructure construction. Collective bargaining and pro-labour policies were widely accepted in the public and corporate spheres, and bargaining agreements influenced wages and working conditions across much of the economy. Product market regulation – including financial – was fairly extensive. After World War II, the state also promoted the expansion of global trade as a tenet of its growth strategy. Industrial policy in the US was less overt than in other advanced economies, but quite extensive in certain sectors, especially those related to defence (Vogel 1996). The Democratic New Deal coalition – the urban working class, southerners, farmers and much of the middle class – and its policy preferences dominated this era.

In the powerful manufacturing sector, Fordism and large, vertically integrated firms dominated. This model relied on unskilled and semi-skilled workers, and was thus compatible with a general skills-based training system (Thelen 2007). It was complemented by weak forms of stakeholder corporate governance and an acceptance of unionized labour, made possible in part by regulated product markets, US global dominance in certain sectors and the high degree of managerial autonomy – and thus indifference to financial market demands – arising from the generally dispersed and passive nature of corporate ownership (Davis 2009). It was also during this era that corporate provision of 'welfare' in the form of health insurance and defined benefit pensions came to be the norm, also made by possible in part by relatively muted market and financial pressures on corporate managers.

While these were undoubtedly real institutional complementarities, in retrospect they may not have been that strong and their maintenance depended as much on political factors (voluntary compliance more than legal requirement) as on economic efficiency gains. With the onset of product market deregulation in the late 1970s, the competitiveness problems of US industry in that same decade, the decline of the supporting New Deal coalition (due in good part to the defection of southern Democrats from the party), shifts in technology and other structural economic conditions, a rapid shift occurred in preferences of employers regarding labour relations and finance/corporate governance during the 1980s. In this decade the large, integrated firm model began to unravel, as hostile takeovers led by Wall Street brought the break up and restructuring of many firms. This was partly in an effort to regain growth and competitiveness but also an effort by financiers to extract greater value (profits) from the real economy. Investors were no longer passive and corporate managers were pressured, then induced through incentive-based pay (stock options), to drop stakeholder in exchange for shareholder corporate governance (Davis 2009).

In the political realm, the transformation took off in the early 1980s with Reagan's anti-government movement (Prasad 2006: 67–70; Block 2011). Deregulation and a smaller state, i.e., freer and more markets, were touted as the solution to the economic ills of the 1970s and early 1980s. Thus, with the combination of simultaneous changes in the corporate sector and political arena, the great era of liberalization began.

As this brief summary will show (see Table 1), the greatest institutional change occurred in the financial domain and industrial relations. In both domains decentralized market competition was increasingly pursued as an end in itself, as well as a means to greater prosperity. While the American welfare state expanded during this time as a percentage of gross domestic product (GDP) and the federal budget, here too market solutions are increasingly emphasized (Pontusson 2005:, 145). By the late 1990s the US model had clearly coalesced around a new model based on a different set of complementarities (Campbell 2011): deregulated and decentralized labour markets combined with shareholder-oriented finance and corporate governance to

Table 1 United States: institutional overview

Institutional domain	Typology	Direction of change/major reforms	Timing of major reforms
Financial system	Market-oriented	Intensification of market finance • Deregulation of banking • Deregulation of securities markets • Increased emphasis on disclosure regulation	1980: Depository Institutions Deregulation and Monetary Control Act 1982: Garn-St. Germain Depository Institutions Act 1999: Financial Services Modernization Act 2000: Commodity Futures Modernization Act 2010: Dodd–Frank Wall Street Reform and Consumer Protection Act
Corporate governance	Shareholder-oriented	• Shift from weak notion of stakeholder to strong shareholder-oriented model • Managerialism slightly weakened • Strong market for corporate control	Rise of shareholder value occurs without major reforms 2002: Sarbanes–Oxley Act
Industrial relations	Pluralism	• 'Employment-at-will' doctrine weakens via growth of anti-discrimination law • Collective bargaining coverage erodes • Strikes decline while disputes rise	Early-to-mid-1980s (1981 PATCO Strike) 'Policy drift'
Education and skill creation	Market-based Fragmented Minimal apprenticeship	• Some increased federal training subsidies associated with trade agreements (NAFTA) or mid-1990s welfare reform • Increased emphasis on university training	No major reforms.

Welfare state	Liberal Means-tested Low replacement rates	• Individualization of risk, especially in private pensions • Reduced public pension benefits; increased retirement age • Expansion of healthcare insurance • Adoption of welfare-to-work principle	1983: Social Security Act Amendments 1996: Personal Responsibility and Work Opportunity Reconciliation Act 2003: Medicare Prescription Drug, Improvement and Modernization Act 2010: Patient Protection and Affordable Care Act
Industrial policy	Regulative Technology promotion Passive measures	Defence-driven (procurement; DARPA) Tax subsidies • Sectoral deregulation • From public to private R&D spending	Early 1980s

produce a system with a highly flexible allocation of productive resources – regarded within the US and also by VoC theory as a chief competitive advantage of an LME. The American model was no longer organized by and around large integrated firms, but by markets guided by financial imperatives (Davis 2009).

The remainder of this section summarizes very briefly the key institutional changes across the five non-finance domains addressed by this project. Particular attention is given to establishing the institutional complementarities that may operate across them and constitute a distinctive model of capitalism.

2.1. Corporate governance

It is important to note corporate law in the US is largely under state jurisdiction.[1] To the extent that the federal government regulates corporate governance, it largely does so through securities market regulation and focuses on transparency (disclosure) regulation of listed firms. There are two key moments in corporate governance reform since 1980. The first period was the mid- to late 1980s. In this period, US corporate governance shifted from a system of managerial dominance with a weak norm of stakeholder governance to a system of shareholder value governance (Lazonick and O'Sullivan 2009). Within the firm, external financial actors gained greater influence over management via takeover activity, use of performance pay and shareholder activism (driven in part by the rise of institutional investors). The shift during the 1980s cannot be attributed to any single, major reform. Rather, it was more a result of the new leveraged buyout wave and pressure from activist buyout funds; this was facilitated further by regulatory and tax rulings favouring the use of stock options for executive compensation. Intellectual backing for these moves came from financial economy theories rooted in principal–agent analysis (Jensen and Meckling 1976) and the efficient market hypothesis, which suggested that financial markets were the most efficient allocators of capital (Davis 2009). The second major reform was the Sarbanes–Oxley Act of 2002 – a populist political reaction (with support from both parties) to a wave of high-profile corporate scandals. The main thrust of legislation was to strengthen further financial reporting and oversight requirements, but this also marked the first federal efforts to go beyond disclosure regulation to 'structural regulation', including mandates regarding internal board structure (Cioffi 2010).

2.2. Industrial relations

From the early 1950s to the early 1970s, the unionization rate in the US hovered around 30 per cent of the labour force. The rate began declining during the 1970s and accelerated rapidly during the 1980s (it now stands at roughly 12 per cent overall and 7 per cent in the private sector [Godard 2009; Lehne 2006]). The degree of union decline in the US is unique among advanced economies, and it also cannot be linked to major formal reforms.

This was possible because the period of relatively peaceful co-operation between management and labour from the 1950s into the 1970s rested to a considerable degree on management's voluntary acceptance of organized labour representation.

The decline, then, occurred to a great degree through anti-labour interpretations and enforcement of existing labour laws and regulations by the president, federal bureaucracy and courts. A crucial turning point and signal event occurred in 1981 when Ronald Reagan fired striking air traffic controllers and hired replacement workers. Hiring replacement workers was not illegal under US labour law but also not widely practised by employers until after this action (Cramton and Tracy 1998). The rise of shareholder value ideas reinforced this anti-union shift in corporate sentiment. Unions were also hurt by massive job losses in traditionally unionized sectors owing to rapid de-industrialization. Godard (2009) argues that the comparatively dramatic decline in US labour was also owing to the narrowly self-interested character of the business unionism that predominated in the US. This inhibited the deep incorporation of labour into the broader progressive politics movements and limited general public sympathy to unions. Today there are few statutory or normative restrictions on layoffs by employers and the US has the most flexible labour force in the Organization for Economic Co-operation and Development (OECD).[2] Labour and wage flexibility are further enhanced by the comparatively low replacement rate and duration for unemployment insurance.[3]

2.3. Education and training

In comparative perspective, the US education and training system places greater emphasis on the production of general (transferable) skills (Thelen 2007) that is consistent with LME's reliance on general rather than specific assets. The federal role in vocational training is largely defined by subsidies to state-run programmes, with some minimal federal effort to co-ordinate or harmonize programmes across states. Consequently, one cannot speak of a national system of apprenticeship and vocational training. In addition to supporting universities, most states support vocational training schools and community colleges. It is difficult to argue that there has been a major reform of the US education and training system, though there have been frequent minor reforms at the state and federal level. Firm-based training is common, but generally unregulated and voluntary.

2.4. Welfare state

The US has always had a liberal welfare state, with comparatively low social insurance and replacement rates, means testing and greater reliance on market mechanisms to encourage individual risk provision (Pontusson 2005). In the early 1980s Reagan conducted a much-publicized campaign against the welfare state and had some success in curbing means-tested but not universal programmes (Prasad 2006: 82–96). More generally, though, over the last 30 years US policy-makers have attempted to curb the growth of welfare state spending by encouraging market-based solutions and the individualization of risk (Hacker 2006).

A prime example is the case of pensions: at beginning of 1980s, about 80 per cent of large- and medium-sized firms in the US offered defined benefit retirement plans to employees; 25 years later less than one-third did (Hacker 2006: 112). Most of these firms shifted to defined contribution programmes, in part owing to tax benefits granted to such plans. Employers also switched as the financial obligations of defined benefit plans became increasingly burdensome under conditions of intensified product market pressures, corporate restructuring and pressure from shareholders for higher returns on capital (Davis 2009). This shift was further aided by the decline of unions that helped secure defined benefit plans (Hacker 2006: 119). The major implication of this change is that the pension risk shifted from employers to employees, but most Americans save much too little to adequately fund retirement (Hacker 2006: 119). The growth of these plans also helped drive the dramatic expansion of institutional investors and securities markets in the US, thus promoting financialization. Since defined contribution plans remain with the employee when switching jobs, this change contributes to increased labour market mobility in the US.

In contrast to the pension situation, the continued reliance in the US on employer-provided health insurance (subsidized by the tax code) may hinder labour market mobility, as employees are reluctant to switch jobs if it means reduced benefits. However, over the last 30 years more and more employers have dropped health insurance coverage, opted for less generous insurance coverage and shifted the cost of premiums increasingly onto employees. In contrast to shrinking private health insurance coverage, over the last decade the federal government expanded healthcare coverage for senior citizens (the 2003 prescription drug expansion) and to populations presently without health insurance via the 2010 Patient Protection and Affordable Care Act. While not creating a true universal healthcare system, the Act is expected to dramatically expand the percentage of citizens with health insurance.

2.5. Industrial policy

Given the comparatively strong anti-statist ideology of US business, most US aid to industry is funnelled through tax deductions rather than overt forms of intervention (Vogel 1996). Though certain sectors of the economy have received explicit and extensive government support for decades, notably agriculture, defence, computers and information technology, and construction (homes and highways). Promotion of the defence industry also largely served as the US technology policy, and more than half of research and development (R&D) spending in the first post-war decades came from government sources (in 1960, the share of R&D spending was roughly two-thirds government, one-third private sector; by 2003 these shares were reversed; see Lehne [2006:

272]). During this era there was also extensive government market regulation – typically price but also market entry regulation – in several sectors of the economy, including utilities, airlines, transportation, telecommunications, finance and agriculture. The international dimension of US industrial policy consisted largely of a free trade agenda.

As in other institutional domains, there was a significant shift in US industrial policy beginning in the late 1970s, when a deregulation and anti-monopoly movement began. Initially conceived as a pro-consumer reform, deregulation was transformed under Reagan into a pro-business reform and supplemented with efforts to weaken 'social regulation', such as environmental, consumer and worker protections (Prasad 2006). Yet, at the same time, massive de-industrialization fostered extensive debate in the US over a more activist industrial policy. By the 1990s, however, a resurgent US economy swept aside any notions of activist industrial policy and there was a renewed push for increasing free trade (the North American Free Trade Agreement was signed in 1994). In sum, US industrial policy came to rest heavily on promoting free trade, select technologies and politically influential sectors, and globalization, while relying on the private sector to lead innovation.

3. UNDERSTANDING AMERICAN CAPITALISM AS FINANCE CAPITALISM

The central feature of change in American capitalism is without doubt the financialization of its economy over the last 30 years. The financial sector itself expanded as a portion of GDP – from 1975 to 2004 total stock and bond market capitalization grew from 102 per cent to 289 per cent of GDP (Deeg 2010: 316); the portion of corporate profits accruing to financial firms and to financial investments of non-financial firms rose dramatically from around 10 per cent in the early 1980s to 40 per cent in the early 2000s (Krippner 2005, 2011); the influence of financial firms over corporate management decisions expanded through the rise of shareholder value principles (Perry and Nölke 2005); institutional investors and non-bank financial institutions ('shadow banking') became major pillars of the industry; the financial behaviour of households changed dramatically, as pension funds and mutual funds became the central vehicle for saving and investment; and yet households saved less and less over time while borrowing more and more to finance consumption (Davis 2009; Langley 2008).

The central question of interest, then, is why did the US go so far in market liberalization and, specifically, develop an economic model dominated by financial capital? As suggested at the outset, varieties of capitalism (VoC) theory is a good starting point: VoC predicts that, under increased competitive pressure, LMEs such as the US will liberalize markets and that financial actors will be a primary mechanism for spreading liberalization pressures (Hall and Soskice 2001). This theory also emphasizes that liberalization spreads because actors will seek to institute complementary institutional arrangements across domains of the economy, and this dynamic is an important part of understanding the evolution of the US model (Campbell 2011). However, VoC cannot readily explain why the US went so much further in liberalizing its markets than other advanced economies, nor why some complementarities emerge and others do not. While VoC emphasizes economic functionalism in its explanation, other theories emphasize the political functionalism of financialization in the US.

Krippner (2011), for example, argues that the US was confronted by three crises as economic growth slowed during the 1970s. First, there was a *social crisis* of heightened distributional conflicts. Second, there was a *fiscal* crisis as the growing cost of promised benefits increasingly outstripped state capacity to generate revenue to pay for them. Finally, there was a *legitimation* crisis for the state, given its inability to handle social and fiscal crisis, leading to a loss of trust in government. The state's *ad hoc* responses to these crisis led to three interrelated policy shifts that created a macro environment conducive to financialization: first, deregulation of financial markets in the 1970s; second, increasing dependence/reliance on foreign capital to finance deficits (starting in the 1980s); and third, a radical change in monetary policy under Volcker. These policy shifts led to increased credit in the US economy that stimulated more consumption and investment while increasing foreign capital flows to finance US deficits. The expansion of private consumption and resulting growth allowed the US government to avoid difficult decisions about how to allocate limited resources among competing interests. Thus, a self-reinforcing political dynamic of financialization ensued.

Schwartz (2009) argues that the creation and growth of a residential mortgage-backed securities (RMBS) market in the 1990s, a product of both private sector initiative and government policy, boosted demand for mortgages, in turn driving rates and quality down while allowing consumers to use their houses as 'ATMs' and increase their consumption. Simultaneously, global disinflation made US-originated RMBS an attractive investment for global capital which helped offset the otherwise rising US current account deficit. Together these produced a strong demand stimulus during the 'long 1990s' (1991–2005) and high economic growth rates. The comparatively high growth of the US economy boosted overseas investment by US multinationals and purchases of financial assets abroad by banks, ultimately boosting US structural economic power in the global economy. Thus, like Krippner (2011), Schwartz (2009) sees the financialization dynamic as driven in large part by the *unintended* outcomes of policy choices and structural changes that yielded superior economic results, which, in turn, reinforced policy-makers' belief that the US model of financial capitalism was a superior and durable model.

These structural theories do highlight important contributors to financialization in the US, perhaps most importantly the role of positive feedback effects between economic growth (and demand/credit expansion) and subsequent policy choices. Schwartz (2009) in particular also highlights the US's unique position as the world's largest economy and global reserve currency which facilitated a growth strategy based on leverage and huge inflows of foreign capital:

this is surely another structural variable that helps explain why financialization could proceed as far as it did in the US.

Yet, like most structural explanations, they are prone to excessive functionalism in their accounts. Krippner's (2011) theory also embodies a strong path dependency argument, with the trajectory of the US model largely set by the mid-1980s. From a comparative perspective, Krippner's argument also does not help us understand why other advanced economies, faced with the same set of crises during the 1970s, liberalized to a much lesser degree. Also, both Krippner and Schwartz's argument rest on the significance of increased cheap capital (i.e., borrowing) as the salve that solved political problems for US politicians. While there is much evidence in favour of this, borrowing by governments and private leverage as a political solution is common cross-nationally and comparatively (contemporary Greece comes to mind as a good example), yet is not necessarily associated with such extensive financialization as in the US. Thus, we need to go further in order to understand the unique degree of financialization in the US and the historically contingent events that turned broad structural forces into specific and distinct outcomes.

While this contribution is too short to develop a full theoretical and empirical account, we suggest that the structural factors highlighted by Krippner (2011) and Schwartz (2009) and the role of complementarities highlighted by VoC be combined with a historical-institutional (HI) account which allows for greater indeterminacy in the evolutionary path of US capitalism and thus highlights the politics behind it (see also Campbell 2011). The HI account adds two important variables to explaining the outcome, namely the institutional character of the US legislative and regulatory structure on the one hand and social and political coalitional dynamics on the other. These other two variables help us understand why some liberalization measures were resisted for long periods of time, even by the financial sector, and how both the Democratic and Republican parties became proponents of financialization because of electoral strategies and shifting ideology, and not simply because of the positive functionality of financialization. Moreover, there were several contingent events in the 1980s and 1990s – financial crises – that might well have derailed the deregulation movement and understanding why these did not requires a historical account.

3.1. The mid-century regulated finance model

Going into the 1980s, the US financial system was characterized by fragmentation, deconcentration, banking specialization, and interest and product regulation. Fragmentation and deconcentration were largely products of the fact that most US states severely limited branching across state lines and, in many states, branching within states. Thus, both state and nationally chartered banks operated within severely constrained geographic market segments. Banking specialization resulted from the Glass–Steagall Act, passed in response to the banking failures of the Great Depression, which separated commercial from investment banking. The 1956 Bank Holding Act also forbade banks from underwriting insurance. Prior to the 1980s state and federal regulators also imposed deposit rate regulation, while states, via usury laws, imposed lending rate ceilings.

In securities, legislation passed during the 1930s established the regulatory structure that is largely in place to this day. [4] First, the Securities and Exchange Commission (SEC) is the primary regulator of securities markets and oversees a series of self-regulatory organizations (SROs), including the stock exchanges, and the Financial Accounting Standards Board (established in 1973), thus creating a system of public–private regulation. Second, securities market regulation is focused primarily on financial transparency and disclosure regulation. Both features of securities market regulation remain largely unchanged and reforms over the last three decades have largely focused on improving transparency.

3.2. The great transformation

The critical juncture that set the US economy on the road to finance capitalism and a strongly liberal market order was during the Reagan presidency (1981–88). On the political side, the breakdown of the New Deal coalition, which had dominated national politics and supported a more 'managed' (co-ordinated) capitalism from the 1930s to the 1970s, opened the door to a neoliberal shift in the US approach to its economy. The coalition broke down largely as a result of the realignment of southern Democrats to the Republicans in wake of civil rights actions of 1960s, the decline and disaffection of the working class and the defection of many middle class voters to Republicans (Edsall and Edsall 1992).

In 1980 Ronald Reagan campaigned and won the election on a strong anti-government, anti-tax rhetoric. While some segments of the business community were early supporters of this neoliberal turn, his success rested in good part on winning over substantial segments of working- and middle-class voters (Prasad 2006). For them the Reagan agenda was sold as a solution to the stagflation of the 1970s and early 1980s. The Reagan era marked the rise of neoliberals within the Republican Party and the decline of so-called 'Rockefeller Republicans' (centrists). By the time of his re-election in 1984, Reagan had built a strong electoral coalition spanning the upper and middle classes, with a good deal of working-class support as well. In short, from the early 1980s to the early 1990s the centre of American politics shifted significantly to the right (Abramowitz and Saunders 1998); this strengthened support for the neoliberal policies pushed by the Republican party and forced centrist Democrats to largely embrace them as well.

Beyond these shifts in voter preferences and the party system, two institutional aspects of the American system arguably contributed to a high degree of financialization. The first is the well-known fragmented nature of the legislative process and strong influence of special interests; the second is the fragmented financial regulatory structure. In the 1980s increasingly global financial markets intensified competition for capital and financial services which US financial interests repeatedly used as a successful argument with legislators to further deregulation (Kapstein 1996; Suarez and Kolodny 2011). In addition to key legislative reforms, fragmentation of regulators meant that a deregulatory move by one regulator often begat a process of 'competitive deregulation,' i.e., 'competing' regulators usually came under pressure from the banks they regulated to match the first (Deeg and Lütz 2000). The naming of Alan Greenspan as head of the Federal Reserve Bank (Fed) in 1987 was very important in accelerating this dynamic, as Greenspan was a firm believer in the self-regulatory capacity of markets and thus was a staunch advocate for financial deregulation.

Deregulation during the 1980s was marked by two key changes. The first was price deregulation via the 1980 Depository Institutions Deregulation and Monetary Control Act. This permitted banks to set their own interest rates on deposits (seen as a boon to savers at a time of high interest rates). The second was the gradual dismantling of product and market segmentation among financial institutions that ultimately paved the way for very large ('too big to fail') financial institutions to emerge. The first step in this direction actually began in the mid-1970s when some states began deregulating branching restrictions. This, in turn, set off a cycle of competitive deregulation among states that culminated in the federal 1994 Riegle–Neal Act which permitted bank holding companies to merge across borders. Another key step came in 1982, when thrifts (savings and loan banks) were also substantially deregulated, partly in an effort to expand commercial lending during the 1981–82 recession, but also as part of the Reagan administration's deregulatory agenda.

But the most significant and most contentious reforms centred on dismantling the barriers between commercial and investment banking established by the Glass–Steagall Act of 1932. The elimination of these barriers was far from inevitable and occurred piecemeal over a period of nearly 20 years. The gradual elimination of these barriers had a profound effect on the US financial system: it facilitated the growth of 'too big to fail' financial institutions; enabled banks to engage in much riskier business and expose depositors to those risks; and facilitated the growth of the 'shadow' banking system (e.g., with banks acting as prime brokers to hedge funds). The push for elimination began during the 1980s when major US commercial banks, which had been doing investment banking activities in overseas markets (primarily London) for many years, began pressuring regulators in the US to permit banks to enter into such business at home (Deeg and Lütz 2000; Helleiner 1994). Federal Reserve Chairman Alan Greenspan was strongly in favour of this petition and soon after taking office used the Fed's regulatory authority to permit Bank Holding Companies – primarily supervized by the Federal Reserve – to engage in limited investment banking activities. Over the next decade Greenspan increased these permitted activities as a percentage of bank assets in several steps because repeated attempts at formal reform were blocked in Congress by opposition from investment banks and insurance firms which did not want competition from commercial banks (Suarez and Kolodny 2010). In short, division among segments of the financial industry and their ability to exploit the fragmented legislative process stifled this liberalization dynamic for many years.

Other events during the late 1980s might well have halted or slowed financial liberalization had they not been managed effectively by regulators and Congress. The first was the savings and loan crisis that began in the mid-1980s and stretched into the 1990s. Upon their deregulation in the early 1980s, savings and loans rapidly expanded their lending, notably in real estate. But the banks were poorly regulated and many overexposed their balance sheets during the real estate boom of the 1980s. In the late 1980s and 1990s hundreds of savings banks were closed or taken over by an agency set up by the Federal government. Despite costing taxpayers billions of dollars, the diversion of this problem into an independent agency and the drawn out nature of the crisis minimized the political backlash against deregulation (Cassell 2003).

The second was the stock market plunge in October 1987 that set off widespread panic among investors. But Greenspan deftly managed this crisis by flooding the financial system with liquidity and taking other measures to calm markets and prop up asset prices. In effect, he rescued Wall Street and thereby reassured the public and politicians that financial deregulation could continue. This was the first of several 'Wall Street rescues' by Greenspan that, after the financial crisis, came to be viewed by many as a major contributor to moral hazard in the finance industry and the excessive leverage and risk-taking that built up in the US financial system during his term.

By the early 1990s Greenspan had achieved reverential status among both Republican and Democratic members of Congress, and the principle of market liberalization had become the widespread norm among the business community, regulators and both political parties. Democrat Bill Clinton won the 1992 election and this required him to campaign and govern as a centrist, and in 1994 the Republican Party gained control of both houses of Congress for the first time in 40 years. Thus, rather than reversing some of the neoliberal reforms of the Reagan era, he largely subscribed to the deregulation ideology and reappointed Greenspan as Fed chair and populated the Treasury Department and other key posts with Wall Street insiders.

The economic success of the American economy under Clinton, including the dot.com boom during the late 1990s, was seen in the US as validation of its emphasis on deregulated markets. Political leaders and regulators also came to see the US as – and to a great degree it was – the global standard setter in financial regulation, accounting, corporate governance and labour market regulation (Posner 2009). Given this context, the second half of the 1990s brought another wave of reforms that accelerated the expansion of finance capitalism. The two most significant reforms were the 1999 Financial Services Modernization Act (FSMA) and the Commodity Futures Modernization Act (CFMA) of 2000.

The FSMA formally ended the regulatory separation of commercial and investment banking (Glass–Steagall) that had held sway since the 1930s. This reform fully opened the door to universal banking and increased capital ties between commercial banks and other non-banking financial institutions. In practical terms this meant that large banks could expand their securities business and proprietary trading – a very profitable, but risky source of income – and also channel funds to private equity and hedge funds. After some two decades of failed repeal efforts, the passage was finally possible when investment banks and insurance firms decided that, in light of changed business opportunities stemming from previous liberalizations and market developments, they would now stand to gain more than they would lose from a repeal (Suarez and Kolodny 2011).

The Commodities Futures Modernization Act was a cornerstone in the legislative edifice that codified *laissez-faire* and created the financial boom and bust of the 2000s. The Act circumscribed – rather than enhanced – the ability of regulators to regulate a wide range of the financial derivatives that were rapidly growing on Wall Street. The most significant move to regulate came from the head of the Commodity Futures Trading Commission (CFTC), Brooksley Born. In 1998 she released a concept paper laying out her concerns that the rapid growth of derivatives traded off regulated exchanges (over the counter [OTC]) was creating an unacceptable systemic risk, and she suggested that the CFTC might move to regulate them (CFTC 1998). This paper touched off a rapid and powerful response by a coalition of *laissez-faire* advocates that included not only Republicans like Fed Chair Alan Greenspan, but also key players in the Clinton government – notably Treasury Secretary Robert Rubin and his deputy, Larry Summers. Joining them was Chair of the Securities and Exchange Commission, Arthur Levitt – a rival regulator to the CFTC. In Congress, the anti-regulation coalition was led by Republican Senator Phil Gramm. Even though the near collapse and Fed-orchestrated rescue in 1998 of the Long Term Capital Management hedge fund clearly showed the systemic risks emanating from the growth of unregulated derivatives, there was little political support for regulation. While some investor groups and multi-national enterprises (MNEs) supported Born's position in congressional hearings, the large majority of lobbyists representing both financial and non-financial firms came down on the anti-regulation side (US Congress 1998).

While the CFMA decision not to regulate was supported by a strong political majority, there was another critical regulatory failure in this era that was possible because a minority interest could control key levers of influence (veto points) in the fragmented legislative process. This failure pertained to Fannie Mae and Freddie Mac, two government-sponsored financial firms that, since the mid-1990s, were huge players in mortgage-backed securities (RMBS) markets. The growth of RMBS was a big part of financialization in the US and at the heart of the 2007–9 crisis. Pushed for years by administrative officials and powerful members of Congress to expand home ownership among the middle and lower classes, these two firms gradually lowered lending standards and drastically expanded their business. Both firms were so poorly run and regulated by a special regulatory agency that even Alan Greenspan thought they needed more regulation. During the 2000s Bush government Treasury officials and influential members of Congress attempted to strengthen regulatory oversight but each time were thwarted by Fannie Mae and Freddie Mac's ability – both were notoriously heavy lobbyers of Congress – to win enough supporters in key congressional committees (Thompson 2009).

Altogether these deregulatory measures or failures to regulate helped fuel the very rapid growth of securitization and derivatives markets, including the mortgage-backed derivatives at the heart of the crisis. They were in no small part the product of a convergence between Democratic and Republican party leaders on a policy preference of *laissez-faire* (Suarez and Kolodny 2011). Beyond ideological convergence and the success of industry lobbying, it is worth highlighting that the dramatic growth of defined contribution pension and mutual funds since the early 1980s has also created a structural interest among American households in financialization because their economic security is ever more dependent on financial market returns (as opposed to wage income).[5] For much of the late 1990s and early 2000s average Americans benefitted from financialization, as disinflation, rising equity markets and innovations in housing finance made cheap borrowing to fuel consumption possible (Langley 2008; Schwartz 2009). Leveraged consumption also compensated to a significant degree for the stagnant or declining real wages for much of the working population (Davis 2009).[6]

Not surprisingly, the financial crisis in 2007–9 led the public and most politicians to call the *laissez-faire* approach to financial regulation into question. As in most other countries, a legislative process to rewrite financial regulation was initiated, with the primary product being the Dodd–Frank Wall Street Reform and Consumer Protection Act of 2010. The law was passed while the Democrats controlled both houses of Congress, though it also received notable Republican support. The Act represents a broad-sweeping reform of financial regulation that reverses – if only partially – the decades-long movement in the US toward deregulation of financial markets.

The most important change in the Act for the structure of regulation was the creation of the Financial Stability Oversight Council whose function is to counter emerging threats to the overall stability of the financial system. The Council may designate non-bank financial companies for supervision by the Federal Reserve Board (Fed) and make recommendations for enhanced prudential standards applicable to such companies, as well as to large ('mega') bank holding companies. In turn, the Fed is required to regulate mega bank holding companies and designated non-bank financial companies through, *inter alia*, risk-based capital and leverage limits that include off-balance-sheet activities and are countercyclical, increasing in times of economic expansion and decreasing during economic contractions. The Act also imposed certain limitations or prohibitions on proprietary trading activities by banks and generally prohibits them from sponsoring or retaining any equity, partnership, or other ownership interest in a hedge fund or a private equity fund (Fein 2010).

The long-term effects of the Dodd–Frank Act on financialization processes are not easily predicted, and there are reasons to believe that this crisis will not lead to a new institutional trajectory in US capitalism (see also Block 2011). For while there are indeed more regulations, including for derivatives, financial firms are returning to many of their prior practices, and undoubtedly will develop new ones to circumvent new regulations. The legislation also leaves a large rule-making mandate for regulators to fill in the broader framework goals of the Dodd–Frank Act. This, in turn, has opened the door for financial lobbyists to fend off the most onerous regulations (Carpenter 2010). Moreover, many of the current regulators were supporters of the light-touch approach to regulation before the crisis, and it is unclear how much their fundamental convictions have really changed. Finally, while countless American households have been burned by the financial crisis, their increased dependence on financial markets suggests that they will continue to prefer policies that foster the expansion of markets and higher returns on financial investments (Davis 2009).

4. CONCLUSION

At the outset of the 1980s it was not a foregone conclusion that US model would evolve into the strongly liberalized financial capitalism we find in the present. While the Reagan presidency was critical in starting down this path, the present form of capitalism is the result of many subsequent changes in both formal and informal institutions. Many of the outcomes were intended, some unintended. This reflects in part the fact that major reform happens infrequently in the US due to its fragmented legislative process. Rather, reforms tend to occur cumulatively and often in a haphazard fashion, shaped by court decisions, legislative measures at the federal or state level, or through regulatory decisions. Thus, institutional change tends to be evolutionary, marked by processes of displacement and drift. There are also undoubtedly some institutional complementarities that acted as important causal sources. As discussed in Section 2, for example, the rise of shareholder value in finance and corporate governance during the 1980s almost certainly accelerated corporate efforts to weaken or break unions as part of the major corporate restructuring wave undertaken in the 1980s. And even though the American welfare state has expanded during this period in some dimensions, the increased reliance on tax-subsidized private pension savings added significant impetus to financialization.

During the economic boom years of the 1990s, powerful private sector lobbies were successful in pushing state policies toward even more radical deregulation, or, in the case of finance, to non-regulation. It is this very 'vulnerability' of the legislative process that has enabled the American financial sector to beat back most of the post-crisis regulation that might have significantly altered financial markets, especially for derivatives. In this respect the US model of capitalism as it evolved over the last 30 years has largely survived the crisis and the basic American faith in the virtue of markets is still largely intact. There is, however, another key element of this model that is still in jeopardy;

namely, for most of the last 20 years growth depended to a considerable extent on high levels of personal consumption fed by cheap and easy money that is no longer sustainable at that level (Schwartz 2009). Thus, the search for new sources of growth may, in the longer run, lead to a substantially different American model of capitalism.

Biographical note: Richard Deeg is Professor and Head of the Department of Political Science at Temple University, Philadelphia, USA.

ACKNOWLEDGEMENTS

I am grateful to Sandra Suarez, Howard Gospel, Robin Kolodny, participants in the Institutional Changes and Trajectories of Socio-Economic development Models (ICaTSEM) project meetings, as well as two anonymous referees for most helpful comments, and to Ashish Vaidya for research assistance. The research in this contribution was supported by the European Union's Seventh Framework Programme (FP7/2007-2011) under grant agreement no. 225349 (ICaTSEM project).

NOTES

1 More than 50 per cent of all publicly traded and 63 per cent of the Fortune 500 firms have their legal home in Delaware which has the most management-friendly corporate laws; see http://www.delaware.gov/topics/incorporateindelaware (accessed 12 October 2011).
2 The US has the lowest employment protection index score and shortest average employment tenure of all the OECD countries (Pontusson 2005: 120).
3 Most states provide six months of unemployment benefits. However, during recessions the federal government often provides additional funds to states to lengthen the term of benefits.
4 The primary enabling statutes include the Securities Act of 1933, Securities Exchange Act of 1934 and Commodities Exchange Act of 1936.
5 In 1980, about 6 per cent of US households held mutual fund investments; by 2000, nearly half did (Davis 2009: 18).
6 From 1973 to 2000, real US household income of the bottom quintile rose just 10 per cent; the second quintile just 15 per cent; while the highest quintile gained over 60 per cent (Pontusson 2005; 35).

REFERENCES

Abramowitz, A.I. and Saunders, K.L. (1998) 'Ideological realignment in the US electorate', *Journal of Politics* 60(3): 634–52.
Block, F. (2011) 'Crisis and renewal: the outlines of a twenty-first century new deal', *Socio-Economic Review* 9(1): 31–57.

Campbell, J.L. (2011) 'The US financial crisis: lessons for theories of institutional complementarity', *Socio-Economic Review* 9(2): 211–34.

Carpenter, D. (2010) 'Institutional strangulation: bureaucratic politics and financial reform in the Obama administration', *Perspectives on Politics* 8(3): 825–46.

Cassell, M. (2003) *How Governments Privatize: The Politics of Divestment in the United States and Germany*, Washington, DC: Georgetown University Press.

Cioffi, J. (2010) *Public Law and Private Power: Corporate Governance Reform in the Age of Finance Capitalism*, Ithaca, NY: Cornell University Press.

Commodity Futures Trading Commission (1998) 'Over-the-counter derivatives: concept release', *Federal Register* 63(91), Tuesday 12 May 1998: 26114–27.

Cramton, P.C. and Tracy, J.S. (1998) 'The use of replacement workers in union contract negotiations: the U.S. experience, 1980–1989', *Journal of Labor Economics* 16(4): 667–701.

Davis, G.F. (2009) *Managed by the Markets: How Finance Reshaped America*, Oxford: Oxford University Press.

Deeg, R. (2010) 'Institutional change in national financial systems', in G. Morgan *et al.* (eds), *Oxford Handbook of Comparative Institutional Analysis*, Oxford: Oxford University Press, pp. 309–34.

Deeg, R. and Lütz, S. (2000) 'Internationalization and regulatory federalism in financial systems: the United States and Germany at the crossroads?', *Comparative Political Studies* 33(3): 374–405.

Edsall, T.B and Edsall, M.D. (1992) *Chain Reaction: The Impact of Race, Rights and Taxes on American Politics*, New York: W.W. Norton.

Fein, M.L. (2010) 'Dodd–Frank Wall Street Reform and Consumer Protection Act', mimeograph, available at http://ssrn.com/abstract=1357452 (accessed 16 January 2012).

Godard, J. (2009) 'The exceptional decline of the American labor movement', *Industrial and Labor Relations Review* 63(1): 82–108.

Hacker, J. (2006) *The Great Risk Shift: The Assault on American Jobs, Families, Health Care, and Retirement*, Oxford: Oxford University Press.

Hall, P. and Soskice, D. (2001) *Varieties of Capitalism: The Institutional Foundations of Comparative Advantage*, Oxford: Oxford University Press.

Helleiner, E. (1994) *States and the Reemergence of Global Finance: From Bretton Woods to the 1990s*, Ithaca, NY: Cornell University Press.

Jensen, M.C. and Meckling, W.H. (1976) 'The theory of the firm: managerial behavior, agency costs and ownership structure', *Journal of Financial Economics* 3(4): 305–60.

Kapstein, E. (1996) *Governing the Global Economy: International Finance and the State*, Cambridge, MA: Harvard University Press.

Krippner, G. (2005) 'The financialization of the American economy', *Socio-Economic Review* 3(2): 173–208.

Krippner, G. (2011) *Capitalizing on Crisis: The Politics Origins of the Rise of Finance*, Cambridge, MA: Harvard University Press.

Langley, P. (2008) *The Everyday Life of Global Finance: Saving and Borrowing in Anglo-America*, Oxford: Oxford University Press.

Lazonick, W. and O'Sullivan, M. (2000) 'Maximizing shareholder value; a new ideology for corporate governance', *Economy and Society* 29(1): 13–35.

Lehne, R. (2006) *Government and Business: American Political Economy in Comparative Perspective*, Washington, DC: CQ Press.

Perry, J. and Nölke, A. (2005) 'International accounting standard setting: a network approach', *Business and Politics* 7(3), Article 5, available at http://www.bepress.com/bap/vol7/iss3/art5 (accessed 14 September 2011).

Pontusson, J. (2005) *Inequality and Prosperity: Social Europe vs. Liberal America*, Ithaca, NY: Cornell University Press.

Posner, E. (2009) 'Making rules for global finance: transatlantic regulatory cooperation at the turn of the millennium', *International Organization* 63(4): 665–99.

Prasad, M. (2006) *The Politics of Free Markets*, Chicago, IL: University of Chicago Press.

Schwartz, H. (2009) *Subprime Nation: American Power, Global Capital, and the Housing Bubble*, Ithaca, NY: Cornell University Press.

Suarez, S. and Kolodny, R. (2011) 'Paving the road to "too big to fail": business interests and the politics of financial deregulation in the United States', *Politics and Society* 39(1): 74–102.

Thelen, K. (2007) 'Skill formation and training', in G. Jones and J. Zeitlin (eds), *The Oxford Handbook of Business History*, Oxford: Oxford University Press, pp. 559–80.

Thompson, H. (2009) 'The political origins of the financial crisis: the domestic and international politics of Fannie Mae and Freddie Mac', *The Political Quarterly* 80(1): 17–24.

US Congress (1998) 'Over-the-counter derivatives', Senate Committee on Agriculture, Nutrition and Forestry, 30 July (S. Hrg. 105-998).

Vogel, D. (1996) *Kindred Strangers: The Uneasy Relationship between Politics and Business in America*, Princeton, NJ: Princeton University Press.

Index

Note:
Page numbers in **bold** type refer to figures
Page numbers in *italic* type refer to tables
Page numbers followed by 'n' refer to notes

For Product Safety Concerns and Information please contact our EU
representative GPSR@taylorandfrancis.com Taylor & Francis Verlag GmbH,
Kaufingerstraße 24, 80331 München, Germany

Printed and bound by CPI Group (UK) Ltd, Croydon, CR0 4YY

01/05/2025
01858355-0012